NHCPL

DESIGNING SOLUTIONS FOR MICROSOFT® SHAREPOINT® 2010

Discard
HCL

DESIGNING SOLUTIONS FOR
Microsoft® SharePoint® 2010

Making the Right Architecture and Implementation Decisions

Todd Baginski (FRESH TRACKS CONSULTING, LLC)

Robert Bogue (THOR PROJECTS)

Chris Keyser (MICROSOFT)

Jason Lee (CONTENT MASTER LTD)

NEW HANOVER COUNTY
PUBLIC LIBRARY
201 CHESTNUT STREET
WILMINGTON, NC 28401

Copyright and Terms of Use

ISBN: 978-0-7356-5608-6

This document is provided "as-is." Information and views expressed in this document, including URL and other Internet Web site references, may change without notice. You bear the risk of using it.

Some examples depicted herein are provided for illustration only and are fictitious. No real association or connection is intended or should be inferred.

This document does not provide you with any legal rights to any intellectual property in any Microsoft product. You may copy and use this document for your internal, reference purposes.

© 2010 Microsoft. All rights reserved.

Microsoft, Windows, Windows Server, Windows Vista, Visual C#, SQL Server, Active Directory, IntelliSense, Silverlight, MSDN, Internet Explorer, and Visual Studio are trademarks of the Microsoft group of companies. All other trademarks are property of their respective owners.
Printed in Canada

Contents

Foreword

Here at Microsoft, we have been fortunate to see organizations of all sizes build fantastic solutions on SharePoint, from Internet presences, to departmental workflows, to business intelligence portals, and much more. Reviewing these solutions with a wide range of developers has shown us that the key success factors for SharePoint development are the same as those for any software development project:

- A strong development team that invests in learning the technologies and best practices.
- A solid architecture plan that has been validated through design reviews and prototypes.
- A design, development, and testing process that is appropriate for the complexity of the project.

SharePoint has come a long way in the last decade. The success of SharePoint is due in no small part to its empowerment of end users. More than ever before, the platform allows users to build sites for sharing, collaborating, searching, and communicating without the involvement of developers or the IT team. This flexibility makes business teams more effective by improving their ability to innovate and adapt quickly to changing business needs. However, at some point, many organizations reach a stage where they want functionality beyond the capabilities that SharePoint provides out of the box. Because SharePoint makes it so easy to build solutions without any coding, people often mistakenly believe that custom SharePoint development is more straightforward than custom development for other platforms.

When you decide that you need a custom SharePoint solution, you should first be sure that there isn't a built-in approach that can meet your needs. In many cases, developers will build a custom solution without realizing that the desired functionality is already built into the platform. If you do proceed with a custom solution, make sure your developers invest some time to understand the fundamentals of SharePoint development. Rather than risk introducing errors or unexpected behavior, it's a good idea to understand the architectural concepts, good practices, and key decision areas relevant to SharePoint application development.

This patterns & practices book, and the related MSDN release, *Developing Applications for SharePoint 2010*, are two of the most effective ways to help your developers and architects understand the choices they face in designing and developing SharePoint solutions, and the consequences of their choices. The book and the accompanying guidance provide real-world examples and reference implementations that illustrate how to apply the techniques, approaches, and good practices described in the content. The material is useful as an end-to-end guide for those who want to gain a comprehensive understanding of key decision areas, and as a reference for guidance on specific issues. In short, it's an essential tool to help developers and architects design and develop better applications for SharePoint 2010.

Jeff Teper
Corporate Vice President

Preface

This book came about because of a Microsoft® patterns & practices project to produce guidance for Microsoft SharePoint® developers. *Developing Applications for SharePoint 2010* marked the third release of patterns & practices guidance for SharePoint in less than two years. This release was particularly exciting. We started scoping the release while we were still completing the August 2009 release on Microsoft Office® SharePoint Server (MOSS) 2007. By the time the SharePoint Conference in October arrived, we had a beautifully detailed and stack-ranked backlog, derived from interviews with customers, MVPs, and field-facing Microsoft partner teams. Imagine how surprised I was when at the review meeting our advisors turned our priorities completely upside down! What had happened? Our advisors had spent the month leading up to the conference working on SharePoint 2010 and had realized that many of the new features caused fundamental changes in how applications are built. Experts in MOSS 2007 were struggling in some cases to make the right design decisions in SharePoint 2010. Explaining how to think about and relate the pieces of an application with SharePoint 2010 became a priority, and we shifted to "Application Archetypes" (or as I like to call them, models) as the primary focus of this release.

While providing answers in guidance is always helpful, in the real world problems are nuanced and require deviation from any generic guidance we could provide. Thus, our top-level objective was to help you think about the problem rather than prescribe what to do. We strove to provide the knowledge and understanding in a way that helps you, whether you're a developer or architect, make decisions and understand their consequences. This book represents much of the core content we shipped in the online release of *Developing Applications for SharePoint 2010* on MSDN®, and complements the reference implementations and library we included as part of that release. With each release, we've tuned our approach to the guidance to make it more accessible. In this release, we've broken the examples into multiple reference implementations that are targeted to a single area, thereby maximizing the return on the time you invest to learn a specific area.

A great release is a team effort, and this release represents the combined work of many individuals. We have been moving at a furious pace of back-to-back releases, and I've been fortunate to work with some of the most talented, yet humble teammates throughout those releases. I don't think we could have had a more distributed team, with members from Philadelphia to Seattle and several points in between, and across the globe from Argentina, to India, to the UK. This accomplishment is a testament to the dedication and positive attitude of the entire team. Without a great team, our pace would have been impossible to sustain. And what productivity we realized! We shipped more than six hundred pages of documentation, over twenty-five How-Tos, eight reference implementations, and a reusable library.

I would especially like to thank my two project-lead colleagues in patterns & practices with whom I have worked on every release. Hanzhong (Hanz) Zhang did a superb job running test while also driving many aspects of project management for the release. Francis Cheung led development where he did a superb job of balancing practicality and complexity and providing a constant calming force for the team. Without them, the project could not have succeeded. Working with Hanz and Francis has made my job a lot easier, and much more enjoyable. They are great colleagues and friends.

Jason Lee organized many of the concepts and wrote the high-quality prose in the book and guide. Jason's combination of deep SharePoint skills, superb writing, and high productivity were crucial to this release and to the book. His calm attitude and British sense of humor were a welcomed addition to our virtual team room. Jason also contributed to technical decisions on the design aspects of the reference implementations and library.

We had a fantastic group of advisors throughout all of the releases, and with this release we were fortunate enough to have two of our advisors join the team. Robert Bogue and Todd Baginski, both SharePoint MVPs, provided deep expertise to guide the team. Rob and Todd wore many hats, from reviewer, to developer, to advisor, to writer during the release. Their knowledge and passion for the subject infused the whole team with energy, and they were the team's constant ambassadors to the wider SharePoint community.

VenkataAppaji Sirangi has been a tester on the team since the first release. Appaji ran a virtual team from India for the release, working closely with Hanz in Seattle. Not only did he run the test team, he also took on many additional tasks including creating the installation scripts for the reference implementations. Appaji has a positive can-do attitude, especially helpful during the inevitable crunch every test team faces at the end of a release.

Shawn Beeson came on late to the team as a developer and dove right into the effort. He is a very productive SharePoint developer with tremendous energy. Shawn worked with Francis and played a key role in figuring out how to use new features, and in the developing and designing a broad range of examples. He entered into each new area with vigor, and was constantly challenging himself and the team on the right technical approaches.

I'd like to also thank the many others on the test and development team whose contributions were essential to delivery, including Sateesh Babu Chakka, Hernan de Lahitte, Mariano Grande, Durga Mohan Palika, and Venkata Siva Krishna Yellapragada.

This project produced a lot of content, both written and images. The editing team always gets crunched at the end of a project. The exceptional quality, speed, and flexibility of the editing team to handle late-breaking documentation were essential to our on-time release. The team of Tina Burden, RoAnn Corbisier, Sharon Smith, and Nancy Michell made sure we stayed on track with the quick turnaround of complex topics. A special thanks as well to Nancy for editing the book content, as always with a great attitude , very timely responses, and great suggestions on structure and approach, and to RoAnn for driving the production process. Richard Burte has the tough job of being on the very end of every project in patterns & practices with the production release, and kept us on our toes. Rob Nance and Katie Niemer did a great job of producing a large volume of high-quality images throughout. I would also like thank Hanz, who organized and drove the entire coordination effort around documentation production in a way that I am just not capable of doing.

Our advisors are essential to making sure the content we produce is accurate, complete, and consumable. I'd like to call out the contributions of three advisors who truly went above and beyond for this release. Eric Schupps and Darrin Bishop reviewed nearly every document, attended almost every review call, and provided invaluable input. Reza Alirezaei provided great feedback during development and created a demonstration site containing all of the reference implementations for public consumption. I'd also like to thank J. Dan Attis, Todd C. Bleeker, Jackson Chackungal, Eric Charran, Michael Chorey, Andrew Connell, Spencer Harbar, Scot Hillier, Mike Huguet, Vesa Juvonen, Balakrishnan Krishnamoorthy, Roger Lamb, David Mann, Matthew McDermott, Chris O'Brien, Maurice Prather, Paul Schaeflein, Trent Swanson, Erwin van der Valk, Ethan Wilansky, and Andrew Woodward for their reviews and input.

We could not have produced this guidance without the many reviews and input from the product team. I would like to recognize Rob Howard, Maxim Lukiyanov, and Mike Ammerlaan from the SharePoint team for their reviews, for responding to many questions quickly and in detail, and for their overall encouragement during the development. Mike Morton from the Microsoft Visual Studio® team helped us figure out some complicated problems and was a tremendous supporter. Peli de Halleux, from Microsoft Research, who has to be the most innovative, intelligent, and productive developer I know, helped us with unit testing and made significant improvements in unit testing for SharePoint during the life of our project. I'd like to also than the many additional valuable contributors from the product team including Paul Andrew, Juan Balmori, Phillip Beish, Sumant Bhardvaj, Michael Cheng, Reza Chitsaz, Gabe Hall, Ivan Han, Eilene Hao Klaka, Peter Harwood, Randall Isenhour, Daniel Roth, Yimeng Li, Andrew May, Thomas Mechelke, Elisabeth Olson, Adam Outcalt, Iouri Simernitski, Brad Stevenson, and James Sturms.

Last, but not least, I have the luxury of thanking my family since I am writing the attributions. I was definitely a man on a mission on this release, and the patience of my family was essential. I'd like to thank my wife Donna, and my two kids, Chris and Rachel, for putting up with me during many long days and weekends during the development of the guidance. I'm sure that others on the team made similar sacrifices and had similar support from home, and I would like to thank all of the family members for their patience.

I am fortunate to have an unusual job where I can explore so many interesting areas and develop guidance that I hope will help many developers and architects build better SharePoint applications. The development of the guidance and book has been a long, yet enjoyable journey. I hope you find this book and the accompanying guide useful, and that you enjoy reading and applying it as much as I enjoyed developing it.

Chris Keyser
Principal Program Manager – *patterns & practices*
Microsoft Corporation
Redmond, September 2010

Introduction

Microsoft® SharePoint® 2010 is the fourth incarnation of the popular collaboration and content management platform from Microsoft. With each release, the reach and capabilities of SharePoint products and technologies have grown, offering new tools to organizations and new opportunities to developers. With SharePoint 2010, you can build multi-tenant, hosted applications on an infrastructure that is scalable, secure, and stable.

Let's take a brief look at some of the new functionality. SharePoint 2010 introduces the concept of sandboxed solutions whereby you can deploy solutions directly to a site collection without access to the server or the involvement of the IT team. To safeguard the performance and security of the farm as a whole, SharePoint restricts the functionality and throttles the resources available to sandboxed solutions. SharePoint 2010 also provides many new ways of working with data. For the first time, you can configure relationships and constraints between SharePoint lists, which goes some way towards bridging the gap between the capabilities of relational databases and the capabilities of SharePoint lists as a data source. New concepts, such as external content types and external lists, make it easier to consume and manipulate external data from within the SharePoint environment. The new LINQ to SharePoint provider enables you to replace your CAML queries with more user-friendly LINQ expressions. Finally, SharePoint 2010 introduces substantial support for client applications that interact with SharePoint sites and lists. Client object models for JavaScript, Silverlight, and managed Microsoft .NET clients provide client applications with strongly typed access to SharePoint objects and collections, while a REST-based Web service provides platform-independent access to SharePoint list data.

The new features, operational models, and configuration tools in SharePoint 2010 introduce fresh opportunities and challenges for developers and architects. To design effective SharePoint solutions, you need a deep technical understanding of the platform. For example, you'll want to understand the benefits and limitations of targeting your applications to the sandbox execution environment. You will want to know whether you should implement a data model using SharePoint lists or a relational database. You may want to know how to avoid hitting list query throttling limits when you write LINQ to SharePoint expressions, and you'll likely want to know how you can take advantage of the data binding capabilities of the Microsoft Silverlight® platform when you develop client applications for SharePoint. This book will help you answer all these questions and more.

Rationale

There are many books available that describe how to get started with SharePoint development. The product documentation, together with any number of blog posts and other online resources, provide comprehensive instruction on how to complete particular development tasks. What's harder to find is technically rigorous guidance on the design and architecture of SharePoint applications. For this reason, the patterns & practices team at Microsoft produced the *Developing Applications for SharePoint 2010* online guidance and download. Over several months, the team worked with leading industry experts and Microsoft product teams to gather deep knowledge of the capabilities, nuances, and limitations of SharePoint 2010 as a developer platform. They documented key design choices and decision points, established best practices, and developed reference implementations that demonstrate robust approaches to common SharePoint development scenarios. They also updated the SharePoint Guidance Library—a reusable class library that makes it easier for developers to manage application configuration data, log events, and manage dependencies between classes in SharePoint applications—to provide optimal support to developers working with SharePoint 2010.

This book draws much of its core guidance and technical reference material from the *Developing Applications for SharePoint 2010* release and presents it in a single volume. If you're looking for a general introduction to SharePoint development, this probably isn't the book for you. However, if you already have some experience developing applications for the SharePoint platform, this book can help you take your knowledge and expertise to the next level.

Note: *The Developing Applications for SharePoint 2010 online guidance is available at http://msdn.microsoft.com/ library/ff770300.aspx. We encourage you to download the associated resources, as the examples and components reinforce many of the concepts described in this book.*

Who Should Read This Book?

This book is intended primarily for developers and architects who have some knowledge or experience with SharePoint products and technologies. It offers technical insight, guidance, and design patterns for developers who know the basics and want to extend their skills to the design of robust, enterprise-scale applications. No prior knowledge of the 2010 version is assumed. However, to get the most out of this book you should have some familiarity with the core concepts of SharePoint configuration and development. For example, you should have:

- An understanding of the core logical architecture elements in SharePoint, such as farms, Web applications, site collections, and sites, together with their object model representations.

- An understanding of key SharePoint data concepts, such as lists, fields, content types, and metadata management.

- An awareness of the different execution options for custom SharePoint code, such as Web Parts, timer jobs, event receivers, and workflows.

- An understanding of SharePoint features and solution packages, including deployment, activation, and retraction.
- Some familiarity with security and authorization in SharePoint, including process accounts, farm administrators, SharePoint users and groups, and permissions management.
- A basic awareness of the infrastructure associated with SharePoint server farms, including Web front-end servers and application servers, Microsoft Internet Information Services (IIS) Web sites, and content databases.

You will need a basic working knowledge of C#, since code examples are presented in C#. A familiarity with .NET Framework concepts such as generics, anonymous types, and LINQ expressions, while not essential, will help you understand some of the concepts and examples presented here.

What's Inside?

This book is divided into four broad areas of design and development for SharePoint 2010 applications: execution models, data models, client application models, and application foundations. Each represents a key area of architectural decision making for SharePoint developers, as illustrated by Figure 1. Each area is described below.

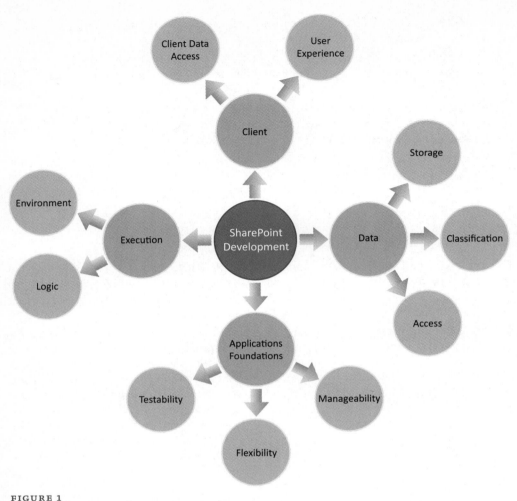

FIGURE 1
Key architectural decision drivers in SharePoint 2010

Execution Models illustrates how different types of SharePoint solutions are managed and executed. The section describes how you can develop effective applications in different operating environments and under a variety of constraints. In particular, it provides deep technical insight into the new sandboxed solution model, and explains the different ways in which you can extend the sandbox environment with various types of full-trust functionality. Figure 2 illustrates the key decision points in this area.

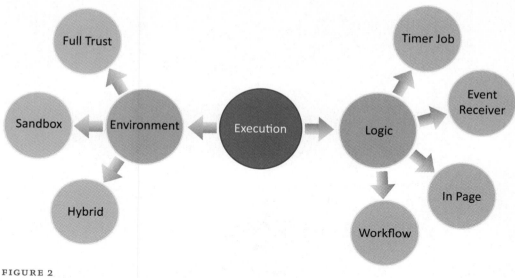

FIGURE 2
Execution model decision points

Data Models addresses the challenges involved in consuming and manipulating data in SharePoint applications. SharePoint 2010 includes a great deal of new functionality with respect to data, particularly with the introduction of external content types, external lists, and the ability to build relationships and constraints between SharePoint lists. This section of the book provides insights that can help you choose between standard SharePoint lists and external data sources as a platform for your SharePoint applications, and it offers approaches and patterns that you can use to mitigate the performance degradation associated with large lists. It also provides detailed insights into data access techniques, including the new LINQ to SharePoint capability. Figure 3 illustrates the key decision points in this area.

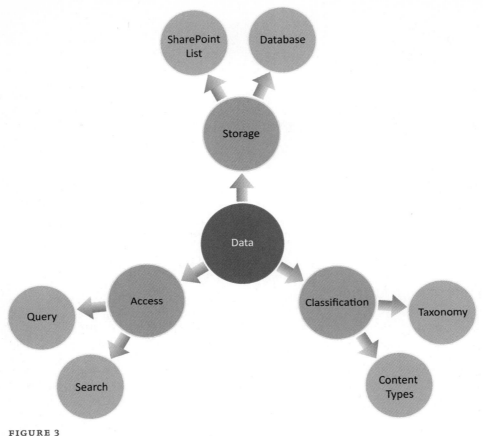

FIGURE 3
Data model decision points

Client Application Models shows how you can make effective use of the new client-side development features in SharePoint 2010. These features include several new mechanisms for data access, such as client-side APIs for JavaScript, Silverlight, and managed clients, as well as a Representational State Transfer (REST) interface. The SharePoint 2010 platform also provides more out-of-the-box support for rich Internet application (RIA) technologies such as Ajax and Silverlight. Figure 4 illustrates the key decision points in this area.

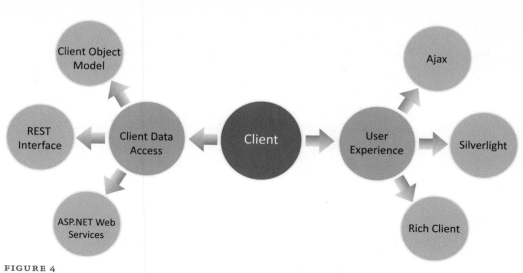

FIGURE 4
Client-side development decision points

Application Foundations shows how best to meet common development challenges in SharePoint applications, such as achieving effective isolation of classes and services, managing application configuration settings, logging events and trace information, and performing unit and integration testing. Addressing these challenges enables you to build flexible, robust, and modular solutions that are easy to maintain as your applications evolve. The concepts described in this section of the book should underpin everything you do in the areas of execution models, data models, and client-side development.

The scope of technical material that falls under the umbrella of SharePoint development grows increasingly broad with each release, thus several decisions were made to constrain the scope of this guidance. In the client section, the guidance concentrates on new opportunities for building RIA user interfaces with Silverlight and Ajax. Microsoft Office® client development also includes many new areas of functionality, but this area is worthy of its own book and is too broad a topic to include here. In the data section, the guidance concentrates on lists and libraries, external data, and data access. While site structure is also an important component of an effective SharePoint deployment, in many ways it's more of an operational issue than a development issue and as such is not included in the guidance. Taxonomy and search are omitted for the same reason. The new service application model in SharePoint is powerful, but as most organizations will not need to build their own service applications, the guidance also does not address this area.

PART ONE
EXECUTION MODELS

1   Understanding SharePoint Execution Models

Extensibility has always been one of the key advantages of the Microsoft® SharePoint® platform. Developers can enhance the functionality of SharePoint sites in any number of ways and by creating many different types of solutions, such as Web Parts, workflows, event receivers, and timer jobs. Each type of solution presents the developer with a unique set of decisions, opportunities, and limitations. Each is deployed to different locations, is loaded by different processes, and is subject to different execution conditions and constraints. In addition to these different types of solutions, Microsoft SharePoint 2010 introduces new options for the execution environment in which you want your code to run. In particular, the introduction of the sandboxed execution environment allows you to deploy solution packages directly to a site collection without access to the server. These solution packages run in a strictly controlled environment to help protect the performance, stability, and security of the SharePoint environment as a whole.

If you want to design and build robust, effective SharePoint solutions, you'll need an in-depth understanding of the different SharePoint execution models together with an awareness of the benefits and drawbacks of each approach. In this chapter, you'll find an overview of the key approaches to execution and deployment. In particular, the chapter can help you answer the following questions:

- What are the key approaches to execution and deployment in SharePoint 2010?
- When is it appropriate to use a particular execution model?
- Which SharePoint processes run each different type of solution?
- Which execution models are compatible with each type of solution?

The remaining chapters in Part I build on this chapter to provide more detailed insight into each of the core approaches to execution and deployment in SharePoint 2010.

> **Note:** *Part I focuses on server-side execution models. You can also interact with a SharePoint environment from client platforms such as Microsoft Silverlight®, Windows® Presentation Foundation (WPF), or JavaScript through the new SharePoint client object model. Part III provides an insight into client-side development for SharePoint 2010.*

Introducing the Sandbox

In earlier versions of SharePoint, there were limited options for deploying custom solutions to a SharePoint environment. You would deploy assemblies either to the global assembly cache or to the Web application's bin folder within the Internet Information Services (IIS) file structure. You would deploy other resources, such as images, configuration files, user controls, and SharePoint features, to the SharePoint file structure (commonly referred to as the "SharePoint root") on each server. In order to manage the installation, deployment, and retraction of these assemblies and resources over multiple servers, you would use a SharePoint solution package (WSP). The solution package would have to be placed on a file system available to a SharePoint server in the farm, installed using the **stsadm** command line tool, and then deployed to one or more Web applications from either the command line or the SharePoint Central Administration Web site.

This approach works well, as long as you meet the following criteria:

- You have server-side access to the SharePoint farm.
- You are a member of the Farm Administrators group.
- You have the confidence of the IT team.

This is increasingly unlikely to be the case. Many large companies provide a single, centrally managed SharePoint platform and simply provision site collections for disparate divisions, departments, and teams as required. Many smaller companies look to hosting companies to provide a SharePoint environment, which is also typically provided on a per-site collection basis. In both cases, developers who are looking to provide custom solutions are unlikely to have the server-side access they need to deploy their solutions. Hosting companies in particular may be understandably reluctant to permit anyone to deploy code that may jeopardize the performance, stability, or security of the SharePoint farm and, therefore, their other tenants.

In response to the market need to allow developers to create code that can be run in shared environments, SharePoint 2010 supports an additional deployment and execution model: the sandboxed solution. This model allows users who do not have access to the server file system to deploy managed code applications into individual site collections. Sandboxed solutions are deployed using a SharePoint solution package to a specialized gallery (document library) in the root site of the site collection.

These applications run in an environment of reduced trust—the *sandbox*—and are executed within an isolated process. When you develop solutions that target the sandbox execution model, you are restricted to using a subset of the SharePoint APIs and your code must observe more stringent code access security (CAS) policies for the rest of the Microsoft .NET Framework base class libraries. These constraints offer additional safeguards to the IT team, because the inherently lower trust environment reduces the risk of a security exploit by the sandboxed application. In return, the sandbox execution model offers developers the opportunity to customize and extend the functionality of their SharePoint sites in circumstances in which the deployment of custom code would otherwise be prohibited, such as hosted solutions or large, regulated corporate deployments.

In order to balance this newfound freedom to deploy managed code without the involvement of the IT team, SharePoint 2010 includes various safeguards against inefficient or resource-intensive sandboxed applications. In addition to the restrictions on the APIs that are available to the developer, the sandboxed solution framework monitors the execution of sandboxed applications and can terminate code that runs for too long or consumes too many resources. Administrators may configure a points-based system to throttle the system resources that are made available to sandboxed applications. This contributes to the overall stability of the system.

What Are the SharePoint Execution Models?

In terms of execution models, there are two principal types of solutions in SharePoint 2010: farm solutions and sandboxed solutions. Within each type of solution, there are various execution models available to you. Farm solutions can include components that run in a full-trust environment or components that run under code access security policy restrictions. Sandboxed solutions can include components that run entirely within the sandbox environment as well as hybrid approaches that can include various full-trust components.

FARM SOLUTIONS

A farm solution is a collection of resources that you deploy through the server-side file system in your SharePoint environment. These resources execute within the same process space as the SharePoint application, which means that your code can use the full SharePoint object model and has access to all the same resources as SharePoint itself.

When you deploy a farm solution, you can choose from two different execution models: the full-trust execution model and the bin folder/code access security (bin/CAS) execution model. These models will already be familiar to you if you have worked with Microsoft Office® SharePoint Server 2007 and Windows SharePoint Services 3.0.

The Full-Trust Execution Model

When you use the full-trust execution model, the assemblies in your solution are deployed to the global assembly cache on each Web front-end server and application server in the server farm. The SharePoint Web application process loads the assembly from the global assembly cache and your code runs with full trust—in other words, it runs without any code access security restrictions (see Figure 1).

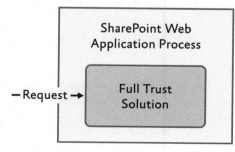

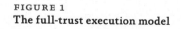

FIGURE 1
The full-trust execution model

Because the assemblies are deployed to the global assembly cache, you can make your solution available to any Web application on the server farm.

The Bin/CAS Execution Model

The bin/CAS approach is a partial-trust execution model. When you use the bin/CAS execution model, you deploy your assemblies to the bin directory associated with a SharePoint Web application. The worker process associated with the SharePoint Web application loads the assembly from the bin directory (see Figure 2). However, the operations your code may perform are restricted by the code access security policies that are applied in the Web.config file to assemblies in the bin directory.

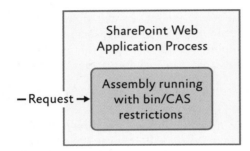

FIGURE 2
The bin/CAS execution model

Because the assemblies are deployed to the bin folder of a specific Web application, your solution is, by definition, scoped to that Web application instead of to the farm as a whole.

In terms of deployment, the only differences between the full-trust execution model and the bin/CAS execution model are the location where you deploy your assemblies and the code access security policies associated with that location. In both cases, any non-compiled items, such as ASP.NET markup files, XML files, or resource files, are typically deployed to the SharePoint root on each Web front-end server. If you want to deploy a farm solution using either of the farm solution execution models, you must have access to the server file system and be a member of the Farm Administrators security group.

Sandboxed Solutions

Sandboxed solutions are new to SharePoint 2010. A sandboxed solution is a collection of resources that you deploy directly to a specialized gallery (library) in the root site of a site collection. This library is referred to as the Solutions Gallery. Just like a farm solution, you package a sandboxed solution as a SharePoint solution package (WSP). However, you can deploy a sandboxed solution without physical access to the server file system and without the involvement of the IT team by directly uploading the WSP through the Web user interface (UI). Instead, the site collection administrator determines who has permissions to add sandboxed solutions to his or her site collection.

To counterbalance this newfound freedom to deploy solutions without the explicit approval of the IT team, SharePoint includes several constraints that restrict what you can do with a sandboxed solution. The following are some examples:

- Your code has access to a limited, "safe" subset of the SharePoint object model.
- Your assemblies are loaded by an isolated process.
- The solution framework terminates your code if it does not respond to requests within a specified duration.

The IT team allocates a resource quota to each site collection that defines the boundaries within which the sandboxed solution must operate. The solution framework shuts down all sandboxed solutions within a site collection if the site collection uses up its daily resource quota for sandboxed solutions. Within an individual site collection, administrators can review the resources consumed by individual sandboxed solutions from the site collection user interface.

There are two approaches to execution using the sandboxed solution environment. You can deploy a solution that runs entirely within the sandbox environment, which is referred to as the sandbox execution model. However, the sandbox environment also allows you call out to full-trust components under certain conditions. For example, you can consume specially developed, fully trusted, global assembly cache-deployed classes from your sandboxed solutions via a full-trust proxy. These approaches are referred to as hybrid execution models.

It's important to draw a distinction between components that you can deploy within a sandboxed solution and components that actually execute in the sandbox environment. For example, you can deploy a declarative workflow in a sandboxed solution. However, the workflow logic actually executes with full trust. Any calls to the SharePoint object model actually execute with full trust. These concepts are explained in greater detail later in Part I.

The Sandbox Execution Model

When a SharePoint Web application process receives a request that invokes your sandboxed solution, the Web application process does not directly load your assembly. Instead, the Web application process loads an execution wrapper that loads your assembly into an isolated sandbox process (see Figure 3).

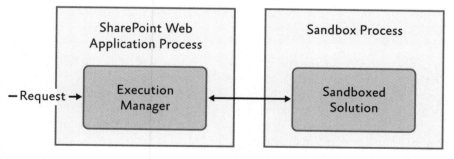

FIGURE 3
The sandbox execution model

When you use the sandbox execution model, your solution is limited in scope to the site collection in which it is deployed. In addition to the constraints outlined previously, the solution cannot access content or resources from other site collections.

Hybrid Execution Models

There are times when the benefits of the sandbox approach are appealing to an organization, but the limitations of the sandbox environment prevent you from creating a complete solution. In these cases, a hybrid approach may offer an attractive solution. Sandboxed solutions can access full-trust components through various mechanisms. For example, sandboxed solutions can do the following:

- They can use a full-trust proxy to access logic that runs with full trust, such as calls to APIs that are not permitted in the sandbox or calls to external services.
- They can use a declarative workflow to access a code-based custom workflow activity.
- They can use an external list to access external data through Business Connectivity Services (BCS).

These full-trust components could be developed in parallel with the sandboxed functionality, or they might be developed and deployed by the IT team to make additional functionality available to sandboxed solution developers. For example, the SharePoint Guidance Library includes a full-trust proxy that you can use to enable sandbox developers to log events and trace information from their sandboxed solutions.

In the first hybrid approach described in this chapter, you can execute global assembly cache-deployed full-trust code from a sandboxed solution by using a full-trust proxy. The full-trust proxy is a controlled exit point that allows your sandboxed code to make a synchronous call out to logic that executes outside of the sandbox process (see Figure 4).

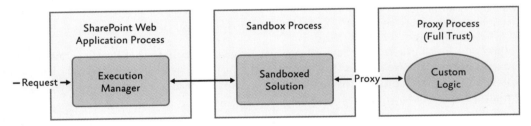

FIGURE 4
Hybrid execution using a full-trust proxy

It is important to understand that the full-trust proxy is implemented by the fully trusted component, rather than by the sandboxed solution. If sandboxed solution developers could use a proxy to run any global assembly cache-deployed code, this would subvert the restrictions placed on the sandbox environment. In order to provide services to sandboxed solutions, your fully trusted classes must inherit from the **SPProxyOperation** abstract class. After your full-trust proxies are deployed to the global assembly cache, they can be consumed from any sandboxed solution in the SharePoint farm.

Before creating a full-trust proxy, you should carefully consider your options. Any full-trust proxy can increase the potential for sandboxed applications to cause security or performance issues. Generally speaking, you should aim to keep the functionality that you expose to sandboxed applications through a full-trust proxy to the minimum required.

In the second hybrid approach described in this chapter, the full-trust component is a custom workflow activity that is deployed to the global assembly cache. You can consume the custom workflow activity in a declarative workflow from your sandboxed solution (see Figure 5).

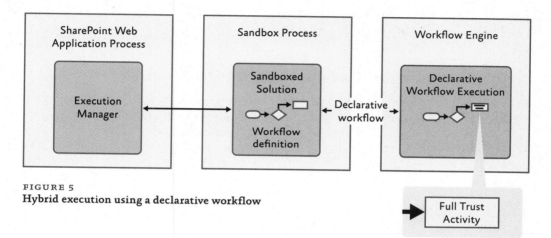

FIGURE 5
Hybrid execution using a declarative workflow

Using this approach, the fully trusted logic in the custom workflow activity is invoked asynchronously when the sandbox process executes the declarative workflow.

In the final hybrid approach described in this chapter, the full-trust component is an external content type defined in the BCS. The sandboxed solution includes an external list that connects to the external content type. As a result, the sandboxed solution can access data from other applications through the external list, even though the sandbox is prohibited from directly making an external connection (see Figure 6).

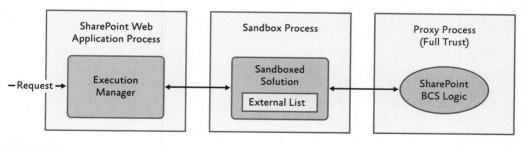

FIGURE 6
Hybrid execution using an external list

External content types and external lists: External content types and external lists The external content type is a new SharePoint 2010 feature that enables you to define a connection to an external data source. External content types can also define a set of CRUD (Create, Read, Update, and Delete) operations that allow you to manipulate that external data from your SharePoint environment. External lists connect to external content types and provide a SharePoint list wrapper around external data, so that you can access and manipulate that external data from the familiar format of a SharePoint list.

Which Execution Model is Right for My Solution?

Before you take a detailed look at the functionality and constraints of each execution model, it is worth taking some time to review some high-level examples that illustrate when each model might be appropriate. There are several factors that should influence your choice of execution model. In some cases, the decision may be made for you. If your code will be deployed to a shared or hosted environment, you may well be limited to the deployment of sandboxed solutions. If you are designing a third-party application, targeting the sandbox environment could make your product viable to a wider audience. In other cases, despite the inherent benefits to the overall stability, security, and performance of the farm as a whole, sandboxed solutions may not allow you to do everything you need to. The intended scope of your solution is another important factor—sandboxed solutions are constrained to a single site collection, bin/CAS solutions are restricted in scope to a single Web application, and full-trust solutions are available to the entire server farm.

Typical Scenarios for Farm Solutions

You can use the full-trust farm solution approach to deploy absolutely any combination of functionality and resources from the entire spectrum of SharePoint development. However, that does not mean that the full-trust model is always the best choice. When you deploy a solution that uses the full-trust execution model, you lose all the safeguards that are offered by the sandbox and hybrid approaches. Typically, you might choose to deploy a full-trust farm solution when the functionality you need is not available in the sandbox environment and the additional effort of building a hybrid solution is not justified. You might also consider full-trust solutions for high-volume, public-facing sites where the performance impact of using a sandboxed solution is unacceptable.

When you consider a bin/CAS deployment, remember that code access security policies can be difficult to get right and difficult to maintain. With the introduction of the sandbox environment, the combination of sandboxed solutions with full-trust components where necessary is preferred to the use of the bin/CAS approach in most cases. However, there are still some circumstances in which you may want to consider using the bin/CAS execution model. For example, if you have a high-volume site and you want to take advantage of granular security for your application, the bin/CAS model might meet your requirements. The bin/CAS approach cannot be used to run feature receivers, coded workflow activities, timer jobs, or service applications. These components must be deployed to the global assembly cache.

Common scenarios for full-trust farm solutions include the following:

- **Asynchronous timer jobs for large, regular batch operations**. For example, you might want to aggregate data from lists and sites on different site collections. Alternatively, you might want to run a bulk import or export of external data on a daily or weekly basis.

- **Fully coded workflows or activities**. You can model many business processes by creating your own custom workflow activities and consuming these activities from declarative workflows. However, in some cases, only a fully coded workflow will provide the functionality you need, particularly if you require complex or parallel branching logic. For example, suppose you implement a process to create swipe cards for secure access. The workflow must connect to an external security system to create the user record and request card production. You might use a fully coded workflow to support a parallel approval process with the Human Resources department and the security team.

Typical Scenarios for Sandboxed Solutions

In many cases, the sandbox execution model may be the only option available to you. This is particularly likely if you want to deploy a solution to a highly regulated environment, such as a shared or hosted deployment, or if your organization cannot justify the management costs of an environment that allows full-trust solutions. However, there are also many scenarios in which the sandbox execution model might be your preferred approach, regardless of the options available to you. In addition to the farm-wide benefits of stability, security, performance, and monitoring, sandboxed solutions offer benefits to solution developers. For example, you can upload your sandboxed solutions through a Web interface and without the involvement of the IT team; this enables hassle-free deployments and faster development iterations. If the capabilities of the sandbox environment meet the requirements of your application, the sandbox execution model will often be an attractive choice.

Common scenarios for sandboxed solutions include the following:

- **Data aggregation**. For example, you might want to create a Web Part or a Silverlight control that shows a summary of all tasks assigned to the current user from across the site collection or that aggregates sales data from individual team sites.

- **Data capture**. Suppose you are responsible for organizing and posting job vacancies at your organization. You might deploy a content type and an InfoPath form to collect and organize the information. You could also include a declarative workflow to manage the process through the received, approved, and posted phases.

- **Document management**. Imagine that you need to create a document repository for resumes. You might create a solution package that includes a document template and a content type. You deploy the document template to a document library and you include feature receiver classes to register the content type with the library.

TYPICAL SCENARIOS FOR HYBRID SOLUTIONS

Hybrid approaches can offer an attractive choice when the sandbox execution model alone does not provide all the capabilities that you need. You can use a hybrid approach to minimize the amount of full-trust code in your solution, both to maximize the performance and stability benefits you gain from the sandbox environment and to limit the management and review costs associated with the deployment of full-trust code.

Hybrid approaches also enable you to make additional functionality available to sandboxed solution developers across your organization. For example, you could develop and deploy a full-trust proxy that provides logging functionality. Other developers could then use your full-trust proxy in sandboxed solutions, from any site collection, without exceeding the limitations of the sandbox environment.

Common scenarios for hybrid approaches include the following:

- **Interaction with external services**. For example, suppose you create a sandboxed solution that tracks help desk requests from external customers. Your solution might use a full-trust proxy to submit each customer's location details to a geo-coding service. The geo-coding service returns a latitude and longitude, which your sandboxed solution can use to calculate the nearest available engineer for each customer.

- **Full-trust workflow activities**. Imagine, for instance, you want to extend the job postings data capture example from the sandbox scenarios. You might create and deploy a full-trust workflow activity that takes the data from a posting form and then uses a Web service to publish the information to an external job board Web site. You can consume this workflow activity from the declarative workflow within your sandboxed solution.

- **Extension of sandbox capabilities**. Suppose you want to allow sandboxed solution developers to use personalization. You might create a full-trust proxy to expose properties from the profile store. Similarly, you might create proxies to enable sandboxed solution developers to use logging functionality or read configuration settings from the farm-scoped property bag.

- **Integration with business data**. Let's say you want to show a list of custom activities from your customer relationship management (CRM) system alongside a proposal workspace in SharePoint 2010. You could create an external content type to enable SharePoint solutions to interact with the CRM data. External content types are full-trust components. Within the sandboxed solution, you could create an external list that binds to the CRM external content type and enables you to query customer data.

HOW DOES MY EXECUTION LOGIC AFFECT MY CHOICE OF MODEL?

Before you make design decisions about how to build a SharePoint application, it is important to understand how various SharePoint components execute their logic. First, knowing where your logic will execute can provide a useful context when you choose an implementation strategy. The following table maps SharePoint components to the actual processes in which they execute.

	IIS worker process	Sandbox worker process	Timer job process	Service application processes
Declarative components	✔			
Web Parts	✔	✔*		
Web pages	✔	✔		
Event receivers	✔	✔*		
Coded workflow activities	✔	✔*	✔	
Full-trust assemblies	✔		✔	
Fully coded workflows	✔		✔	
Timer jobs			✔	
Service applications				✔

Restrictions and caveats apply. These are discussed in more detail throughout Part I of this book.

It's not always obvious which process will run your code. Workflows are a case in point. Typically, workflows run in the IIS worker process when they are first initiated. After re-hydration, they execute within the same process as the event that triggered the rehydration. For example, if there is a timed delay in the workflow, the workflow will be re-started from the timer process when the timer fires. If an approval causes the workflow to rehydrate, the workflow runs in the IIS worker process where the approval was received from the user. In some circumstances, workflow activities may also run in the sandbox worker proxy process. For example, if sandboxed code creates an item in a list, and this triggers a workflow activity, then the workflow activity will run in the sandbox worker proxy process.

In addition to understanding where logic executes, it is important to know which SharePoint components are supported by each execution model. The following table shows which execution models you can use with various custom components.

	Sandboxed solution	Hybrid solution	Full-trust farm solution
Declarative components	✔	✔	✔
	✔*	✔	✔
Content pages	✔	✔	✔
Application pages		✔	✔
Event receivers	✔*	✔	✔
Coded workflow activities	✔*	✔	✔
Full-trust assemblies		✔	✔
Fully coded workflows		✔	✔
Timer jobs		✔	✔
Service applications		✔	✔

Restrictions and caveats apply. These are discussed in more detail throughout Part I of this book.

Some components are subject to restrictions when they run within a sandboxed solution. Standard Visual Web Parts cannot be used in the sandbox because they require the deployment of ASCX files to the server. However, the Microsoft Visual Studio® 2010 SharePoint Power Tools provide an item template for a sandbox-compatible Visual Web Part. The sandbox-compatible Visual Web Part generates a source file from the user control and compiles this file as part of the assembly. This approach eliminates the need to deploy the ASCX file for the user control. Event receivers that run within the sandbox are limited to events that occur within the boundaries of the site collection, and they can only be registered declaratively.

Full-trust coded workflow activities can only be used within sandboxed solutions when they are consumed by a declarative workflow. You can also create sandboxed code that is invoked by a wrapper workflow activity provided by SharePoint.

Conclusion

This chapter provided an introduction to execution models in SharePoint 2010. The following models were introduced and discussed:

- **The full-trust execution model**. Assemblies are deployed to the global assembly cache and non-compiled components are deployed to the server file system. The solution runs using the same process and permissions as the SharePoint application and is available to the entire server farm.

- **The bin/CAS execution model**. Assemblies are deployed to the bin folder for the SharePoint Web application in the IIS file structure and non-compiled components are deployed to the server file system. The solution runs using the same process as the SharePoint application, but its permissions are restricted by the code access security policy specified by the Web.config file. The solution is available to all sites within the SharePoint Web application.

- **The sandbox execution model**. The solution package, including assemblies and non-compiled components, is deployed to the solutions gallery in a site collection. The solution runs using an isolated, low-privilege process. Sandboxed assemblies have access to a restricted subset of the SharePoint API and are subject to significant CAS restrictions. Access to system resources is monitored and throttled to prevent adverse effects on the wider SharePoint environment. The solution is only available within the site collection to which it is deployed and cannot access resources from outside the site collection.

- **Hybrid approaches to execution**. You can extend the functionality of sandboxed solutions by consuming various permitted full-trust components. You can develop a full-trust proxy to expose functionality to the sandbox, you can consume full-trust workflow activities from a declarative workflow deployed in a sandboxed solution, and you can use external lists within sandboxed solutions to retrieve external data through the BCS.

The chapter also described examples and typical scenarios in which each execution model might be appropriate. It identified the process accounts that load different types of custom SharePoint components, and it explained which execution models you can use with each of these components. The remaining chapters in Part I provide a closer look at the functionality, advantages, and limitations of each model.

2 Execution Models for Farm Solutions

If you've worked with Microsoft® Office® SharePoint® Server 2007 or Windows® Share-Point Services 3.0, you'll be familiar with farm solutions even if you're not familiar with the term itself. A farm solution is a collection of resources that you deploy through the server-side file system in your SharePoint environment. These resources can include Microsoft .NET Framework assemblies together with non-compiled components such as Web pages, images, and configuration files. Before the advent of the sandboxed solution gallery in SharePoint 2010, the farm solution approach was the only way you could deploy custom functionality to a SharePoint environment.

Typically, farm solutions are packaged as SharePoint solution package (WSP) files that contain assemblies, other non-compiled components, and an XML manifest file. A farm administrator uses Windows PowerShell™, the STSADM command-line tool, or the SharePoint Central Administration Web site to install solution packages to the server environment. After a solution package is installed, the farm administrator can activate the solution to a specific Web application (or multiple Web applications, if you use the full-trust model).

As described in the previous chapter, you can configure your farm solutions to use a full-trust execution model or a bin/CAS execution model. When you use the full-trust approach, the solution package deploys your assembly to the global assembly cache on each Web server. When you use the bin/CAS approach, the solution package deploys your assembly to the bin folder of a specific Web application in the Internet Information Services (IIS) file structure on each Web server. In both cases, the solution package can deploy other components such as resource files, ASCX user controls, and ASPX Web pages to the SharePoint directory structure on each Web server (commonly referred to as the "SharePoint root").

This chapter explains the technical details behind the execution models for farm solutions, and it identifies some of the key execution issues that you should consider when you work with them. The chapter focuses primarily on the full-trust execution model, because the bin/CAS model is no longer considered a recommended approach.

How Does the Full-Trust Execution Model Work?

The precise details of a how a full-trust farm solution executes will vary slightly according to the type of SharePoint component you have deployed. For example, Web Part assemblies and most event receivers are loaded by an IIS worker process (W3wp.exe), while timer jobs are loaded by the SharePoint timer job process (Owstimer.exe). However, the concepts remain broadly the same (although the timer process typically runs under an account with higher permission levels than the IIS worker process). In this case, suppose you have deployed a Web Part. A request that invokes your Web Part logic is directed to the IIS worker process that manages the Web application associated with the request. The IIS worker process loads the appropriate assembly from the global assembly cache. Because the assembly is located in the global assembly cache, and as such is not subject to code access security (CAS) policies, it has unrestricted access to the SharePoint object model and to any other APIs that are accessible from the worker process. The assembly is also able to access remote resources such as databases, Web services, and Windows Communication Foundation (WCF) services. Figure 1 shows the various components of full-trust execution.

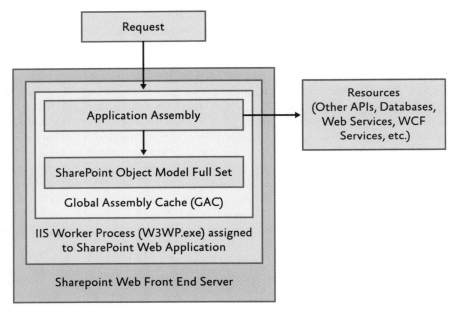

FIGURE 1
The full-trust execution model

How Does the Bin/CAS Execution Model Work?

When you deploy a farm solution using the bin/CAS execution model, the assembly is added to the bin folder in the IIS file structure for your SharePoint Web application. As a result, the assembly can be loaded only by the IIS worker process associated with that Web application (in contrast to the full-trust execution model, in which your global assembly cache-deployed assemblies can be loaded by any process). This difference precludes the use of bin/CAS solutions to deploy various SharePoint components, such as timer jobs, event receivers, service applications, and workflows, which require your assemblies to be available to other processes.

Requests that invoke your code are directed to the IIS worker process that runs the Web application associated with the request. The IIS worker process loads the appropriate assembly from the Web application's bin folder in the IIS file system. Because the assembly is located in the bin folder, it is subject to the code access security policies defined in the configuration file for the Web application. These policies define the degree to which your assembly can use the SharePoint object model as well as other APIs, databases, and services. Figure 2 shows the various components of bin/CAS execution.

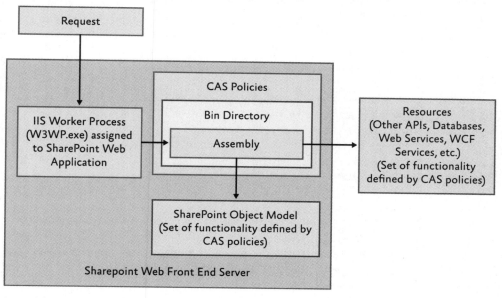

FIGURE 2
The bin/CAS execution model

What Can I Do with Farm Solutions?

Full-trust farm solutions have no limitations in terms of functionality or scope. You can deploy every type of SharePoint component with a full-trust solution, and you can make your components available to site collections across the server farm.

Bin/CAS solutions are more limited. Scope is restricted to the target Web application, and functionality is constrained by the code access security policies that are applied to the Web application. Bin/CAS solutions are also unsuitable for the deployment of timer jobs, event receivers, service applications, and workflows, as these components require assemblies to be deployed to the global assembly cache. In other words, the bin/CAS approach is only suitable for components that are loaded by the IIS worker process (W3wp.exe), such as Web Part assemblies, as only the IIS worker process has access to the bin folder. In some cases developers use a hybrid approach whereby Web Part assemblies are deployed to the bin folder and other assemblies are deployed to the global assembly cache where assemblies can be loaded by any process and the CAS policy does not apply.

What Are the Core Issues for Farm Solutions?

Each execution model creates a different set of challenges for the developer. Farm solution development creates particular issues in the areas of deployment, capabilities, stability, and security that you must consider.

DEPLOYMENT

When you create a full-trust farm solution, there are no limits to the types of resources that you can deploy. Nor are there restrictions on the locations within the server file system to which you can add these resources. However, your organization may limit or prohibit the deployment of farm solutions due to security or performance concerns. In many cases, your application may also have to undergo a formal code review before you can deploy the solution to the server environment.

CAPABILITIES

Full-trust farm solutions execute without any code access security restrictions and run using the same process identity as the code that invokes your solution. Typically, your code will run in the IIS worker process (W3wp.exe), the SharePoint Timer process (Owstimer.exe), or a service application process, depending on your execution logic. As a result, your code executes without any restrictions—in other words, your code can do whatever the SharePoint platform itself can do. In cases where security or stability are not significant issues, or where the application undergoes a high level of functional and scale testing, a farm solution is an appropriate choice. Otherwise, consider running only the components that specifically require a farm solution deployment within a farm solution. Components that can run within the sandbox environment should be deployed in a sandboxed solution.

STABILITY

Farm solutions are not subject to any monitoring or resource allocation throttling. Poorly written code in a farm solution can jeopardize the performance and stability of the server farm as a whole. To prevent these issues, you should carefully review your farm solution code to identify issues that could cause memory leaks or process timeouts. For example, developers often encounter the following pitfalls that can adversely affect performance:

- Failure to dispose of **SPSite** and **SPWeb** objects after use.
- Iterating through items in large lists instead of executing queries on the lists.
- Using **for** or **foreach** loops to aggregate data, instead of using **SPSiteDataQuery** or other recommended data aggregation methods.
- Using recursive method calls to iterate through information in every site within a site collection.
- Failure to close connections to external systems after use.
- Failure to trap timeouts when connecting to external systems.
- Overuse or improper use of session state.

This is not an exhaustive list. Instead, it simply illustrates that there are many different ways in which you can unnecessarily slow your SharePoint environment. To minimize risks to farm stability, you should review your solution code against all best practice guidance in the relevant functional areas.

SECURITY

Farm solution code runs in the same process space as SharePoint itself. These processes run using privileged accounts. Both of these factors increase the scope for harm if your code is compromised or exploited. Even if you deploy your code using the bin/CAS approach and apply restrictive code access security policies, the risk of a damaging security exploit is substantially higher than you would encounter through a sandboxed solution. You should take care to review your code for security vulnerabilities before your deploy your solution.

Conclusion

This chapter provided insight into the execution of farm solutions in a SharePoint 2010 environment. The following aspects of farm solution deployment and execution were discussed:

- **Processes and mechanisms**. Full-trust solutions operate with the permission set of the host process, whereas bin/CAS solutions are subject to the CAS policies specified by the Web.config file.
- **Capabilities**. Full-trust solutions are unrestricted in terms of functionality. You cannot use bin/CAS solutions to deploy timer jobs, event receivers, service applications, or workflows, as these components require an assembly to be deployed to the global assembly cache.

- **Core issues**. It may not be possible to deploy a farm solution to every SharePoint environment, especially if the environment is hosted or centrally managed. This is an important consideration if you are developing third-party components, since creating a farm solution will restrict the number of scenarios in which your components can be used. As farm solutions are not subject to monitoring or resource throttling, you must take care to ensure that your solutions do not jeopardize the stability or security of the wider SharePoint environment.

See It in Action: The Farm Solution Reference Implementation in the Developing Applications for SharePoint 2010 online guidance is a fully documented downloadable solution that illustrates many key aspects of farm solution design and deployment. The reference implementation uses a timer job to aggregate list data across site collection boundaries. It also illustrates other common tasks for farm solutions, such as deploying custom application pages to the Central Administration Web site and managing configuration data for timer jobs. You can deploy the reference implementation to a SharePoint 2010 test environment and explore the source code at your leisure in Microsoft Visual Studio® 2010.

For more information, see Reference Implementation: Farm Solutions at http://msdn.microsoft.com/en-us/library/ff798362.aspx.

3

Execution Models for Sandboxed Solutions

In Microsoft® SharePoint® 2010, the introduction of the sandbox execution environment enables you to deploy custom solutions to SharePoint site collections when other solution deployment options are unavailable or undesirable. Sandboxed solutions are packaged as SharePoint solution package (WSP) files that contain assemblies, other non-compiled components, and an XML manifest file. A site collection administrator, or another user with sufficient permissions, uploads the solution package to a specialized library—the solution gallery—in the root site of the site collection. Every sandboxed solution is executed in a unique application domain. Because the application domain is unique to your solution, SharePoint is able to monitor your solution for performance issues and resource use, and it can terminate your code if it exceeds the boundaries set by the IT team. The application domain runs within an isolated process, using an account with a lower set of permissions than the Web application service account, and is subject to various restrictions on functionality and scope.

This chapter explains the technical details behind the execution model for sandboxed solutions. It describes in detail what you can and cannot do in the sandbox environment, and it explains how IT professionals can manage, configure, and constrain the execution of sandboxed solutions. It also identifies some of the key execution issues that you should consider when you work with sandboxed solutions.

How Does the Sandbox Execution Model Work?

When your solution runs within the sandbox environment, requests that invoke your code are first directed to the Internet Information Services (IIS) worker process that runs the Web application associated with the request. The request is handled by the Execution Manager, a component that runs in the same application pool as the Web application.

The Execution Manager routes the request to a server that runs the SharePoint User Code Service (SPUCHostService.exe). Depending on your farm configuration, this could be a Web front-end server or it could be a dedicated application server. When the user code service receives a request, it will either start a new sandbox worker process (SPUC-WorkerProcess.exe) or route the request to an existing sandbox worker process. More specifically, the execution manager routes the request to a specific sandbox worker process if that process is already hosting an application domain for the solution in question.

If no loaded application domain is found, the execution manager will route the request to the sandbox worker process that is under the least load. The worker process then creates a new application domain and loads the solution assembly. If the worker process has reached the maximum number of application domains it is configured to host, it unloads an existing application domain before it creates a new one.

After the sandbox worker process loads the solution assembly into an application domain, it executes your code. Because the assembly runs in the context of the sandbox worker process, it has a limited set of permissions to use the SharePoint object model and it is prevented from interacting with any other APIs, services, or resources.

The code access security (CAS) policies that limit access to the SharePoint object model are described by the configuration file associated with the sandbox worker process. When your sandboxed code makes calls into the permitted subset of the SharePoint API, the sandbox worker process forwards these requests to a proxy process (SPUCWorker-ProcessProxy.exe) that executes the SharePoint object model code. A sandbox worker process and a sandbox proxy process always work as a pair.

Figure 1 shows the various components of the sandbox execution architecture.

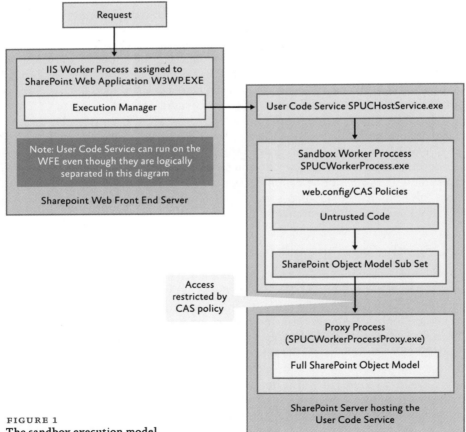

FIGURE 1
The sandbox execution model

The execution of sandboxed solutions is driven by the following three key processes:

- **User Code Service (SPUCHostService.exe)**. This is responsible for creating the sandbox worker processes that execute individual sandboxed solutions and for allocating requests to these processes. You must start this service through the SharePoint Central Administration Web site on each server that will host sandboxed solutions.

- **Sandbox Worker Process (SPUCWorkerProcess.exe)**. This is the process in which any custom code in your sandboxed solution executes. When a sandbox worker process receives a request that invokes a particular solution, it loads an application domain for that solution (unless it is already loaded). If the worker process reaches the limit on the number of application domains that it can host, it will unload one of the application domains for another solution and load the application domain required to serve the current request. The sandbox worker process monitors the resources accessed by your solution and destroys processes that take too long to execute or exceed other limits. Each sandbox worker process is monitored by the SharePoint environment against the criteria specified by the IT team.

- **Sandbox Worker Process Proxy (SPUCWorkerProcessProxy.exe)**. This provides a full-trust environment that hosts the SharePoint API. This enables sandboxed solutions to make calls into the subset of the SharePoint object model that is accessible to sandboxed solutions. These calls are actually executed in the proxy process.

Note: *These executable files can be found in the folder 14\Usercode on each SharePoint server.*

What Can I Do with Sandboxed Solutions?

When you develop solutions that target the sandbox execution model, you need to understand the constraints that apply to the sandbox environment. This section reviews some common SharePoint development scenarios for their compatibility with the sandbox execution model. The following table shows several common development scenarios together with the execution models that are available to you in each case. This is not an exhaustive list, but it serves to give you a feel for the types of scenarios that you can implement with a sandboxed solution.

Scenario	Sandbox	Hybrid	Full trust
Create a Web Part that aggregates data from multiple SharePoint lists within the same site collection. *	✔	✔	✔
Create a Web Part that aggregates data from multiple SharePoint lists from different site collections within the same SharePoint farm.		✔	✔
Create a Web Part that aggregates data from multiple SharePoint lists from different site collections from different SharePoint farms.		✔	✔
Create a Web Part that displays data from an external list.		✔	✔
Create a Web Part that interacts with a Web service or a Windows® Communication Foundation (WCF) service.		✔	✔
Create a workflow in SharePoint designer.	✔	✔	✔
Create a sandbox workflow action (a method call).	✔		
Create a full-trust workflow activity.		✔	✔
Create a workflow in SharePoint designer that uses a full-trust custom coded workflow activity.		✔	✔
Create a fully coded workflow.			✔
Deploy a new list definition.	✔	✔	✔
Deploy a new list definition with list item event receivers.	✔	✔	✔
Deploy a list definition with list event receivers.	✔	✔	✔
Deploy a site definition.	✔	✔	✔
Create a content type.	✔	✔	✔
Create an external content type.**			✔
Create a new ribbon element.	✔	✔	✔
Create a new **Site Actions** menu item.	✔	✔	✔
Create an instance of a SharePoint list.	✔	✔	✔
Programmatically create a SharePoint subsite.	✔	✔	✔
Bind a content type to the home page of a SharePoint subsite.		✔	✔
Deploy a new application page.			✔
Create a timer job.			✔
Create a service application.			✔

*The Visual Web Part supplied with Microsoft Visual Studio® 2010 will not run in the sandbox environment, although a Sandboxed Visual Web Part template is now available. See text for further details.

**External content types are typically created by using the External Content Type Designer in SharePoint Designer 2010. However, they must be deployed and configured using a farm solution or through the Central Administration Web site.

The standard Visual Web Part template is not supported in the sandbox environment. The reason for this is that Visual Web Parts effectively host an ASCX user control within the Web Part control. The ASCX file is deployed to the _controltemplates virtual directory in the physical file system on each Web front-end server. The sandbox environment does not allow you to deploy files to the server file system, so you cannot use a sandboxed solution to deploy a Visual Web Part based on the Visual Studio 2010 Visual Web Part project template. However, a Visual Studio Power Tool is available that addresses this issue. A Power Tool is a plug in for Visual Studio. The tool will generate and compile code representing the user control (ASCX) as part of the assembly. This avoids the file deployment issue. The further information section at the end of this chapter provides more information on how to obtain the Visual Studio 2010 SharePoint Power Tools.

To determine whether your application code is running in the sandbox process, check whether the application domain name has the text "Sandbox" contained within it. You can use the following code to accomplish this:

```C#
if(System.AppDomain.CurrentDomain.FriendlyName.Contains("Sandbox"))
{
    // Your code is running in the sandbox.
}
```

CODE ACCESS SECURITY RESTRICTIONS

The execution of sandboxed solutions is governed by a restrictive code access security policy. This limits sandboxed solutions to the use of a specific subset of the **Microsoft. SharePoint** namespace. The code access security policy also prevents sandboxed solution code from accessing external resources or systems. The Web.config file in the 14\Usercode folder specifies the CAS policies that apply to sandboxed solutions as a trust level. In the SharePoint 2010 SDK, each class-level entry indicates whether the class is available in the sandbox. The product documentation also includes a complete list of the namespaces and classes that are available in the sandbox environment. The further information section at the end of this chapter includes links to this documentation and other useful reference material.

There are various nuances that apply to these API restrictions:

- Within the sandbox, you can use an assembly that includes blocked types and methods, as long as those blocked types and methods are not used within the sandbox environment.
- Any methods that are called from the sandbox must not include any blocked types or methods, even if those blocked types or methods are not actually invoked when the method is called from the sandbox environment.

If you attempt to use a SharePoint method that is not permitted in the sandbox environment, the method call will throw a **MissingMethod** exception at run time. This occurs for all methods in the blocked namespaces. If you want to catch these errors before you deploy your solutions, the Visual Studio 2010 SharePoint Power Tools include a Sandbox

Compilation extension that generates build errors when the sandbox solution project uses types that are not permitted.

Permission Restrictions

In addition to code access security policy restrictions, the sandbox worker process uses an account with a limited permission set. Using a low-privileged account further limits the amount of harm that a compromised sandboxed solution can do within the production environment. This further restricts the actions that you can perform from sandboxed code.

Because sandboxed code is executed in a partial-trust environment, any assembly that contains code that will be called from the sandbox must include the attribute **Allow PartiallyTrustedCallersAttribute**.

Retrieving User Identity

Within your sandboxed solutions, you can programmatically retrieve the **SPUser** object associated with the current request. However, you cannot access the underlying authentication token for the current user. In most cases, this is not a problem because the restrictions of the sandbox environment generally prevent you from performing operations in which the underlying identity is required, such as impersonating a user in order to access an external system.

Using Event Receivers

You can create event receiver classes within sandboxed solutions for events that fire on list items, lists, and individual sites—in other words, events that fire within the boundaries of a site collection. Specifically, you can only create event receivers that derive from the following classes:

- **SPItemEventReceiver**
- **SPListEventReceiver**
- **SPWebEventReceiver**

You cannot use the object model to register event receivers within sandboxed solutions. For example, you cannot use a feature receiver class to register an event receiver on feature activation. However, you can register event receivers declaratively in your feature elements file.

Accessing External Data

Broadly speaking, there are two main approaches that you can use to access external data in SharePoint 2010 solutions. You can use:

- **Business Data Connectivity Object Model** (BDC OM). Use this to work with external content types and external lists.
- **SharePoint Object Model**. Use this, namely the **SPList** API, to work with external lists.

You can use both the BDC OM and the **SPList** API to access data from external lists. In fact, the **SPList** API actually uses the BDC OM to perform CRUD (Create, Read, Update, and Delete) operations on external list data. However, the **SPList** API is available in the sandbox environment, whereas the BDC OM is not.

The **SPList** API performs well when the external list contains simple field types and when the built-in BDC formatter is able to "flatten" (serialize) more complex types. However, there are certain scenarios in which the **SPList** API will not work; for example, it will not work when you need to retrieve custom data types or binary large objects (BLOBs), when a list has bi-directional associations, or when the back-end system uses non-integer identifier fields. In these cases, you must use the BDC OM. The BDC OM is not directly available within the sandbox environment; instead, you need to create a full-trust solution or a hybrid solution that uses a full-trust proxy to access the BDC APIs. For more information about this approach, see Chapter Four, "Hybrid Approaches to Execution."

The BDC OM is present in SharePoint Foundation 2010, SharePoint Server 2010, and Office 2010.

USING WORKFLOWS

You can use sandboxed solutions to deploy declarative workflows that were created in SharePoint Designer. These declarative workflows are stored in the content database. Like with any declarative logic, declarative workflows execute with full trust, regardless of whether you define them in a sandboxed solution or a farm solution. However, you cannot deploy coded workflows to the sandbox environment.

As you probably already know, you can define custom-coded workflow activities that run in the full-trust execution environment. You can also create sandboxed code that is invoked by a workflow action.

> *Workflow activities and workflow actions are related concepts. A workflow activity is any class that derives from* **System.Workflow.ComponentModel.Activity**. *A workflow action is a SharePoint Designer concept that describes any activity or group of activities that can be composed into a human-readable sentence in the SharePoint workflow engine. A workflow action is represented by an* **Action** *element in a feature manifest file or an* **.actions** *file, as you will see in the code examples that follow.*
>
> *Technically, you cannot create a workflow activity that runs in the sandbox. However, you can create a sandboxed method that is packaged as a workflow action. In the case of sandboxed workflow logic, the workflow activity is the SharePoint-provided wrapper class that calls your sandboxed code. For the sake of readability and simplicity, this topic refers to sandboxed code that is invoked by a workflow action as a sandboxed workflow action.*

To create a sandboxed workflow action, you must create a class with a method that accepts an **SPUserCodeWorkflowContext** as the first parameter. You can also have additional parameters, which will be defined in the Elements.xml file for the solution. For example, a sandboxed workflow action that copies a document library between sites might have the following method signature:

C#
```csharp
public Hashtable CopyLibraryAction(SPUserCodeWorkflowContext context, string
libraryName, string targetSiteUrl)
{
    // This is the logic to copy a library to a target site.
}
```

The action is then defined in the Elements.xml file, which tells SharePoint about the action and the implementing class. It also enables SharePoint Designer to use the activity in a declarative workflow for the site collection.

XML
```xml
<Elements xmlns="http://schemas.microsoft.com/sharepoint/">
  <WorkflowActions>
    <Action Name="Copy Library"
            SandboxedFunction="true"
            Assembly="..."
            ClassName="..."
            FunctionName="CopyLibraryAction"
            AppliesTo="list"
            UsesCurrentItem="true"
            Category="patterns & practices Sandbox">
      <RuleDesigner Sentence="Copy all items from library %1 to site %2">
        <FieldBind Field="libraryName" Text="Library Name" Id="1"
                   DesignerType="TextBox" />
        <FieldBind Field="targetSiteUrl" Text="Target Site" Id="2"
                   DesignerType="TextBox" />
      </RuleDesigner>
      <Parameters>
        <Parameter Name="__Context"
                   Type="Microsoft.SharePoint.WorkflowActions.WorkflowContext,
                   Microsoft.SharePoint.WorkflowActions"
                   Direction="In" DesignerType="Hide" />
        <Parameter Name="libraryName"
                   Type="System.String, mscorlib"
                   Direction="In" DesignerType="TextBox"
                   Description="The library to copy" />
        <Parameter Name="targetSiteUrl"
                   Type="System.String, mscorlib" Direction="In"
                   DesignerType="TextBox"
                   Description="The URL of the target site" />
      </Parameters>
    </Action>
  </WorkflowActions>
</Elements>
```

The workflow execution environment calls the method specified in the **Action** element to launch your sandboxed workflow action.

Suppose that you have deployed a declarative workflow and a sandboxed workflow action to the sandbox environment. SharePoint executes the declarative workflow with full trust, because all the actual run-time code invoked by the workflow is deployed with full trust; therefore, it is considered safe. SharePoint defines a *sandboxed activity wrapper* that executes with full trust and provides a wrapper for all sandboxed actions. The sandbox activity wrapper makes the method call into your sandboxed method. The method defined in the sandboxed solution—**CopyLibraryAction** in the previous example—actually executes within a sandbox worker process. This is illustrated in Figure 2. Details of the user code service processes have been omitted for brevity.

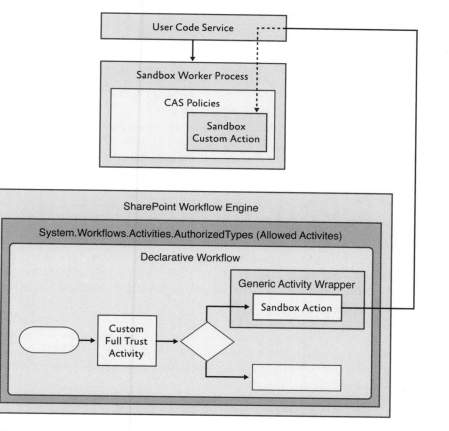

FIGURE 2
Using a sandboxed workflow action from a declarative workflow

When you create the declarative workflow, SharePoint Designer hides the relationship between the sandbox activity wrapper and the sandboxed action implementation. Share-Point Designer also enables you to define parameters and field bindings as inputs to the custom sandbox action.

Sandboxed workflow actions offer advantages in many scenarios, particularly because you can deploy these actions as sandboxed solutions without access to the server environment. However, there are limitations on the tasks that a sandboxed workflow action can perform. Declarative workflows can also use certain approved full-trust workflow activities. For information about how to add custom full-trust workflow activities that can be consumed by a declarative workflow, see Chapter 4, "Hybrid Approaches to Execution."

How Do I Manage Sandboxed Solutions?

Farm administrators can customize many aspects of how sandboxed solutions are executed, validated, and monitored. As a solution architect or a senior developer, it is important to have an awareness of these features because they can impact how your solutions behave and perform.

UNDERSTANDING OPERATIONAL MODES

The IT team can configure the SharePoint farm to execute sandboxed solutions in one of two operational modes. The operational mode determines where the sandbox worker process that executes each sandboxed solution actually resides:

- When the farm is configured in local mode, each sandboxed solution executes on the Web front-end server that receives the request.
- When the farm is configured in remote mode, sandboxed solutions can execute on servers other than the server that receives the request.

When you configure the farm to run sandboxed solutions in remote mode, you can use dedicated application servers to run sandboxed solutions. Alternatively, the server farm can use load balancing to distribute the execution of sandboxed solutions across Web front-end servers. You must start the user code service on each Web front-end server that will run sandboxed solutions.

Figures 3 and 4 illustrate the difference between these approaches. When your farm is configured in local mode (Figure 3), sandboxed solution code executes on the Web front-end server that receives the request. The Web front-end server (WFE in the figures) will spin up a new sandbox worker process and load the solution, unless a process already exists for that solution's unique application domain.

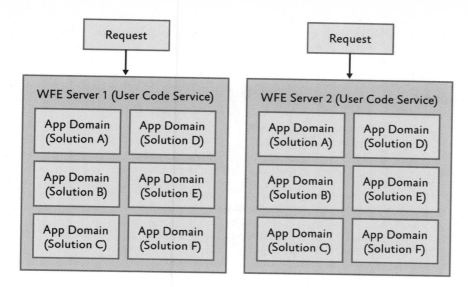

FIGURE 3
Sandbox execution in local mode

When your farm is configured in remote mode with dedicated sandbox servers (Figure 4), the Web front-end server that receives the request will first establish whether any of the sandbox servers are already running a sandbox worker process that contains an application domain for the required solution. If there is an appropriate application domain available, the Web front-end server will route the request to that sandbox server. This is known as solution affinity. If the process is not running on any of the sandbox servers, the Web front-end server will route the request to the sandbox server currently experiencing the least load. This sandbox server will spin up a sandbox worker process and load the solution.

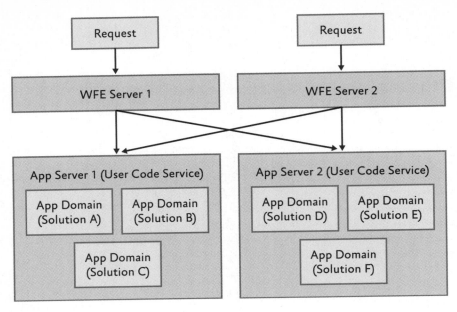

FIGURE 4
Sandbox execution in remote mode with dedicated sandbox servers

When your farm is configured in remote mode, and the user code service is running on more than one Web front-end server (see Figure 5), the Web front-end servers will distribute requests that invoke sandboxed solutions according to server load. If one of the Web front-end servers is already running a sandbox worker process that has loaded the required solution into an application domain, the request is routed to that server. If the solution is not loaded on any of the Web front-end servers, the request is routed to the Web front-end server currently experiencing the least load. This server will spin up a new application domain in the sandbox worker process and load the solution.

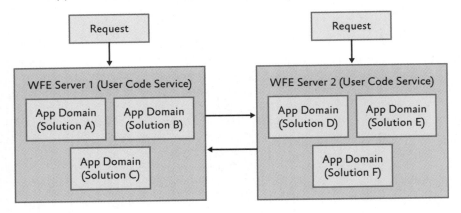

FIGURE 5
Remote mode with Web front-end servers hosting the user code service

The IT team should use capacity planning to select the best operational mode for a particular SharePoint environment. In general, it is recommended you use remote mode. However, if you expect a small number of sandboxed solutions, and response latency is a major concern, local mode may be preferable. This is because there is a minor latency cost in cases where the request is received on one server and the sandbox processes run on a different server.

As your server farm grows larger, or the expected number of sandboxed solutions increases, remote mode can become increasingly advantageous. When more than one server runs the user code service, load balancing and solution affinity mean that each server needs to host only a subset of the deployed sandboxed solutions. This is important because every server that runs the user code service can host only a finite number of sandbox worker processes and application domains. When a server hits these limits, what happens when it receives a request for a sandboxed solution that is not already loaded? To serve the request, it must recycle an existing application domain to be able to load the new application domain. This results in requests queuing for a free application domain and increased recycling of application domains. In addition, it becomes increasingly unlikely that there will be an already loaded ("warm") application domain for particular solutions. These factors can substantially impact server performance and response times. Using remote mode to distribute application domains across multiple servers clearly mitigates these issues.

In addition to simply setting the operational mode to local or remote, the IT team can make various configuration changes that will impact on the performance issues described here. For example, farm administrators can configure the number of sandbox worker processes and application domains that can be hosted on each server that runs the user code service. They can also constrain the number of connections allowed per process. Finally, the user code service includes a flag named **AlwaysRecycleAppDomains**. By default, this is set to **false**. When it is set to **true**, the user code service recycles application domains after every request. This reduces the response time of the server as a "warm" application domain is never available, but it can reduce the risk of data crossover in poorly designed sandboxed solutions.

Deploying and Upgrading Solutions

Sandboxed solutions are deployed as SharePoint solution package (WSP) files to the solutions gallery, a specialized library in the root site of each site collection. You can find the solutions gallery at the site-relative URL _catalog/solutions. The site collection administrator can activate and deactivate the solutions within the gallery.

If you need to deploy a sandboxed solution to multiple site collections, you must upload it to each site collection gallery separately. Alternatively, you could create a central repository for sandboxed solutions and register a custom solution provider with the solution galleries on each site collection. Site collection administrators can then choose which centrally-available solutions they want to activate on their individual site collection. The custom provider approach essentially allows you to upload and manage a solution in a single location while making it available to multiple site collections.

You can upgrade sandboxed solution packages through the user interface. If you upload a solution package with a new file name but the same solution ID as an existing solution, SharePoint will prompt you to upgrade the existing solution. Alternatively, you can use the **Update-SPUserSolution** command in Windows® PowerShell™ to upgrade your solutions. However, this requires access to the server environment, which is not necessarily available to sandboxed solution developers or site collection administrators.

Understanding Solution Monitoring

SharePoint 2010 monitors the performance and resource use of your sandboxed solutions through a system of *resource points*. Farm administrators can set limits on the number of resource points that a site collection containing sandboxed solutions may consume daily. Because these limits are set on a per-site collection basis, the available resources are effectively shared between every sandboxed solution in the site collection. Site collection administrators can monitor the resource points used by individual solutions from the site collection solution gallery. If the solutions in a site collection exceed the daily resource point allocation for that site collection, SharePoint will take every sandboxed solution in the site collection offline for the rest of the day.

Resource points are calculated according to 14 different measurements known as *resource measures*, including CPU execution time, memory consumption, and unhandled exceptions. Each resource measure defines a property named **Resources per Point**. This is the quantity of that particular resource that constitutes an individual resource point. For example, suppose you deploy a solution named Contoso Project Management (CPM) to the sandbox environment. The following table shows a hypothetical example of the resources it consumes across two sample resource measures.

Resource measure	Resources per point	Used by CPM solution in one day	Points consumed
SharePointDatabaseQueryCount	20 queries	300 queries	15
SharePointDatabaseQueryTime	120 seconds cumulative	240 seconds cumulative	2

SharePoint counts the most expensive resource measure toward the total for the solution, instead of the sum of all measures. In this example, because the number of database queries represents the highest resource point usage, the Contoso Project Management solution consumes 15 resource points from the total allocated to the site collection.

To prevent rogue sandboxed solutions from causing instability, SharePoint also monitors individual sandboxed solutions per request. Each of the 14 resource measures includes an **AbsoluteLimit** property that defines a hard limit of the resources that a sandboxed solution can consume in a single request. If an absolute limit is exceeded, SharePoint terminates the request by stopping and restarting the Sandbox worker process. For example, the CPU execution time resource measure has a default absolute limit of 60 seconds. If a single request takes more than 60 seconds to execute, the user code service will stop and restart the sandbox worker process that is executing the request. Individual solutions will not be disabled for violating an absolute limit, although the utilization will count toward the resource points for the site collection; therefore, they will be expensive.

In addition, the user code service includes a property named **WorkerProcess ExecutionTimeout** with a default value of 30 seconds. If this time limit is exceeded during a single request, the user code service will recycle the application domain in question and the request will return an error. These two settings are measured independently by different parts of the system, but they effectively measure the same thing. In general, the **WorkerProcessExecutionTimeout** is preferred over the absolute limit because it will only recycle the application pool instead of the entire process. Exceeding an absolute limit will result in a worker process recycle. When a worker process is recycled, any requests running within the process will fail. In production installations, it is likely that multiple solutions will be running within multiple application domains within one process, so a single rogue solution can disrupt users of more benign solutions.

Farm administrators can use Windows PowerShell to change the **Resources Per Point** for a **Resource Measure**. However, the default measurement weightings were carefully chosen, and understanding the impact of adjustments to these weightings can be complex. You should carefully consider the impact of changing these weightings before you make any modifications.

You can also use Windows PowerShell to investigate how many resource points are being used by specific individual solutions. Resource point consumption depends on the capacity of your server farm and on how you configure measurement weightings, so it is hard to provide an absolute recommendation on where to cap resource point allocations for sandboxed solutions. Instead, you should determine limits by testing against a representative production environment.

On a final note, farm administrators can use the Central Administration Web site to block poorly performing or otherwise undesirable sandboxed solutions. This ensures that the solution in question cannot be deployed to any site collection in the farm.

UNDERSTANDING SOLUTION VALIDATION

In SharePoint 2010, farm administrators can install *solution validators* to provide additional verification of sandboxed solutions. SharePoint 2010 runs these solution validators when you attempt to activate a sandboxed solution package. Each solution validator can run various validation checks on the solution package and can block activation if your solution fails any of these checks.

By default, SharePoint 2010 includes a single default solution validator that simply sets the **Valid** property of each solution to **true**. To create your own custom solution validator, you must create a class that inherits from the **SPSolutionValidator** abstract class. This class includes two key methods:

- **ValidateSolution**. This method validates the solution package and its contents. It has access to the name of the solution package and any files that the package contains.

- **ValidateAssembly**. This method validates each assembly in the solution package.

Both methods enable you to set an error message, together with an error URL to which the user should be directed if validation fails.

To register a solution validator with the SharePoint farm, you can use a feature receiver to add your class to the **SolutionValidators** collection in the local **SPUserCode-Service** object.

What Are the Core Issues for Sandboxed Solutions?

Sandboxed solutions introduce a fresh set of challenges for SharePoint developers. When you develop a sandboxed solution, you should pay particular attention to issues and limitations in the areas of scope and capabilities, authentication, performance, logging, configuration management, and deployment.

SCOPE AND CAPABILITIES

Sandboxed solutions can only interact with resources within the site collection in which they reside. If your application must access data in multiple site collections, you can rule out a sandboxed solution at an early stage in the design process. Similarly, the restricted capabilities of the sandbox environment may prohibit the use of a sandboxed solution.

SECURITY (AUTHENTICATION)

Sandboxed solutions do not maintain the full identity of the user originating the request, and they cannot impersonate a different user account or provide credentials to authenticate to other systems. The **SPUser** object is maintained, but the related security tokens are not. With this in mind, you should consider whether a sandboxed solution is capable of accessing the data or resources that your application requires.

In particular, the constraints on authentication prevent you from executing your code with elevated permissions. In farm solutions, developers will often use the **SPSecurity. RunWithElevatedPrivileges** method to execute a method with full control privileges, even if the user has a lesser set of permissions. However, you should consider carefully whether elevated permissions are really necessary before you reject a sandboxed approach altogether. Although there are scenarios in which you need to elevate permissions, there are also many cases where proper management of user groups and permission sets within the SharePoint site allow your logic to execute from the sandbox environment.

PERFORMANCE (THROUGHPUT)

If a sandbox worker process runs for more than 30 seconds, the user code service will terminate the process. If you need to use long-running processes to deliver your functionality, a sandboxed solution is unlikely to be the best choice. In these circumstances, you should probably be using an asynchronous execution mechanism instead. For example, use a timer job, a workflow, or a service application to execute your logic as a background task within a farm solution.

Executing code within the sandbox environment also incurs a small amount of performance overhead. This is likely to have a noticeable impact only in high-volume applications, such as in Internet-facing portal environments. In these cases, you may want to consider deploying your code within a farm solution.

Logging

Logging functionality is unavailable within the sandbox environment. Sandboxed solutions cannot write entries to the Windows Event log or the Unified Logging Service (ULS) trace log, nor can they create or retrieve diagnostic areas or categories. This should not come as too much of a surprise—writing to the Windows Event log has always required a relatively permissive code access security policy, and creating diagnostic areas requires access to the Windows registry.

The need to expose logging functionality to sandboxed solutions is a good example of a scenario in which you might consider creating a full-trust proxy. For example, the logger component in the patterns & practices SharePoint Guidance Library includes a full-trust proxy to enable developers of sandboxed solutions to use the full range of logging features in SharePoint 2010.

Configuration Settings

Your ability to read and write configuration settings is somewhat restricted in the sandbox environment. The following limitations apply:

- You cannot read configuration settings from or write configuration settings to the Web.config file.
- You can store and retrieve settings in the **SPWeb.AllProperties** hash table, but you cannot use property bags at any level of the SharePoint hierarchy.
- You cannot read or write settings to the hierarchical object store, because you do not have access to an **SPWebApplication** object or an **SPFarm** object.
- You can read or write settings to a SharePoint list within the same site collection as your sandboxed solution.

Deployment

Sandboxed solutions are deployed and activated to a single site collection. If you need to deploy a solution to multiple site collections, the sandbox approach can be less convenient. You can either manually distribute solution packages to individual site collection administrators, or you can implement a custom centralized solutions gallery to make solutions available to individual site collection administrators.

One of the key restrictions of sandboxed solution deployment is that you are not permitted to deploy any files to the server file system. To work around this issue, use a **Module** element to deploy your files to the content database. In each **File** child element, you should specify a **Type** attribute value of **GhostableInLibrary** if the file will be stored in a document library. If your file will not be stored in a document library—for instance, if you are adding custom forms to a regular SharePoint list—you should specify a **Type** attribute value of **Ghostable**.

For example, you cannot deploy JavaScript files or modal dialog Web pages to the server file system. Instead, you might choose to deploy Web pages to the Pages document library and scripts to a subfolder within the Master Page Gallery. By deploying JavaScript files to the Master Page Gallery, you ensure that all users, even anonymous users, have the permissions required to access the file at run time. This approach is especially useful in Internet-facing deployments where anonymous users have read access to the site.

Understanding the Ghostable and GhostableInLibrary Attribute Values

When you add a **File** element to a feature module, you can specify a **Type** attribute value of **Ghostable** or **GhostableInLibrary**. For example, the following feature manifest deploys a .webpart file to a site collection Web Part gallery:

```XML
<Elements xmlns="http://schemas.microsoft.com/sharepoint/" >
  <Module Name="AggregateView" List="113" Url="_catalogs/wp">
    <File Path="AggregateView\Sandbox-AggregateView.webpart"
          Url="Sandbox-AggregateView.webpart"
          Type="GhostableInLibrary">
      <Property Name="Group" Value="P&amp;P SPG V3" />
    </File>
  </Module>
</Elements>
```

The **Type** attribute tells the SharePoint environment how to handle the file. In a farm solution, the attribute values are interpreted as follows:

Ghostable: The file is stored in the server file system. The content database simply includes a link to the file, thereby making it available through SharePoint's virtual file system, but IIS serves the file from the server file system. If a user customizes (unghosts) the file, the modified copy of the file is stored in the content database. When the user requests the modified file, SharePoint serves the file from the content database.

GhostableInLibrary: The file is stored in the server file system and linked to from a document library in the virtual file system. IIS serves the file from the server file system. Just like the **Ghostable** attribute, if a user customizes (unghosts) the file, the modified copy of the file is stored in the content database. When the user requests the modified file, SharePoint serves the file from the content database.

Not specified (unghostable): The file is deployed to the content database in its entirety. When the user requests the file, it is always served from the content database.

In other words, in a farm solution, ghosted files are served from the file system, whereas unghosted and unghostable files are served from the content database.

Unfortunately, these definitions become somewhat clouded when you're deploying files to the sandbox. You already know that you can't use a sandboxed solution to deploy any files to the server file system. As such, you might think that the **Type** attribute should be omitted (implicitly set to unghostable. However, this is not the case because SharePoint always deploys files to the content database when in the sandbox. When you use a sandboxed solution to deploy files, you should continue to use a **Type** attribute value of **GhostableInLibrary** if you're deploying to a document library, or **Ghostable** if you're deploying to the virtual file system. Although the file is never actually deployed to the server file system, SharePoint will ensure that it is made available from the content database.

Conclusion

This chapter provided an insight into the execution of sandboxed solutions in a SharePoint 2010 environment. The following aspects of sandboxed solution deployment and execution were discussed:

- **Processes and mechanisms**. Sandboxed solutions are executed in an isolated application domain by a dedicated sandbox worker process. The sandbox worker process works in conjunction with a sandbox worker proxy process, which runs with full trust. The sandbox worker proxy process enables the sandboxed solution to access any resources that are permitted by the sandbox environment's CAS policy.

- **Capabilities**. The sandbox execution environment is subject to many restrictions to ensure that solutions do not jeopardize the performance, stability, or security of the server farm as a whole. It is important to understand the nuances of these restrictions in order to develop effective sandboxed solutions.

- **Management**. Farm administrators can configure many aspects of how sandboxed solutions are monitored and executed. A server farm can execute sandboxed solutions in local mode, in which each Web front-end server hosts an application domain for every sandboxed solution, or in remote mode, in which application domains are distributed across Web front-end servers or application servers. The resource consumption of sandboxed solutions is monitored by 14 different resource measures, and farm administrators can configure how many resource points the solutions in particular site collections are permitted to use. You can also create custom solution validators that verify whether new sandboxed solutions meet arbitrary criteria before they are allowed to run.

- **Core issues**. Sandboxed solutions are limited in scope to the site collection to which they are deployed. The capabilities of sandboxed solutions are restricted both by the limited permissions of the sandbox worker process and by the CAS policy that applies to the sandbox execution environment. You cannot impersonate user accounts, authenticate to external systems, or execute code with elevated privileges within a sandboxed solution. Sandbox worker processes are terminated if they run for more than 30 seconds, and as such sandboxed solutions are not suitable for long-running processes. Sandboxed solutions cannot deploy any files to the server file system.

See It in Action: The Sandbox Reference Implementation in the Developing Applications for SharePoint 2010 online guidance is a fully documented, download-able solution that illustrates how you can create a reasonably complex SharePoint application that runs in the sandbox environment. The reference implementation is based around a list aggregation scenario. However, it also illustrates many other aspects of sandboxed solution design and development, such as effective use of feature partitioning, proper use of query classes, and the use of various design patterns for robust, testable Web Parts. You can deploy the reference implementa-tion to a SharePoint 2010 test environment and explore the source code at your leisure in Visual Studio 2010.

For more information, see Reference Implementation: The Sandbox Execution Model at http://msdn.microsoft.com/en-us/library/ff798341.aspx.

FURTHER INFORMATION

The following resources should prove helpful to you. You can find them in the book's bibliography online at http://msdn.microsoft.com/gg213840.aspx along with more links.

- "Visual Studio 2010 SharePoint Power Tools"
- "Sandboxed Solutions Architecture"
- "Namespaces and Types in Sandboxed Solutions"
- "Using the SharePoint List Object Model and the SharePoint Client Object Model with External Lists"
- "Business Connectivity Services Object Model Reference"
- "Developing, Deploying, and Monitoring Sandboxed Solutions in SharePoint 2010"
- "Performance and capacity management (SharePoint Server 2010)"

4   Hybrid Approaches to Execution

What is a hybrid approach to execution? When describing execution models, the term *hybrid approach* describes applications that run in the sandbox, yet can call out to full-trust code through various mechanisms. In other words, hybrid approaches combine components that execute in the sandbox environment with components that run with full trust and are deployed with multiple solutions. Essentially, you can think of a hybrid approach as two (or more) distinct, loosely coupled components. The sandboxed component is deployed in a Microsoft® SharePoint® solution package (WSP) to a site collection solutions gallery, and the full-trust component is deployed in a WSP to the server farm. These components are typically developed in isolation, often at different times, and a single full-trust component can be consumed by multiple sandboxed applications. In many environments, the full-trust components are built or validated by the central IT team in order to make them available to multiple sandboxed solutions.

Because a hybrid approach involves creating a sandboxed solution and a full-trust solution, it is important to fully understand both the sandbox execution model and the full-trust execution model before you start to work with hybrid approaches. To recap, there are three different types of full-trust components that you can consume from within a sandboxed solution:

- **Full-trust proxies**. You can implement your full-trust functionality in classes that derive from the **SPProxyOperation** abstract class and deploy the assembly to the global assembly cache. These classes expose a full-trust proxy that you can call from within the sandbox environment.

- **External content types**. You can use an external content type (ECT) to retrieve data from line-of-business (LOB) applications and other external sources through Business Connectivity Services (BCS). External content types must be deployed as full-trust solutions. However, you can create external lists from within the sandbox environment that use these external content types to retrieve data.

- **Custom workflow activities**. You can create custom, code-based workflow activities and deploy these activities as full-trust assemblies to the global assembly cache. You can then consume these activities in declarative workflows from within the sandbox environment.

This chapter explains the technical details behind each of these hybrid execution models. It explains in detail how you can use each model, and it identifies some of the key execution issues that you should consider when you work with hybrid solutions.

How Do Hybrid Execution Models Work?

When you use a hybrid approach to solution deployment, the execution process varies, according to the type of full-trust component you use.

Note: *The Developing Applications for SharePoint 2010 online guidance includes downloadable reference implementations that illustrate how to use each of the approaches that follow. More information is provided at the end of the chapter.*

Hybrid Execution with a Full-Trust Proxy

When you use a full-trust proxy from the sandbox environment, requests follow the normal execution path of sandboxed solutions. The code access security (CAS) policy for the sandbox environment allows sandboxed code to make calls to full-trust proxy assemblies, providing that the proxy assembly is registered with the server farm. You can programmatically register a proxy assembly from a feature receiver or by using Windows® PowerShell™.

Your sandboxed code must use the **SPProxyOperationsArgs** class to structure the arguments that you want to pass to the full-trust proxy. When you call the **SPUtility. ExecuteRegisteredProxyOperation** method, the sandbox worker process invokes the full-trust proxy and passes in your arguments. The proxy code executes with full trust in a proxy process. The full-trust proxy then passes any return arguments back to the sandboxed solution, and normal execution within the sandbox environment resumes.

Figure 1 shows the key components of hybrid execution with a full-trust proxy.

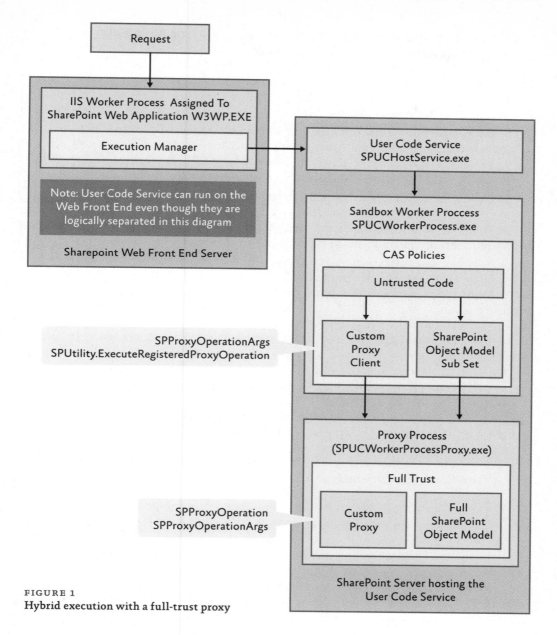

FIGURE 1
Hybrid execution with a full-trust proxy

The following describes the three key code components behind full-trust proxies:

- **SPProxyOperation**. This class provides an abstract base class for full-trust proxies. The class includes a method named **Execute**, within which you can define your full-trust functionality. Your full-trust proxy classes must be deployed to the global assembly cache and registered with the SharePoint server farm, either programmatically or by using Windows PowerShell.

- **SPProxyOperationArgs**. This class provides an abstract base class for the parameter that you pass to the full-trust proxy. To pass arguments to the full-trust proxy, you must create a serializable class that derives from **SPProxyOperationArgs**. Add properties within this class to get and set your arguments.

- **SPUtility.ExecuteRegisteredProxyOperation**. This static method enables you to invoke the full-trust proxy from your sandboxed code. This method requires a string assembly name, a string type name, and an **SPProxyOperationArgs** object. The method returns an argument of type **Object** to the caller.

There are a few key points you need to be aware of when you create a full-trust proxy. First, any types you include in the proxy arguments class must be marked as serializable. Similarly, the type returned by the proxy operation must be marked as serializable. This is because arguments and return values are serialized when they are passed between processes. Second, both the proxy operation class and the proxy argument class must be deployed to the global assembly cache. You cannot pass any types defined in the sandboxed code into the proxy, because the proxy will not have access to load the sandboxed assembly; therefore, it will not be able to load the passed-in type.

The SharePoint context (**SPContext**) is not available within the proxy operation class. If you require contextual information in the proxy operation class, you will need to pass the information required to recreate the context to the proxy. For example, if you need to access a site collection (SPSite) within the proxy, you should pass the site ID as a property on the proxy arguments passed into the proxy operation. The proxy can then recreate the site collection using the site ID, and you can access the **SPUser** instance through **site.RootWeb.CurrentUser**.

Hybrid Execution with External Content Types

When you want to use external content types with sandboxed solutions, deployment constraints alone mean you must use a hybrid approach. External content types must be defined in a farm-scoped feature; therefore, they cannot be deployed as part of a sandboxed solution. You do not need to deploy any fully trusted code to the server. Instead, you can create external content types from the External Content Type Designer in SharePoint Designer 2010 or from the Business Connectivity Services Model Designer in Microsoft Visual Studio® 2010. After the external content types are in place, you can define an external list from within your sandboxed solution to access the external data.

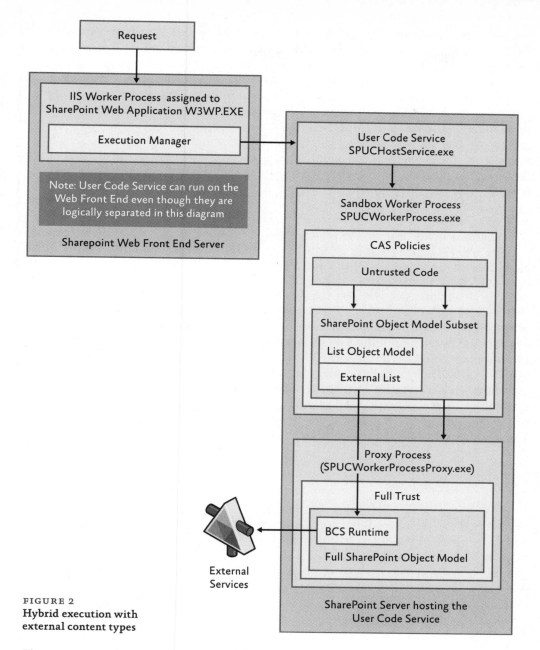

FIGURE 2
**Hybrid execution with
external content types**

The only way you can access external data from custom code in a sandboxed solution is through an external list, by using the **SPList** object model. You cannot use the BCS runtime APIs directly in sandboxed code (see Figure 2).

There are special considerations for securing services for access from the sandbox. When you access external data from the sandbox, it is important to understand how credentials must be configured and used. When code in the sandbox requests access to external data through the external list, the external list implementation calls the BCS runtime. Because this code is part of the internal SharePoint implementation, it will execute within the user code proxy service. For security reasons, SharePoint removes the authentication tokens for the user from the context when it enters the sandbox worker process. As a result, the Windows identity associated with the user is not available in either the sandbox worker process or the sandbox proxy process. Because a Windows identity is not available, the managed account for the sandbox proxy process must be used as the basis for securing calls to an external service or a database through the BCS. All users will authenticate to the service based upon the managed account that runs the user code proxy service. This is an example of the *trusted subsystem* model.

When the BDC runtime receives a request for external data, it determines if the Secure Store Service (SSS) is used to manage credentials to access the service. If the SSS is being used, then the identity of the user associated with the request is typically provided to the SSS, which maps the user (or a group or role to which the user belongs) to a credential that can be used to access the service. Because the user authentication token is not available in this case, the BDC uses *impersonation mode*, which results in the identity of the managed account that runs the user code proxy service being passed to the SSS rather than the identity of the user being passed. In the SSS, the credentials of the managed account are mapped to the credentials that you want to use to access the external system. The SSS returns the mapped credentials to the BDC runtime, which then uses the credentials to authenticate to the external system. Because the BDC runtime does not receive the credentials of individual users, you cannot constrain access to the external system to specific user accounts when the request originates from the sandbox environment. Figure 3 shows this process, using the example of an external vendor management (VM) system.

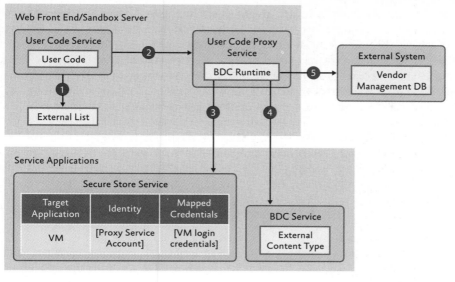

FIGURE 3
Identity flow and external service access

The following describes the numbered steps in Figure 3:

1. Custom user code, executing in the sandbox environment, uses the **SPList** object model (OM) to request data from an external list. The user authentication tokens for the user submitting the request have been removed from the context.

2. The **SPList** OM call is delegated to the user code proxy service. The user code proxy service passes the request to the BDC runtime, which also runs within the user code proxy service process.

3. The BDC runtime calls the SSS. The identity associated with the request is that of the managed account that runs the user code proxy service. The SSS returns the vendor management system credentials that are mapped to the identity of the user code proxy service.

4. The BDC runtime retrieves the external content type metadata from the BDC metadata cache. If the metadata is not already in the cache, the BDC runtime retrieves the external content type metadata from the BDC service. The external content type metadata provides the information the BDC runtime needs to be able to interact with the external vendor management system.

5. The BDC runtime uses the vendor management logon credentials retrieved from the SSS to authenticate to the service and access data from the external vendor management system.

Although the security token of the user, such as the claims token or the Kerberos token, is removed when execution passes to the sandbox process, the SharePoint user (**SPUser**) is still available from the SharePoint context. The security token is required for *authentication*, and without it you cannot pass user credentials to external systems or services. However, the **SPUser** instance is sufficient for *authorization* within SharePoint. SharePoint uses authorization rules to control access to a wide range of resources, including external content types (ECTs). This can be somewhat confusing. The security mechanisms can be summarized as follows:

- The account that runs the sandbox proxy process is mapped to credentials in the SSS, which in turn are used to authenticate to the external system.

- The identity of the current **SPUser** is used to authorize access to specific ECTs within the BDC model. You can configure authorization rules for individual ECTs through the Central Administration Web site.

Hybrid Execution with Custom Workflow Activities

Workflow logic is not executed synchronously in response to a user request. Instead, it is executed asynchronously by the workflow engine. This results in a significantly different execution model.

Within the sandbox environment, you can deploy a declarative workflow that defines connections between individual workflow activities. Many commonly used workflow activities are provided out-of-the-box by SharePoint 2010. The IT team can make additional workflow activities available to your declarative workflow by deploying custom, code-based workflow activities to the global assembly cache as full-trust solutions.

In order to make a full-trust workflow activity available to declarative workflows, the IT team must add an **authorizedType** entry to the Web.config file for the content Web application. This gives your custom activity the same status as the built-in workflow activities that come with SharePoint 2010. The following code example shows the format of an **authorizedType** entry.

```XML
<configuration>
  <System.Workflow.ComponentModel.WorkflowCompiler>
    <authorizedType Assembly="…" Namespace="…" TypeName="*" Authorized="True" />
  </System.Workflow.ComponentModel.WorkflowCompiler>
</system.web>
```

When you add an authorized type, set the **Assembly** attribute to the strong name of your assembly and set the **Namespace** attribute to the fully qualified namespace of your activity class. The downloadable reference implementation described at the end of this chapter provides an example of how to use a feature receiver class to add an authorized type entry for a custom workflow activity.

> **Note:** *As described in Chapter Three, "Execution Models for Sandboxed Solutions," you can also create and deploy custom sandboxed workflow actions. These actions run within the constraints of the sandbox environment. If you need to take advantage of capabilities outside the sandbox, you must deploy your custom workflow activities as full-trust solutions.*

The workflow engine itself always runs in full trust, regardless of whether you deploy your workflow as a sandboxed solution or a full-trust solution. When you deploy a declarative workflow to the sandbox environment, it simply specifies the rules that determine how execution will proceed through the full-trust activities in the workflow.

Figure 4 shows the key components involved in workflow execution. The declarative workflow is loaded from a sandbox solution, whereas custom full-trust workflow activities are loaded from the global assembly cache. However, the workflow is executed entirely in a full-trust environment.

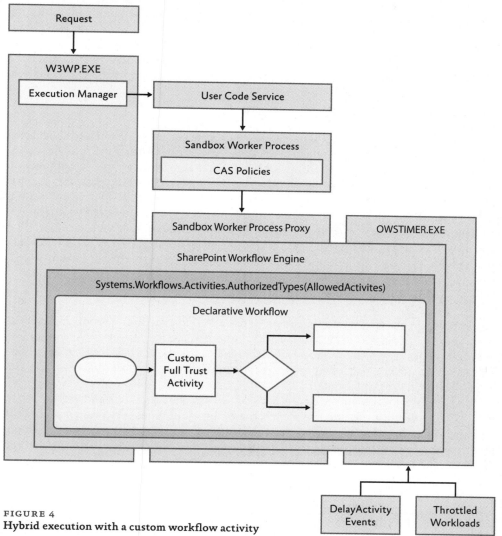

FIGURE 4
Hybrid execution with a custom workflow activity

Note: *The declarative workflow is defined as part of the sandbox solution, but it always executes in a full-trust process such as Owstimer.exe, W3wp.exe, or in the user code proxy process. Generally, the process in which the workflow runs is determined by where the workflow is initiated or where an action is taken that causes the workflow to be "rehydrated" from the database. There are some performance mechanisms that can push execution from W3WP.exe into the timer process under high load conditions. A full-trust custom activity included in the declarative workflow also runs in a full-trust process.*

Declarative workflows cannot be moved between SharePoint Foundation and SharePoint Server. In general, you can create equivalent workflows for each environment, although there are, of course, more activities available for SharePoint Server. Declarative workflows are managed slightly differently on each platform, and the workflow is packaged and deployed with the expectation that the server version is the same. You must develop the workflows on the same SharePoint version that you expect them to run on in production.

What Can I Do with Hybrid Solutions?

Hybrid approaches enable you to bypass the code access security policies and the limited permission set of the sandbox environment. When you create a full-trust proxy or a custom workflow activity, your code runs with full trust and there are no restrictions on what it can do. Any resources consumed by the full-trust code are not counted against the sandbox resource limits of the site collection. However, by definition, hybrid approaches require that your full-trust code is invoked from the sandbox environment. Because sandboxed logic can only run in the context of pages, event receivers, or workflows, hybrid approaches are inherently inappropriate for other application types such as timer jobs or service applications. In these cases, you must look to a full-trust solution.

How Do I Manage Hybrid Solutions?

When you design a SharePoint application to use a hybrid execution model, you will use two or more solution packages to deploy the components to the SharePoint environment. Components that target the sandbox are deployed as sandboxed solutions to a site collection solution gallery, and components that run with full trust are deployed as farm solutions to the server environment.

For example, suppose your solution includes a Web Part that uses an external list to query a LOB application. Behind the scenes, the external list relies on an external content type to provide an interaction with the LOB data source. Figure 5 shows an example where the Web Part is deployed in a sandboxed solution, while the external content type is deployed as a farm solution.

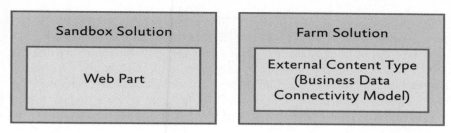

FIGURE 5
Hybrid approach with a Web Part and an external content type

Alternatively, suppose your Web Part uses a full-trust proxy to access parts of the object model that are inaccessible to sandboxed code. Figure 6 shows an example where the Web Part is deployed in a sandboxed solution, while the full-trust proxy is deployed as a farm solution.

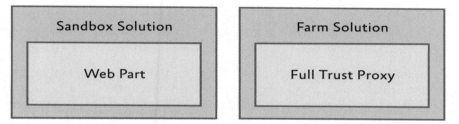

FIGURE 6
Hybrid approach with a Web Part and a full-trust proxy

From an administrative perspective, these types of deployment are managed as two separate solutions. The sandboxed solution is subject to the monitoring, resource throttling, and permission limitations of the sandbox environment, while the farm solution is subject to any organizational constraints on the deployment of full-trust code.

What Are the Core Issues for Hybrid Solutions

When you design your applications to use a hybrid execution model, you will deploy components in both sandboxed solutions and full-trust solutions. As such, you need to consider the issues that relate to each individual solution type in addition to those issues that apply specifically to hybrid approaches. When you develop a hybrid solution, you should pay particular attention to the areas described in the following sections.

SECURITY

Hybrid solutions expose a smaller surface area of full-trust code compared to farm solutions. This can reduce the amount of security review time that you require before deploying your solution. Because some of your solution code runs in full trust, you can impersonate the application pool (in other words, elevate permissions) if necessary. However, the boundaries of the sandbox environment were carefully designed when SharePoint 2010 was developed. You should consider the impact of any full-trust functionality that you expose to the sandbox, because this code runs without the security restrictions that apply to the sandbox environment.

DEPLOYMENT

If you want to use a hybrid approach, your organization must permit you to deploy farm solutions to your SharePoint environment. If you do not have permission to deploy assemblies and other resources to the server environment, you cannot deploy a hybrid solution. Organizations may be more permissive regarding external content types, as you can create an external content type from SharePoint Designer without deploying any managed code.

CAPABILITIES

It is important to understand which components of your solutions can run within the sandbox environment and which components require a full-trust proxy. The full-trust proxy should only include those elements that need to execute with full trust—the other elements should remain within the sandboxed solution. This helps to minimize the surface area of code that you expose to performance or security vulnerabilities. It can also help to reduce the time required for code review, as described in the preceding paragraphs.

LOGGING AND CONFIGURATION

Full-trust proxies can provide a useful way to expose logging and configuration functionality to sandboxed applications. For example, the Microsoft patterns & practices SharePoint Guidance Library contains a logging component that includes a full-trust proxy to enable sandboxed applications to write events to the Windows Event log and the Unified Logging Service (ULS) trace log.

Similarly, a full-trust proxy can provide a sandboxed application with access to configuration settings that would otherwise be unavailable. Full-trust proxies can read and write any data within the Web application and can read data stored in the **SPFarm** object. However, if you create a full-trust proxy to expose additional configuration functionality to sandboxed solutions, take care to include safeguards against improper use of that functionality. For example, developers risk corrupting the content or configuration database if they attempt to persist a non-serializable object to a property bag. In this case, it would be wise to include functionality within the full-trust proxy to verify that the object can be serialized before you proceed with the operation.

Stability

Because full-trust proxies are deployed to the global assembly cache, they are not subject to the resource throttling and monitoring constraints that are applied to sandboxed solutions. It is important to verify that the code in your full-trust proxy performs to a high standard. For example, ensure that your code does not cause excessive memory use or process timeouts, just as you would for code in a farm solution. This can help to ensure that your full-trust proxy does not jeopardize the stability of the farm as a whole.

Performance (Throughput)

As is the case with sandboxed solutions, there is a marginal reduction in performance when you use a hybrid solution instead of a farm solution. This is because of the marshaling of data across application domains.

Conclusion

This chapter provided insights into hybrid approaches to execution for SharePoint 2010 solutions. The following aspects of the design and development of hybrid solutions were discussed:

- **Processes and mechanisms**. There are three key hybrid approaches to execution for SharePoint 2010 solutions. You can create a full-trust proxy to expose additional functionality to sandboxed code, you can consume external data in a sandboxed solution through an external list that connects to an external content type, and you can deploy a declarative workflow that includes custom full-trust activities through a sandboxed solution. Each of these approaches has a unique execution mechanism. However, in each case, the core premise is that a sandboxed solution drives the execution and calls out to full-trust functionality through various means.

- **Capabilities**. There are no restrictions on the functionality that you can include in a full-trust proxy or a full-trust workflow activity. However, by definition, hybrid approaches require that your full-trust code is invoked from the sandbox environment. Since sandboxed logic can only run in the context of pages, event receivers, or workflows, hybrid approaches are inherently inappropriate for other application types such as timer jobs or service applications.

- **Management**. Hybrid approaches are deployed and managed as two or more distinct solutions—one or more containing the sandboxed components, and one or more containing the full-trust components. The sandboxed components are subject to the same security restrictions, resource throttling, and monitoring as any other sandboxed solution. The full trust components run without restriction, just like any other full-trust farm solution.

- **Core issues**. Hybrid approaches require the deployment of some full-trust components, which may not be possible in every SharePoint environment. Any full-trust components run without resource throttling or monitoring and must be subjected to the same testing and approval processes as farm solutions.

See It in Action: The Developing Applications for SharePoint 2010 online guidance includes downloadable reference implementations that illustrate each of the three hybrid approaches to execution in SharePoint 2010. The reference implementations are fully documented and illustrate the key steps and nuances in each approach. You can find the reference implementations at the following locations:

For Reference Implementation: Full-Trust Proxies for Sandboxed Solutions, see http://msdn.microsoft.com/en-us/library/ff798482.aspx.

For Reference Implementation: Workflow Activities, see http://msdn.microsoft.com/en-us/library/ff798330.aspx.

For Reference Implementation: External Lists, see http://msdn.microsoft.com/en-us/library/ff798440.aspx.

You can deploy each reference implementation to a SharePoint 2010 test environment and explore the source code at your leisure in Visual Studio 2010.

FURTHER INFORMATION

For more information on the key classes and methods involved in full-trust proxies for sandboxed applications, see the following pages on MSDN®, or visit the book's bibliography online at http://msdn.microsoft.com/gg213840.aspx for these and more resources.

- "SPProxyOperation"
- "SPProxyOperationArgs"
- "SPUtility.ExecuteRegisteredProxyOperation"
- "Trusted Subsystem Design"

PART TWO
DATA MODELS

1   SharePoint List Data Models

Every custom Microsoft® SharePoint™ application is driven by data in one way or another. Because the SharePoint platform is geared toward managing the flow of information, it's hard to think of a solution development task that doesn't involve either displaying, aggregating, sorting, filtering, manipulating, or creating data. SharePoint 2010 provides SharePoint developers with new ways to work with both internal and external data. For example, you can create relationships between SharePoint lists in the same way that you might create a foreign key relationship between database tables. You can query across these relationships to support moderately complex data aggregation scenarios. You can use new measures designed to protect the performance of data-driven SharePoint solutions, such as throttling list queries to restrict the number of items returned by the query. You can interactively create external content types that define a set of *stereotyped operations* on external databases and services. A stereotyped operation is a data access method that conforms to a common and well-recognized signature, such as **create**, **read**, **update**, and **delete** operations. You can create external lists, which effectively map a SharePoint list to an external content type (ECT). This allows users to interact with external data in the same way as they interact with standard SharePoint list data. Finally, you can use LINQ to SharePoint to query SharePoint list data using the Language Integrated Query (LINQ) syntax. This enables you to build sophisticated queries, such as queries that use joins.

This chapter focuses on how you can use SharePoint data structures to build rich and complex data models. The remaining chapters in Part II examine how you can model data from external data sources, how you can use different data access mechanisms to retrieve and manipulate your data, and how you can use various design patterns to mitigate some of the challenges associated with SharePoint list data.

Understanding List Data in SharePoint 2010

Whenever you design a data-driven application, regardless of the platform, you need to consider how your data is stored and managed. The data model addresses various aspects of data storage and management, including how and where your data is stored, how the relationships between different pieces of information are defined and managed, and how you will access your data.

When you work with SharePoint 2010, one of the first things you should consider is whether you can map your data storage requirements to the built-in data structures provided by the SharePoint platform. SharePoint defines a wide range of lists that can be used without modification or extended according to your needs by creating list templates, defining list instances, or associating content types you create to a list. The following are some examples:

- If you want to store a list of projects, together with descriptive information about each project, you can use a basic list.
- If you want to store statements of work (Word documents) and bid information (Excel workbooks) related to a project, you can use a document library with content types.
- If you want to store image resources for a particular project, you can use a picture library with content types.

This sounds intuitive, but one of the basic challenges of SharePoint development is to understand what SharePoint provides in order to avoid recreating existing functionality. Spend time exploring the list types and content types that are provided by SharePoint 2010, and consider how these components can meet your needs during the data modeling process.

Green Field and Brown Field Scenarios

When it comes to designing data-driven applications, solution architects can find themselves in one of two situations. In one situation, they don't have to worry about anything that exists already and they can start the design process with a blank piece of paper. In the other situation, they have to design the solution around an existing environment, which could include legacy systems and different types of data repositories.

Most architects would agree that not having to deal with legacy systems and preexisting data stores is more fun. This situation is known as *green field development*. You can design the application the way you want it without working around constraints imposed by other systems.

On the other hand, *brown field development* describes scenarios in which you are enhancing an operational system, or integrating with existing systems, such as line-of-business applications, proprietary software, and legacy data stores. As the data management requirements of most organizations evolve continuously over time, you're generally more likely to encounter brown field development scenarios.

Whether your application needs to integrate with other systems and data stores will clearly have a major bearing on the design process. SharePoint 2010 excels as a platform for brown field development scenarios because of its ability to connect to and interact with almost any kind of external system. Although most guidance necessarily ignores the sticky details around integrating existing systems into a solution design, this topic devotes much of its content to the opportunities for integrating with external systems and working with external data.

Structured and Unstructured Data

When it comes to data models for the SharePoint platform, the discussion often leads quickly to structured and unstructured data. Structured data is typically highly organized and tabular, such as the information in a SharePoint list or a database table. Unstructured data contains information, but lacks a rigorous schema, such as the content of a document or an image. For example, the content of this topic is unstructured data. It contains information, but the information doesn't fall into neat categories of rows and columns. Conversely, structured tables may contain columns for notes, videos, or other unstructured information.

At a basic level, you typically use a SharePoint list to store structured data and a SharePoint document library to store unstructured data. However, one of the key benefits of the SharePoint platform is that it allows users to associate some structured data with fundamentally unstructured content. For example, a document will typically have a title and an author, as well as purpose-specific information such as the name of a customer, the due date for an invoice, or the final effective date for a contract. You can add these fields to a SharePoint document library in the same way that you would add them to a Share-Point list, and the SharePoint platform includes features such as *property promotion* that enable you to automatically extract this information from the document in many cases.

This blurring between traditional definitions of structured and unstructured data occurs because conceptually, a document library is simply a list where each item has one—and only one—attachment. SharePoint document libraries include all the same functionality as SharePoint lists, such as the ability to add columns and create different views. This allows users to sort, query, and filter libraries of files and documents in the same way that they would work with regular structured data.

Database Models vs. SharePoint Data Models

A data model describes the real-world pieces of information that your application will work with, together with the relationship between these pieces of information. In the case of a relational data model, this is often represented as an entity-relationship diagram. For example, Figure 1 shows an example of an entity-relationship diagram for a machine parts inventory database.

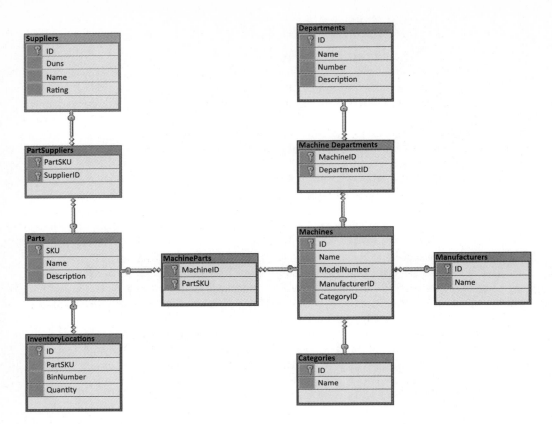

FIGURE 1
Entity-relationship diagram for machine parts inventory database

Today, most developers are familiar with relational databases. In a relational database, the data model is realized using the following constructs:

- A database contains one or more tables. Typically, each table models a logical entity, such as a person, an organization, or a manufactured item. For example, the machine parts inventory database contains tables for machines, parts, suppliers, and other entities.

- Each table contains one or more columns, or *fields*. Each column represents a single item of information about the entity modeled by the table. For example, the table named Machines includes fields named Name, ModelNumber, and ManufacturerId. Each field has a specific data type, such as a string or an integer.

- A table row represents a single entry in the table. For example, the Machines table will include a single row for each machine defined in the table.

- Each table includes a *primary key*. This is a field value, or a combination of field values, that uniquely identifies each entry in the table.

- You can create relationships between tables by linking the primary key of one table to the same field (the foreign key) in another table. This is known as a *foreign key relationship*. For example, the **Id** field is the primary key for the Machines table, while MachineId represents the same field in the MachineDepartment table. As such, a foreign key relationship can be defined between the two tables.

Most database engines, such as Microsoft SQL Server®, also allow tables to execute some programming logic when certain events, known as *triggers*, occur. You might invoke your logic when a row is added, updated, or removed from the table. You can use trigger logic to enforce rules that ensure consistency in the data or to drive updates to applications such as cache refreshes. Typically, database engines use a data definition language (DDL) to represent the data model internally. In Microsoft SQL Server, the DDL is a subset of SQL statements that are used to create the tables and relationships. The database engine stores DDL metadata that describes these structures in a system database. When you query a database, the database engine uses this metadata to determine how to interact with the database in question.

SharePoint allows you to construct data models using constructs that are conceptually similar to those found in a relational database:

- SharePoint lists (and by association, document libraries) are conceptually similar to database tables.
- SharePoint columns are conceptually similar to database table columns.
- SharePoint content types provide an additional layer of abstraction to support reuse and can be compared to the schema for a database table.
- You can create relationships between SharePoint lists using lookup columns that are conceptually similar to the foreign key relationships between database tables.

However, the way in which the data model is stored and implemented differs substantially between SharePoint and a SQL Server database. Although SharePoint uses SQL Server as its underlying data store, it introduces a level of abstraction between the data structures you define and the data store. One key advantage of this additional abstraction is that SharePoint users with sufficient permissions can define and manage their own data structures without the intervention of a database administrator. SharePoint stores the metadata that defines columns, lists, and content types in its content databases, in much the same way that the SQL Server database engine stores data model metadata in its system databases.

SharePoint Columns, Lists, and Content Types

Data models in SharePoint 2010 are implemented using columns, lists, and content types. A full understanding of these constructs underpins every effective data model in SharePoint 2010.

SharePoint Columns

The column, or field, is the core data construct in SharePoint 2010. In the context of the SharePoint platform and SharePoint applications, the terms column and field are used interchangeably:

- Column is preferred in product documentation and is used in the SharePoint user interface.
- Field is often used when referring to declarative markup or object model code. For example, columns are represented as **Field** elements in site or list definitions, as **FieldRef** elements in content type definitions, and by the **SPField** class in the SharePoint object model.

Note: *A **FieldRef** in a ContentType is a reference to an existing site column, instead of a column definition.*

Columns can exist at two different scopes. You can create a *list column,* which exists only within a specific SharePoint list. You can also create a *site column,* which is defined at the site collection level and is made available for use in lists and content types across the site collection, including all subsites. Each site collection includes a site column gallery in which built-in and user-defined site columns are listed. When you create a column, you can define the following information:

- Core details, including the column name and the data type.
- Group details, which can help you organize and find your columns within a site collection.
- Logical details, such as whether a value is required, whether the value must be unique, the maximum length of the value, and a default value, if appropriate.
- Validation details, including a validation formula and an error message.

You can define columns at any site level, although the common practice is to define all site columns in the root site to maximize reuse within the site collection.

The ability to enforce unique column values is new to SharePoint 2010. The unique value constraint applies only at the list instance level. Uniqueness can be defined at the site column level, but it is enforced within each list. Because of the way the unique value constraint works, you must index any columns that enforce uniqueness. You can only apply unique value constraints to columns with certain data types, because some data types cannot be indexed. You can apply the unique value constraint to a column in three ways—interactively through the user interface, declaratively by setting the **EnforceU-niqueValues** attribute in the column definition, or programmatically through the **SPField** class.

Note: *The product documentation provides full details of which SharePoint 2010 data types support unique value constraints. You can find more details on these resources in the Further Information section at the end of this chapter.*

SharePoint Lists

Lists are the storage mechanism in the SharePoint platform. In some ways, lists are conceptually similar to a relational database table, in that they are comprised of columns (or fields) and rows (or list items), and that you can create relationships between lists. SharePoint lists additionally provide a user interface including forms for interacting with the data. Unlike a database table, which typically has a constant predefined set of columns, the SharePoint list also allows users with sufficient permissions to add or remove columns at will.

Although it is possible to define a data model using only lists, the recommended approach is to use content types to define your key data entities.

SharePoint Content Types

Content types were introduced in Windows SharePoint Services 3.0. A content type defines the metadata and behavior for a particular data entity—usually, a business document or item of some kind. Each content type contains references to one or more site columns. You can also associate workflows, information management policies, and document templates with content types. For example, suppose you defined a content type named Contract. This content type might include the following:

- Columns named Customer, Amount, and Final Effective Date
- An approval workflow
- A retention policy linked to the **Final Effective Date** field
- A Word template for a contract document

Content types can be created in three ways. Site collection administrators can create content types interactively through the user interface without developer involvement. Developers can create content types declaratively by using collaborative application markup language (CAML) or programmatically through the **SPContentType** object model.

Content types are defined and managed at the site level, but they are typically defined at the root site in a site collection. In order to use a content type, you must associate it with a list or a document library. You can associate a content type with multiple lists or libraries, and each list or library can host multiple content types. This is useful in scenarios where different types of documents share similar metadata—for example, you might store invoices and sales orders in the same document library, because both share similar fields but might differ in terms of approval processes or retention requirements. The ability to associate behaviors with a content type, such as workflows and event receivers, is comparable to the concept of triggers on a database table. However, because the content type can be applied to multiple locations, you can use content types to define a contract, purchase order, or invoice that has the same metadata—and the same behavior—across the entire organization.

When you associate a content type with a list or library, the content type is attached to the list, together with the site columns, workflows, and policies for that content type. These policies and workflows will apply to any item of that content type in the list. Figure 2 illustrates this.

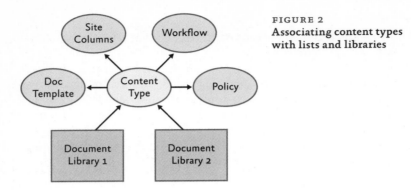

FIGURE 2
Associating content types
with lists and libraries

Content types follow the concepts of inheritance, because many data entities will share common metadata and behaviors. For example, an Invoice content type would inherit from the Document base content type, because an invoice is a type of document and shares certain characteristics with other types of documents. Ultimately, all content types inherit from the Item base content type.

When you associate a content type with a list, the site content type is actually copied to the list and is given a new ID value that identifies it as a child of the site content type. The list content type is then said to inherit from the site content type. As a result, changes to a site content type are not reflected in individual lists and libraries unless you explicitly propagate, or push down, the changes. If you update the content type programmatically, you can use the **SPContentType.Update(true)** method to propagate your changes—the Boolean argument to the **Update** method indicates that your changes should be applied to all child site and list content types. If you update the content type through the site collection user interface, you can select whether your updates should be applied to child content types. You cannot update a content type by changing the declarative (collaborative application markup language, or CAML) content type definition.

Where possible, you should use content types to define data models in SharePoint 2010 instead of using lists directly. Content types enable you to define data structures that can be reused across lists, sites, site collections, and even between farms. This allows you to apply a consistent and identifiable data schema across your entire organization. Note that sharing content types across site collection boundaries is new to SharePoint 2010 and requires you to configure the managed metadata service application.

Creating a Content Type Programmatically
The ability to create and update content types programmatically is new in SharePoint 2010. The key advantage to creating your content types in code is that this allows you to update your content type, together with all its descendant content types, at a later date as the requirements of your organization change. In contrast, defining a content type in CAML creates a permanent data structure that cannot be declaratively updated later. While you can programmatically update a content type that was created using CAML, the definition for the updated content type will be split across the original CAML structure and the programmatically updated version. This adds a certain amount of complexity that

makes content types harder to manage. If it is likely that your content type will evolve, it is often easier to create it programmatically from the start and manage the definition through one block of code.

You can use the following procedure to create a content type:

To programmatically create a content type

1. Check whether the content type already exists. If it does not exist, create the content type and add it to the **ContentTypes** collection for the Web, as shown in the following example.

   C#
   ```
   public static readonly SPContentTypeId myContentTypeId
     = new SPContentTypeId("0x010100FA0963FA69A646AA916D2E41284FC9D9");

   SPContentType myContentType = web.ContentTypes[myContentTypeId];

   if (myContentType == null)
   {
     myContentType = new SPContentType(myContentTypeId,
                                       web.ContentTypes,
                                       "My Content Type");

     web.ContentTypes.Add(myContentType);
   }
   ```

   Retrieve the site columns that you want to add to the content type from the **AvailableFields** collection of the Web. Add each field to the content type by creating a **SPFieldLink** instance for the field, and then adding the field link to the content type, as shown in the following example. Repeat this procedure for each column that you want to add to your content type.

   C#
   ```
   SPField field = web.AvailableFields[MyFieldId];
   SPFieldLink fieldLink = new SPFieldLink(field);

   if (myContentType.FieldLinks[fieldLink.Id] == null)
   {
       myContentType.FieldLinks.Add(fieldLink);
   }
   ```

2. Call the **Update** method on the new content type, as shown in the next example. Specify a parameter value of **true** if you want to push down the changes to content types that inherit from the new content type. For example, specify **true** if you are adding a column to a site content type that is already used in lists.

   C#
   ```
   myContentType.Update(true);
   ```

List Relationships in SharePoint 2010

SharePoint 2010 allows you to create relationships between lists in the same site collection. List instances are related through lookup columns (also known as lookup fields). The real benefit of this functionality is that SharePoint 2010 allows you to use **join** statements, in LINQ to SharePoint or in CAML, to query across lists where lookup column relationships are defined. By default, SharePoint permits a maximum of eight joins per query, although administrators can change this limit through the Central Administration Web site or by using Windows® PowerShell®. However, queries that contain large numbers of join statements are resource-intensive, and exceeding eight joins per query is likely to have a significant detrimental effect on performance.

Although this newly introduced ability to query across lists brings the capabilities of SharePoint data models closer to those of relational databases, SharePoint supports join predicates only where a lookup column relationship exists between the lists. In this regard, the join functionality in SharePoint is less powerful than the JOIN predicate in SQL.

LOOKUP COLUMNS EXPLAINED

Suppose you use a relational database to manage product orders received from your customers. The database might include a table named Orders, which stores the orders you've received, and a table named OrderLines, which stores the individual items that comprise an order (see Figure 3).

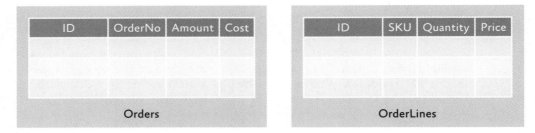

ID	OrderNo	Amount	Cost

Orders

ID	SKU	Quantity	Price

OrderLines

FIGURE 3
Unrelated database tables

To relate the tables, you could add an OrderID column to the OrderLines table, and use this column to define a foreign key relationship between the tables, as shown in Figure 4.

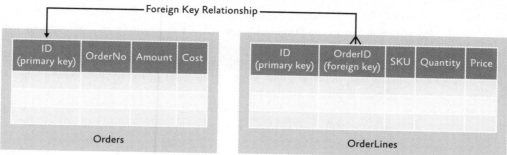

FIGURE 4
Database tables linked by foreign key constraint (primary key)

Alternatively, as shown in Figure 5, you could add an OrderNo column to the OrderLines table, and use this column to define the foreign key relationship (providing that the OrderNo column in the Orders table is subject to a unique values constraint).

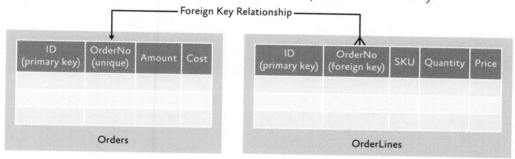

FIGURE 5
Database tables linked by foreign key constraint

Defining the foreign key relationship helps to ensure referential integrity—in the first example, the OrderID column of the OrderLines table can only contain values that are found in the ID column in the Orders table. You can also impose further conditions on the foreign key relationship. For example, when an item is deleted from the Orders table, you can force the database engine to remove corresponding rows from the OrderLines table. Conversely, you can prohibit the deletion of OrderLines items that are linked to an active row in the Orders table.

Lookup column relationships in SharePoint are conceptually similar to foreign key constraints in relational databases, but there are key differences. Suppose you want to implement the previous example in a SharePoint data model. First, you create the Orders list. Next, you define a site lookup column that retrieves values from the Orders list. Finally, you create the OrderLines list and you add the lookup column that retrieves values from Orders. When a user enters a new order line to the OrderLines list, they would select the associated order using the lookup column. You don't get to choose which columns in the Orders or OrderLines lists drive the foreign key constraint. In SharePoint lists, you can view the built in ID column as a permanent, unchangeable primary key, and this is the value that drives the relationship. Instead, you choose the column in the target list that you want to display in the source list, by setting the **ShowField** attribute. When a user adds data to the source list, he or she can select from a list of values in the column you selected on the target list. Figure 6 illustrates this.

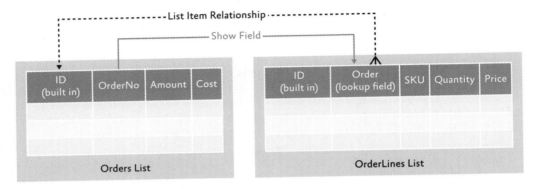

FIGURE 6
Lookup column relationship between SharePoint lists

Another key difference is that in a relational database, you can apply a foreign key constraint to existing data. This is not always good practice, and you would need to take care to remedy any existing data rows that violate the constraint. However, in SharePoint, you do not have this option—you cannot convert an existing column to a lookup column. You must create the lookup column first, and then the user must populate the data by selecting values from the target list. Note that a lookup column definition in itself does not define a relationship until you add it to a list. For example, you can create a lookup field as a site column. The lookup column definition effectively defines one half of the relationship (see Figure 7).

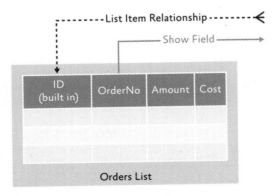

FIGURE 7
Lookup column definition

Whenever you add the site column to a list, you effectively create a unique foreign key relationship between the source list and the target list. In the case of lookup columns, the relationship between lists is managed by SharePoint, not by the underlying database. You can also leave a lookup column blank unless it is marked as a required field, whereas a foreign key constraint always requires a value.

If you want to model a many-to-many relationship using SharePoint lists, you must create an intermediate list to normalize the relationship. This is conceptually similar to the normalization process in database design, where you would also use an intermediate table to model a many-to-many relationship. For example, suppose you want to model the relationship between parts and machines. A part can be found in many machines, and a machine can contain many parts. To normalize the relationship, you would create an intermediate list named PartMachine, as shown in Figure 8.

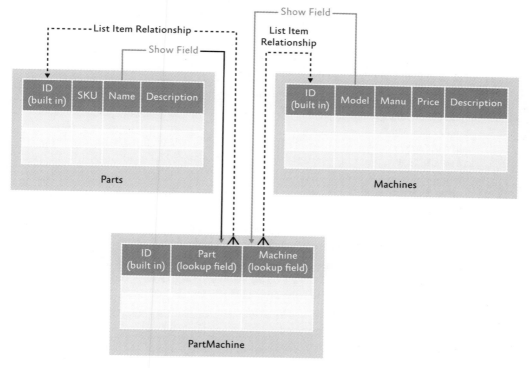

FIGURE 8
Using an intermediate list to model a many-to-many relationship

In this example, the intermediate list, PartMachine, contains lookup columns that link to both lists. To create a relationship between a part and a machine, you would need to create an entry in the PartMachine list. To navigate from a part to a machine, or vice versa, you would have to browse through the PartMachine list. From a user experience point of view, this is less than ideal, so at this point, you would probably add custom logic and custom user interface components to maintain associations between parts and machines.

Relationships between SharePoint lists can be navigated programmatically using either CAML or LINQ to SharePoint. For more information, see Chapter Seven, "Accessing Data in SharePoint 2010".

CREATING AND USING LOOKUP COLUMNS

You can create lookup columns in three different ways: interactively through the SharePoint site settings user interface (UI), programmatically through the **SPFieldLookup** class, or declaratively through CAML. For example, the following CAML code declaratively defines a lookup column named Projects Lookup that returns items from a list named Projects.

```xml
XML
<Field ID="{3F55B8CF-3537-4488-B250-02914EE6B4A8}"
       Name="ProjectsLookup"
       DisplayName="Projects Lookup"
       StaticName="ProjectsLookup"
       DisplaceOnUpgrade="TRUE"
       Group="SiteColumns"
       ShowField="Title"
       WebId=""
       List="Lists/Projects"
       Type="Lookup"
       Required="TRUE">
</Field>
```

The attributes of interest for a lookup column are as follows:

- The value of the **Type** attribute must be set to **Lookup**.

- The **WebId** attribute specifies the internal name of the site that contains the target list. If the attribute is omitted or set to an empty string, SharePoint will assume that the list is on the root site of the site collection.

- The **List** attribute specifies the site-relative URL of the target list. This list instance must exist before the field is defined.

- The **ShowField** attribute specifies the column in the target list that contains the values that you want to display in the lookup column.

Note: *Consider picking a meaningful **ShowField** value for the lookup column that is unlikely to change. For example, choosing a product SKU or a model number is a better foundation for a relationship than a description field.*

LOOKUPS FOR LIST COLUMNS, SITE COLUMNS, AND CONTENT TYPES

You can define a lookup column as a site column or a list column. If you define a lookup column declaratively or programmatically, you must take care to ensure that the target list (in other words, the list that the column refers to) is in place at the appropriate point in the column provisioning process. Regardless of whether you define a lookup column as a site column or a list column, the target list must already exist at the point at which the column is created; otherwise, the column will be unusable. Similarly, if you define a lookup column as part of a list definition, the target list must already exist at the point at which you provision the list containing the lookup column.

Because a lookup column defines a relationship between two list instances, it can often make sense to define your lookup columns at the list level. There are some circumstances in which it makes sense to use site columns and content types. For example, if many similar lists within the same site collection will include a relationship to a list on the root site, you can define a site column for the lookup, include it in a content type, and provision the content type to multiple lists within the site collection.

PROJECTED FIELDS

In addition to the column you identify in the **ShowField** attribute, SharePoint 2010 enables you to display additional columns from the target list in the view of the list that contains the lookup column. These additional columns are known as projected fields. For example, suppose you use SharePoint lists to model the relationship between employees and their departments. You create a Department lookup column for the Employees list. You might also want to display the name of the department manager in the list of employees, as shown in Figure 9.

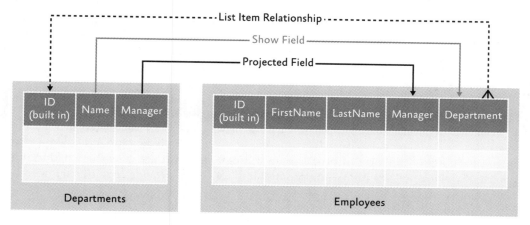

FIGURE 9
Projected fields in SharePoint lists

Note: *This is a somewhat contrived example, because, in reality, the department manager may not be the employee's manager, and the department manager would also be a member of the employees table. However, it serves to illustrate the concept of projected fields.*

ENFORCING LIST RELATIONSHIPS

SharePoint 2010 can help you to maintain referential integrity in your data model by enforcing the relationships defined by lookup columns. Just like foreign key constraints in a relational database, SharePoint allows you to configure restrict delete and cascade delete rules on lookup column relationships.

- Cascade delete rules automatically delete items that reference a record when you delete that record. This rule is typically used to enforce parent-child relationships.
- Restrict delete rules prevent you from deleting a record that is referenced by a lookup column in another list. This rule is typically used to enforce peer-to-peer relationships.

Parent-Child Relationships and Cascade Delete Rules

In a parent-child relationship, some records are children of other records. The child records are meaningless without a valid parent record. For example, an invoicing system might model a relationship between invoices and invoice line items. The invoice line items, which describe the product purchased, quantity ordered, and unit cost, are child records of the invoice item, which describes the customer, the shipping address, the total cost, and so on.

To create the relationship between invoices and invoice line items, you would add a lookup column to the InvoiceLineItems list that retrieves an invoice number from the Invoices list. Because an invoice line item is meaningless without a parent invoice, it would be appropriate to configure the lookup column to cascade deletes. This ensures that when a user deletes an invoice, SharePoint will delete the corresponding line items.

Child items without a valid parent are often referred to as orphans. Cascade delete behavior is designed to prevent orphans from occurring.

Peer-to-Peer Relationships and Restrict Delete Rules

In a peer-to-peer relationship, there is no clear hierarchy between the related entities. For example, in our invoice line items list, you might want to include a lookup column that retrieves an item from a list of products. In this case, the product is neither child to nor parent of the invoice line item—the product lookup simply provides additional information on the invoice line.

Suppose you delete a product record because you no longer sell that product. This damages the referential integrity of your data model, because historical invoice line items will now reference product records that do not exist. A better approach is to mark the product record as inactive if it is no longer available for distribution. In this case, it would be appropriate to configure the product lookup column in the InvoiceLineItems list to restrict deletes. This ensures that a product record cannot be deleted if it has been referenced in an invoice line item.

Making a record inactive while ensuring that it is still accessible for consistency with historical records is often referred to as a *soft delete*.

You can configure list relationship behavior interactively through the user interface or programmatically in a feature receiver class. Because list relationship behavior is specific to individual list instances, you cannot configure this behavior declaratively in column definitions or content types.

Programmatically Setting the Delete Behavior on a Lookup Field

If you use features to deploy the lists and columns that comprise your data model to a SharePoint environment, you may find it convenient to set the required delete behavior programmatically in a feature receiver class. In the SharePoint 2010 object model, lookup columns are represented by the **SPFieldLookup** class. This class includes a **Relationship DeleteBehavior** property that enables you to specify the delete behavior for the column. You must set the **RelationshipDeleteBehavior** property to one of the following **SPRelationshipDeleteBehavior** enumeration values:

- **SPRelationshipDeleteBehavior.Cascade**. Use this value to delete records if the lookup column refers to a row that no longer exists in the related list.
- **SPRelationshipDeleteBehavior.Restrict**. Use this value to prevent users from deleting rows in the related list if those rows are referred to in the lookup column values.

For example, you could call the following method from a feature receiver class to restrict deletions.

C#

```
private void RestrictDeleteOnLookupField(SPWeb web, string listUrl, Guid fieldGuid)
{
  SPList list = web.GetList(GetListUrl(web.ServerRelativeUrl, listUrl));
  SPField field = list.Fields[fieldGuid];
  SPFieldLookup fieldLookup = (SPFieldLookup)field;
  fieldLookup.Indexed = true;
  fieldLookup.RelationshipDeleteBehavior =
    SPRelationshipDeleteBehavior.Restrict;
  fieldLookup.Update();
}
```

Query Throttling and Indexing

A familiar challenge when you work with SharePoint lists is how to address the performance degradation that can occur when your list contains a large number of items. However, SharePoint is capable of managing extremely large lists containing millions of rows. The frequently quoted limit of 2,000 items per list actually refers to the maximum number of items you should retrieve in a single query or view in order to avoid performance degradation. Effective indexing and query throttling strategies can help you to improve the performance of large lists.

WHAT IS INDEXING?

SharePoint enables you to index columns in a list. This is conceptually similar to indexing columns in a database table; however, in the case of SharePoint lists data, the index is maintained by SharePoint instead of SQL Server.

Indexing columns in a list can substantially improve the performance of various query operations, such as queries that use the indexed column, join operations, and ordering operations such as sorting. In any list, you can either index a single column or define a composite index on two columns. Composite indexes can enable you to speed up queries across related values. However, like with database indices, list indexing does incur a performance overhead. Maintaining the index adds processing to creating, updating, or deleting items from a list, and the index itself requires storage space. A list instance supports a maximum of 20 indices. Some SharePoint features require indices and cannot be enabled on a list where there is no index slot remaining. You should choose your indexed columns carefully to maximize query performance while avoiding unnecessary overhead.

Note: *Not all column data types can be indexed. The Further Information section at the end of this chapter includes links to online resources that provide more details.*

WHAT IS QUERY THROTTLING?

Query throttling is a new administrative feature in SharePoint 2010. It allows farm administrators to mitigate the performance issues associated with large lists by restricting the number of items that can be accessed when you execute a query (known as the list view threshold). By default, this limit is set to 5,000 items for regular users and 20,000 items for users in an administrator role. If a query exceeds this limit, an exception is thrown and no results are returned to the calling code. Out of the box, SharePoint list views manage throttled results by returning a subset of the query results, together with a warning message that some results were not retrieved. Farm administrators can use the Central Administration Web site to configure query throttling for each Web application in various ways. For example, farm administrators can do the following:

- Change the list view threshold, both for users and for site administrators.

- Specify whether developers can use the object model to programmatically override the list view threshold.

- Specify a daily time window when queries that exceed the list view threshold are permitted. This enables organizations to schedule resource-intensive maintenance operations, which would typically violate the list view threshold, during off peak hours.

- Limit the number of lookup, person, or workflow status fields that can be included in a single database query.

If the farm administrator has enabled object model overrides, you can also change list view thresholds programmatically. For example, you can do the following:

- Change the global list view threshold for a Web application by setting the **SPWebApplication.MaxItemsPerThrottledOperation** property.

- Override the list view threshold for an individual list by setting the **SPList. EnableThrottling** property to **false**.
- Override the query throttling settings on a specific query by using the **SPQuery ThrottleOption** enumeration.

Query throttling is designed to prevent performance degradation, so you should only programmatically suspend throttling as a temporary measure and as a last resort. Ensure that you restrict the scope of any throttling overrides to a minimum. We recommend against changing the query throttling thresholds. The default limit of 5,000 items was chosen to match the default point at which SQL Server will escalate from row-level locks to a table-level lock, which has a markedly detrimental effect on overall throughput.

List-based throttling applies to other operations as well as read operations. In addition to query operations, throttling also applies to the following scenarios:

- Deleting a list or folder that contains more than 5,000 items
- Deleting a site that contains more than 5,000 items in total across the site
- Creating an index on a list that contains more than 5,000 items

How Does Indexing Affect Throttling?

The list view threshold does not apply simply to the number of results returned by your query. Instead, it restricts the numbers of database rows that can be accessed in order to complete execution of the query at the row level in the content database. For example, suppose you are working with a list that contains 10,000 items. If you were to build a query that returns the first 100 items sorted by the ID field, the query would execute without issue because the ID column is always indexed. However, if you were to build a query that returns the first 100 items sorted by a non-indexed Title field, the query would have to scan all 10,000 rows in the content database in order to determine the sort order by title before returning the first 100 items. Because of this, the query would be throttled, and rightly so because this is a resource-intensive operation.

In this case, you could avoid the issue by indexing the Title field. This would enable SharePoint to determine the top 100 items sorted by title from the index without scanning all 10,000 list items in the database. The same concepts that apply to **sort** operations also apply to **where** clauses and **join** predicates in list queries. Careful use of column indexing can mitigate many large list performance issues and help you to avoid query throttling limits.

Managing Large Lists

Large lists can have a detrimental effect on the performance and efficiency of a SharePoint environment. For example, product guidelines for Windows SharePoint Services 3.0 and Microsoft Office® SharePoint Server (MOSS) 2007 recommended that you prevent users from viewing more than 2,000 list items at a time in order to avoid performance degradation, while in SharePoint 2010 running queries that load more than 5,000 rows from the content database will cause a marked deterioration in performance. As described earlier in this chapter, throttling limits will by default prevent users from executing queries that require more than 5,000 items to be retrieved and processed.

Generally speaking, you should always aim to limit the amount of list data retrieved to only that required by the user to complete the task at hand. In most cases it's not necessary or even useful to display several thousand items at once. However, large lists may be unavoidable in certain scenarios, for example if your lists grow rapidly or organically over time or if you need to migrate data from a large document store. Large lists are not automatically a bad thing. When properly managed, SharePoint can handle millions of items of data in a single list. However, large lists require proactive engagement from developers and the IT team to ensure that they work smoothly in your SharePoint environment.

USING THE CONTENTITERATOR CLASS

In addition to introducing list throttling limits, SharePoint Server 2010 provides a new class named **ContentIterator** that you can use to query lists without hitting these limits. You should consider using this class if you need to run a query that will return more than 5,000 rows of data. Essentially, the **ContentIterator** instance divides the list into chunks and runs the query against one chunk of list data at a time. Each list item is processed asynchronously by a callback method until the query is complete. The following code example illustrates the basic code pattern for using the **ContentIterator** class.

```C#
protected void OnTestContentIterator(object sender, EventArgs args)
{
  SPQuery listQuery = new SPQuery();
  listQuery.Query = "[CAML query goes here]";
  SPList list = SPContext.Current.Web.Lists["MyList"];
    ContentIterator iterator = new ContentIterator();

    iterator.ProcessListItems(list,
                              listQuery,
                              ProcessItem,
                              ProcessError);
}

public bool ProcessError(SPListItem item, Exception e)
{
  // Process the error
  return true;
}
public void ProcessItem(SPListItem item)
{
  // Process the item
}
```

Note: *The use of query classes such as **SPQuery** is described in more detail in the next chapter.*

The **ContentIterator** instance runs through each item in the list, invoking the specified callback method—**ProcessItem** in this example—for each list item. If an error occurs during processing, then a specified error callback method is invoked—in this case, **Process Error**. By using this approach you can execute queries involving large numbers of list items without breaching query throttling limits.

The **ContentIterator** class provides a broad range of additional functionality, such as the ability to order result sets, which is not described in this chapter.

PARTITIONED VIEW

A common approach to managing large amounts of list data is to leave the data in a single large list, but to provide access to the list through targeted views that return smaller segments of data. List data often lends itself to natural segmentation, for example by region, status, date range, or department. Because you're simply providing multiple windows onto one list, rather than splitting the list itself, you can create multiple types of views on the same list. For example, you could create one set of views that partition the list by region and another set of views that partition the list by date range. Figure 10 illustrates this.

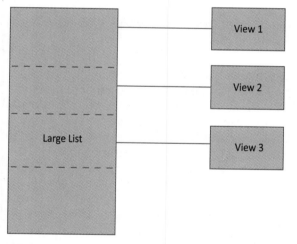

FIGURE 10
View partitioning pattern

In order for partitioning to be effective, the fields that you use to partition the list must be indexed. If the fields are not indexed, SharePoint would need to scan every list item in order to establish which items satisfy the view criteria.

After removing the default views from the list, you can use various approaches to create partitioned views, such as metadata navigation and filtering, custom views based on filtered columns or folders, custom Web Parts, and Content Query Web Parts.

When you evaluate the suitability of a design pattern, it's useful to have a set of criteria in mind. In this chapter, we look at the efficacy of list patterns in four key areas—performance, staleness, storage, and security. For the Partitioned View pattern, these considerations are as follows:

- **Performance**. With proper indexing and carefully managed view sizes, view partitioning performs well. Take care to avoid introducing view queries that evaluate non-indexed fields, as this will undermine the partitioning. Lists with high growth rates need to be monitored to ensure that views remain optimally sized.

- **Staleness**. List data is retrieved in real time, thus stale data is avoided.

- **Storage**. No information is duplicated, so there is no additional storage cost.

- **Security**. In very large lists, there are performance implications to applying item-level permissions. Query performance is affected by both the number of unique permissions on the list and the number of items in the list. There are no hard and fast rules about query performance and unique permissions in a list, but you should aim to minimize the number of unique permissions applied to large lists. A small set of unique permission scopes in a list will have a low impact on performance, and performance will progressively degrade as the number of unique permissions grows. Performance will significantly degrade with more than 5,000 unique permissions, and there is a hard limit of 50,000 unique permissions per list. If a list is performing poorly because of many unique permission scopes, then segmentation of the list into multiple lists—as opposed to view partitioning—may reduce the number of permissions required and improve performance.

Partitioned List with Aggregate View

Another approach to managing large amounts of list data is to divide your data into several smaller lists. In this case, users will typically interact with each list through the default list views, although in some scenarios list items are aggregated across multiple lists into a central view (see Figure 11). In this case you need to choose your segmentation strategy carefully. Once you have segmented the data by a particular field, retrieving data according to different criteria will require cross-list querying and filtering, which becomes costly from a performance perspective as the number of lists increases. For example, if you segment a large amount of list data into individual lists by region, and then you want to retrieve all items across a specific date range, you would need to query across every list and include filter criteria to restrict the date range. As such, there needs to be a natural segmentation of the data for this approach to work well.

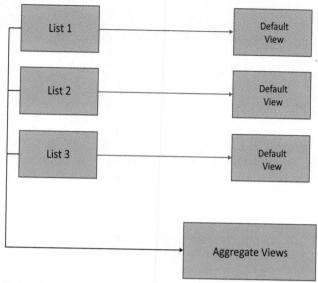

FIGURE 11
Partitioned list with aggregate view pattern

To perform the aggregation, you will need to define a custom view that rolls up data across the individual lists. In most cases, you will create aggregate views either by using the Content Query Web Part or by using the **SPSiteDataQuery** class in a custom Web Part.

The key considerations for the Partitioned List pattern are as follows:

- **Performance**. Since segmented lists are smaller than a single large list, it's easier to avoid throttling limits. However, you may encounter throttling limits on the aggregate view query, although aggregate queries allow you to retrieve up to 20,000 rows from the content database, instead of the default 5,000 permitted for individual lists. If your lists grow at different rates, some lists could become too large over time, and further segmentation may be difficult to achieve since you would need to devise additional partitioning criteria. Cross-list queries are expensive, so you should consider caching aggregate views.

- **Staleness**. If you use the default views on individual lists, data is retrieved in real time. However, caching aggregate result sets can result in stale data.

- **Storage**. No information is duplicated, so there is no additional storage cost.

- **Security**. Since the lists are smaller, the performance cost of item security is mitigated. Segmenting your list data may also help you to avoid creating item-level permissions. For example, consider a single large list where item permissions are applied according to department. If that list is segmented by department into individual lists, you can apply list-level security for each department list rather than using item-level security.

Aggregating List Data

One of the most common development tasks for SharePoint is the aggregation of data from multiple lists. There are several different patterns you can use to approach this task. Each pattern has advantages and tradeoffs in terms of performance and server load, timeliness of data, and security.

AGGREGATED VIEW

An aggregated view uses SharePoint APIs—typically the **SPSiteDataQuery** class or the **SPPortalSiteMapProvider** class—to query data from several sources and aggregate that data into a single view. The key considerations for aggregated views are as follows:

- **Performance.** Performance will vary according to how many items you aggregate. To improve performance and reduce the load on the server, you can use the **SPPortalSiteMapProvider** class to cache queries performed with the **SPSite DataQuery** class. To avoid hitting query throttling limits, ensure that you index columns that are evaluated by your aggregation query. You should also limit the number of items returned to only those required by your specific scenario. Remember that caching query results will increase memory use.

- **Staleness.** List views are populated by retrieving list data in real time. However, caching aggregate result sets may result in stale data. As the cache interval increases, the likelihood of stale query results increases. For this reason, you should only cache results if it is acceptable to display data that may not always reflect the latest changes to a list.

- **Storage.** No additional storage is required since the data is queried dynamically at run time.

- **Security.** Item-level security permissions are enforced when you use the **SPSite DataQuery** class and the **SPPortalSiteMapProvider** class.

SEARCH-AGGREGATED VIEW

A search-aggregated view uses the SharePoint search service to query data from multiple sources and aggregate the results into a single view (see Figure 12). This approach allows you to retrieve data from multiple site collections within the SharePoint farm. However, your view data is only as up-to-date as your last incremental search crawl.

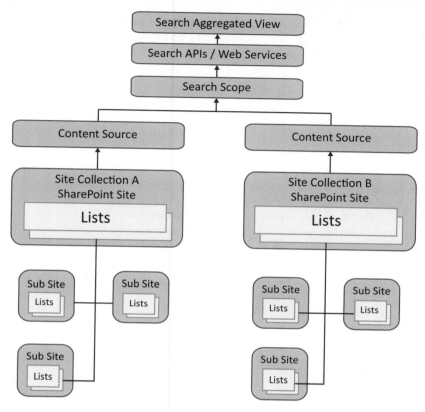

FIGURE 12
Search-aggregated view pattern

You can use the following high-level steps to implement a search-aggregated view:

3. Create content sources for the data you want to aggregate.

4. Run full crawls on each content source and set up crawl schedules.

5. Create search scopes for your content sources, and update the search scopes.

6. Use the search service Web services or APIs to query your search scopes.

The key considerations for search-aggregated views are as follows:

- **Performance**. This approach performs very well, especially when aggregating data across several sites or site collections. This is the best-performing option you can use to query large volumes of data that span site collections.

- **Staleness**. The search engine periodically indexes, or crawls, your content sources. If data in the content sources changes between indexing operations, your search results will be out of date. You should choose the frequency of your incremental search crawls carefully to keep staleness to an acceptable level. Some search engines, such as Microsoft FASTTM Search Server 2010 for SharePoint, allow you to push changes to the index in order to minimize staleness.

- **Storage**. The search index contains information from the list and requires disk space. The search index is propagated from the index server to each query server in the farm.
- **Security**. The search service automatically performs security trimming to ensure that only the items that a user has permission to view are displayed in the results. The content access account that the search service uses to crawl the data must be granted read access to each data source.

UNION LIST AGGREGATION

A union-aggregated list stores information from several lists or data sources, and is typically deployed to a centrally accessible location. The key criterion for a union-aggregated list is that all the data sources have a common schema—in other words, they have the same columns. Union-aggregated lists are usually easy to maintain, as they allow users to manage information from multiple sources in a single location (see Figure 13).

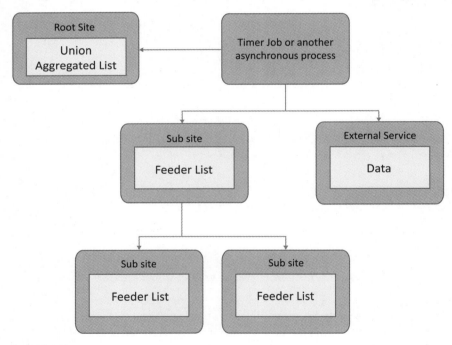

FIGURE 13
Union-aggregated list pattern

Union-aggregated lists are typically populated using custom code, either by a timer job or another asynchronous process. In most cases you'll want to create custom views to filter the data, in order to enhance performance and usability. As with any custom views, you should aim to index columns that are evaluated by the view query to improve the query performance and avoid inadvertently hitting query throttling limits.

You should use the search-aggregated view pattern in preference to the union-aggregated list pattern wherever possible, as the search service maintains the central index for you. However, the union-aggregated list pattern may be preferable in the following circumstances:

- When the search service is not available.
- When you need to perform transformations or calculations on list data.
- When you want to use lookup columns.
- When you want to be able to perform sorting, grouping, or filtering on the entire aggregated data set.
- When you want to be able to use the capabilities of SharePoint lists, such as workflow or the application of information policies, on the aggregated data set.

The key considerations for the union-aggregated list pattern are as follows:

- **Performance**. To avoid any performance degradation associated with large central lists, use views to query the data. You can improve the performance of the view queries by returning only the columns that are specifically required.
- **Staleness**. The aggregated list may contain stale data, depending on how frequently the aggregation process is performed.
- **Storage**. Additional database storage will be needed to store the aggregated list. This will count towards any storage quotas imposed on your site collection.
- **Security.** List items in the aggregated list do not inherit permissions from items in the source lists or data sources. However, you can of course set item-level permissions in the aggregated list. As described earlier, item-level security can have a detrimental impact on list performance. If you have a small number of unique security scopes (or permissions), creating and querying a single aggregated list will typically perform better than dynamically querying multiple sources. However, as the number of unique security scopes increases you will progressively lose this performance benefit, and eventually it could become more expensive to perform this query on the union list than it would be to perform an aggregate query. A common cause of this situation is a large list with a workflow attached to each item, where the workflow grants an individual employee permission to work on each item. If you have 8,000 distinct employees working on the list, then the performance is likely to be poor. From a security perspective, having large numbers of security scopes also makes this type of list harder to manage.

In some cases, union-aggregated lists can make list permissions easier to manage when compared to simple large lists, as you can set list-level permissions on the individual source lists and on the union-aggregated list. For example, suppose you aggregate statements of work (SOWs) from lists on the HR, IT, and Finance departments. You can set permissions on each individual list to ensure that only people in the relevant department can view list data, and you could set permissions on the aggregated list to ensure that only executives can view the aggregated data. This helps you to avoid the overhead of managing item-level permissions on a single large list.

DENORMALIZED LIST AGGREGATION

Much like a union-aggregated list, a denormalized aggregated list stores information from several lists or data sources and is typically found in central locations. However, whereas the data sources for a union-aggregated list have a common schema, the data sources for a denormalized aggregated list have different columns. This type of list is similar to a view in a database (see Figure 14).

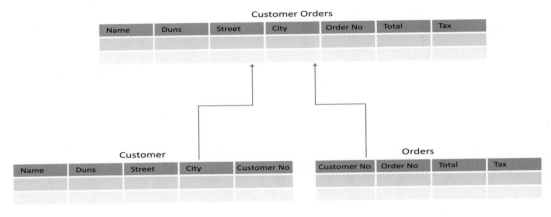

FIGURE 14
Denormalized list aggregation pattern

Denormalized aggregated lists are implemented in a manner similar to union-aggregated lists, and are typically populated by timer jobs or other asynchronous processes. You should make use of list joins, where available, to build the aggregated data set.

> **Note:** *List joins are discussed in more detail in Chapter Seven, "Accessing Data in SharePoint 2010."*

Broadly speaking, the key considerations for denormalized list aggregation are the same as those for union list aggregation. Item-level security can be harder to manage for denormalized aggregated lists, as a row of data from each source list forms a single row of data in the aggregated list. This can add complexity if the security scopes differ between the source lists.

LIST OF LISTS AND LIST OF SITES

A list of lists contains links to other lists, usually in a centrally accessible location. This can include many different scenarios, such as lists of lists in the same site collection, multiple site collections, the same Web application, multiple Web applications, the same farm, and multiple farms. In most cases, these lists are used to provide easy navigation to related lists within the chosen scope. Lists of lists are frequently populated by workflows and are often queried by custom navigation controls such as Microsoft Silverlight® menus.

In terms of implementation, a list of lists is essentially just a list of hyperlinks. The list can be manually maintained or populated automatically by a workflow or a timer job. The key considerations for lists of lists are as follows:

- **Performance**. Lists of lists typically don't contain many records, since their purpose is simply to consolidate links to other lists in order to improve navigation. As a result, performance is not usually an issue.

- **Staleness**. There is no automatic mechanism that keeps track of other lists, so the data may not always be accurate. This can lead to incomplete data or broken navigation connections. To avoid this issue, you can create an automated process to check for link accuracy. This would usually be implemented in the form of a timer job.

- **Storage**. Minimal storage is needed for a list of this type because both the number of items in the list and the number of columns are usually small.

- **Security**. By default, links to other lists will not be security trimmed at run time. Users could see links to lists in other site collections, Web applications, or server farms that they don't have permission to access. You can use item-level permissions or audience targeting to avoid this issue.

A list of sites contains links to other SharePoint sites or external Web sites, and is usually deployed to a centrally accessible location. Just like lists of lists, lists of sites can encompass a variety of scopes, from a single site collection to multiple farms, and are typically used to aid navigation. The same implementation issues and key considerations apply to both lists of lists and lists of sites.

Conclusion

This chapter introduced the new data capabilities of SharePoint 2010 and explored some of the key aspects of modeling data with SharePoint lists. In particular, the following areas were described and discussed:

- **Data models in context**. It's useful to view SharePoint data models in the context of broader data modeling considerations, such as structured or unstructured data and green field or brown field development scenarios.

- **SharePoint data structures**. The key data constructs in SharePoint 2010 are columns, lists, and content types. Columns are conceptually similar to database fields, while lists are conceptually similar to database tables. Content types are a SharePoint-specific concept that supports reusability and metadata management.

- **List relationships**. SharePoint 2010 allows you to create relationships between SharePoint lists. These relationships are conceptually similar to foreign key constraints in relational databases. You can define cascade delete and restrict delete rules between lists in a SharePoint site.

- **Throttling and indexing**. SharePoint 2010 prevents users from running queries that require more than a specified number of rows to be retrieved from the content database. By default, the limit is set to 5,000 rows for a regular site user and 20,000 rows for an administrator. You can mitigate the impact of query throttling through the use of an effective indexing strategy.

- **Managing large lists**. Large lists can have adverse effects on the performance of a SharePoint 2010 environment if they are not managed carefully. There are various approaches you can use to mitigate these effects. You can leave all the list items in a single list and develop multiple views to present smaller subsets of the list data. You can partition the list into smaller subsets according to metadata values, and use an aggregate view to merge list data where appropriate. You can also use the **ContentIterator** class to query large lists. This class uses an asynchronous pattern to avoid hitting query throttling thresholds.

- **List aggregation**. One of the most common tasks faced by SharePoint developers is the aggregation of data from multiple lists. Almost all list aggregation scenarios can be matched to one of a handful of patterns, such as aggregated view, search-aggregated view, union list aggregation, and denormalized list aggregation. Each aggregation pattern has its own benefits and drawbacks.

See It in Action: *The SharePoint List Data Models Reference Implementation in the Developing Applications for SharePoint 2010 online guidance is a fully-documented, downloadable solution that illustrates how you can implement a reasonably complex data model using lists in SharePoint 2010. The reference implementation documentation describes how you can perform more challenging data modeling tasks, such as building many-to-many relationships between SharePoint lists. It also illustrates various data access patterns, which are discussed in Chapter Seven, "Accessing Data in SharePoint 2010." You can deploy the reference implementation to a SharePoint 2010 test environment and explore the source code at your leisure in Microsoft Visual Studio® 2010.*

For more information, see Reference Implementation: SharePoint List Data Models at http://msdn.microsoft.com/en-us/library/ff798373.aspx.

FURTHER INFORMATION
The plethora of new features in SharePoint brings with it many new design options and tradeoffs for the SharePoint application developer. Additional information is available in the documents listed below, and there are more sources referenced in the book's online bibliography at http://msdn.microsoft.com/gg213840.aspx.
- "Building Block: Columns and Field Types"
- "Enforcing Uniqueness in Column Values"
- "Base Content Type Hierarchy"
- "Updating Content Types"

2   External Data in SharePoint 2010

Microsoft® SharePoint® 2010 provides many new and improved ways to work with external data. In SharePoint 2010, you can retrieve, manipulate, and integrate external data from disparate sources while providing a seamless user experience. This chapter examines the architecture that underpins this functionality and provides insights into how to meet some of the design challenges that you may encounter in this area.

Introducing the BCS

In SharePoint 2010, the functionality that enables you to work with external data is provided by Business Connectivity Services (BCS). BCS is an umbrella term—much like Enterprise Content Management (ECM) in SharePoint 2007—that encompasses a broad range of components and services. Each of these components and services provide functionality relating to the modeling, access, and management of external data. Figure 1 shows the key components of the BCS.

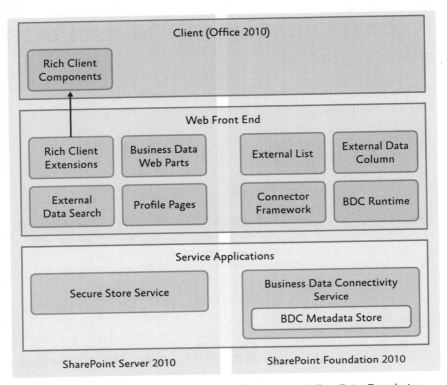

Note: SharePoint Server includes all components that are part of SharePoint Foundation.

FIGURE 1
Business Connectivity Services in SharePoint 2010

The Business Data Connectivity (BDC) service application and the BDC runtime are the core components of the BCS when it comes to modeling, managing, and accessing external data. The Secure Store Service (SSS) supports access to external data by allowing you to map the credentials of SharePoint users or groups to external system credentials. Other BCS components enable users to interact with external data in various ways. For more information about how these components relate from an execution perspective, see **Chapter Four, "Hybrid Approaches to Execution."**

> **Note:** *The Business Data Connectivity service should not be confused with the Business Data Catalog (also referred to as the BDC) in Microsoft Office® SharePoint Server 2007, which was the predecessor to the BCS. In this book, BDC refers to the Business Data Connectivity service application.*

UNDERSTANDING SERVICE PROXY GROUPS

In order to understand the components of the BCS, you need a basic familiarity with the new service application framework in SharePoint 2010. This replaces the shared service provider found in SharePoint Server 2007 and enables third parties to build new service applications for the SharePoint platform. Instead of using a shared service provider to provide collections of services to SharePoint farms and Web applications, each service in SharePoint 2010 is architected as an individual service application. In BCS, both the SSS and the BDC are examples of service applications.

Administrators can create multiple instances of particular service applications. For example, you might configure one BDC instance for an intranet portal and another for a public-facing internet site. In order to use a service application, you must create a service application proxy. Where the service application provides a service, the service application proxy consumes a service. A default configuration of SharePoint 2010 largely contains pairs of service applications and service application proxies, as shown in Figure 2.

Business Data Connectivity Service	Business Data Connectivity Service Application	Started
Business Data Connectivity Service	Business Data Connectivity Service Application Proxy	Started
Excel Services Application	Excel Services Application Web Service Application	Started
Excel Services Application	Excel Services Application Web Service Application Proxy	Started
Managed Metadata Service	Managed Metadata Service	Started
Managed Metadata Service	Managed Metadata Service Connection	Started
PerformancePoint Service Application	PerformancePoint Service Application	Started
PerformancePoint Service Application	PerformancePoint Service Application Proxy	Started
Search Administration Web Service for Search Service Application	Search Administration Web Service Application	Started
Search Service Application	Search Service Application	Started
Search Service Application	Search Service Application Proxy	Started
Secure Store Service	Secure Store Service Application	Started
Secure Store Service	Secure Store Service Application	Started

FIGURE 2
Service applications and proxies in the Central Administration Web site

Each Web application is associated with an application proxy group that contains a collection of service application proxies. This model supports a flexible approach to application proxy management—for example, an administrator may want different Web applications to use different subsets of the available application proxies. You can add a single service application proxy to multiple application proxy groups. Likewise, you can add multiple service application proxies of the same type to an application proxy group. However, the application proxy group will only use one of the proxies, and the proxy instance you want to use must be marked as the default instance of that proxy type for the application proxy group. Having more than one proxy instance for the same service type is an administrative convenience that enables you to easily switch between two instances by changing which is marked as **default**.

This arrangement can lead to confusion for developers who are not familiar with the service application framework. For example, if you add a new instance of the SSS application, and you want to use that SSS application instance in your Web application, you must ensure the following:

- The service application proxy for the service instance is in the application proxy group mapped to your Web application.
- The service application proxy is the default SSS proxy instance in the application proxy group.

Business Data Connectivity Models

When you design a SharePoint application around external data, the metadata for your data model is stored and managed by the BDC service application. This is known as a Business Data Connectivity model, or BDC model. You can interactively create a BDC model in SharePoint Designer 2010, or programmatically in Microsoft Visual Studio® 2010 for more complex scenarios. In a BDC model, data entities are represented by external content types. An external content type models an external data entity, such as a database table or view or a Web service method, and defines a set of *stereotyped operations* on that data entity. In addition to external content types, a BDC model typically includes an external data source definition, connection and security details for the external data source, and associations that describe the relationship between individual data entities. Other BCS components, such as external lists and external data search, enable end users to interact with the external data provided by the BDC model.

> **Note:** *A stereotyped operation is a data access method that conforms to a common and well-recognized signature, such as* **create**, **read**, **update**, *and* **delete** *operations.*

Creating BDC models for your external data sources offers many benefits. First, the BDC model enables you to centrally maintain all the information you need to interact with an external data source. This ensures that the external data source is accessed consistently by applications across your environment. After creating the BDC model, you can work with the external data in several ways without writing any code. The following are some examples:

- You can surface the external data through the out-of-the-box Business Data Web Parts.
- You can interact with the external data through external lists.
- You can crawl and index the external data for search.

Figure 3 shows the basic overall structure of a BDC model.

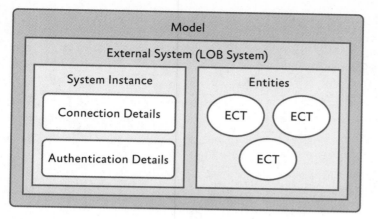

FIGURE 3
Conceptual illustration of a BDC model

As you can see, each model defines one or more external systems or services. These are sometimes known as LOB systems (line-of-business systems) for historical reasons, and are represented by **LobSystem** elements in the BDC model schema. This represents a general view of an external system, its data entities, and its operations. For example, it might represent a particular type of Customer Relationship Management (CRM) system. Within each external system definition, you must define one or more system instances. These represent a specific, individual implementation of the external system, such as a particular installation of a CRM system. The system instance definition defines the connection and authentication information that the BDC service application requires in order to communicate with the external system instance. The other key component of an external system definition is a set of entities, represented by external content types (ECTs). These are described later in this topic.

The metadata that comprises a BDC model is stored as XML. You can import, export, and manually edit BDC models as .bdcm files. However, for many simple BDC models, the interactive tooling provided by SharePoint Designer 2010 will make manual editing of the BDC model unnecessary.

BDC models are stored by the BDC metadata store, a central component of the BDC service application. When a SharePoint client application requests external data, the BDC runtime component on the Web front-end server requests from the BDC metadata store the metadata that defines the BDC model. The BDC runtime then uses the metadata provided to perform data operations directly on the external system. The BDC runtime also caches BDC model metadata on the Web front-end server.

In the case of client computers that use Microsoft Office 2010 to access external systems, the metadata for an application is packaged on the server and deployed with the application for use by the BDC client runtime. The BDC client runtime uses the metadata provided to perform operations directly on the external system instead of going through SharePoint. The BDC client runtime caches both BDC model metadata and the external data itself for offline use. This is illustrated in Figure 4.

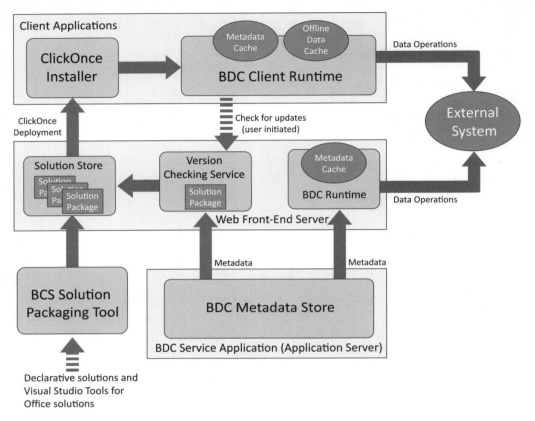

FIGURE 4
Metadata and data access in BDC models

EXTERNAL CONTENT TYPES

An external content type (ECT) is conceptually similar to a regular SharePoint content type (although unrelated in terms of implementation). Just like a regular content type, an ECT is a collection of metadata that models a data entity. External data sources describe data schemas in different ways. For example, Web services describe their data entities and operations using the Web Service Description Language (WSDL), while relational databases describe their data entities and operations using a database schema. When you create a BDC model in SharePoint Designer, these data definitions are translated into ECTs. Each ECT definition includes the following components:

- One or more identifiers that uniquely identify instances of the data entity
- One or more methods (known as operations in SharePoint Designer) that define a particular operation, such as **create**, **read items**, **update**, or **delete**, on the data entity

The methods are the central component of any ECT, and the BDC service application infers the structure of your data entity from the return types of these methods. The methods that make up an ECT are known as stereotyped operations, because they map the external service methods or database queries to standardized data operations that the BCS user interface components can use to display and manipulate the external data. For example, the BDC model supports stereotyped operations that perform the following actions:

- Create an item
- Retrieve all items
- Retrieve an individual item
- Update an item
- Delete an item
- Stream an item

Stereotyped operations offer many advantages, such as enabling SharePoint to crawl and index external data for search and allowing users to manipulate external data through built-in Business Data Web Parts without requiring custom-coded components.

EXTERNAL LISTS

External lists are not part of the BDC model, but they are briefly described here because of their close relationship with ECTs. An external list is a BCS component that provides a SharePoint list-style interface for data entities modeled by an ECT. Unlike SharePoint lists and content types, each external list is mapped to a single ECT. The external list enables users to view, sort and filter, create, update, and delete external data entities in the same way that they would work with data in a regular SharePoint list. An ECT must implement **Finder** and **SpecificFinder** methods to be exposed as an external list. As a developer, you can also use the **SPList** object model to programmatically interact with data through the external list (with some restrictions). However, because external lists don't "own" the external data, they cannot receive events when items are added, updated, or deleted. As such, you can't associate workflows or event receivers with external lists. However, logic in workflows and event receivers that execute on standard SharePoint lists can access items in external lists.

EXTERNAL DATA AND SEARCH

The SharePoint search service uses ECTs to crawl external data sources for search. To support search crawls, the ECT must include the following types of stereotyped operations:

- An **IdEnumerator** method. This type of method returns the identity values for each instance of an ECT entity. You can support incremental indexing by configuring the **IdEnumerator** method to return a field that represents the last modified date and time, because this enables the search service to establish whether an item has been modified since the last search crawl.

- A **SpecificFinder** method. This type of method returns a single entity instance when provided with the unique identifier for that item.

The Further Information section at the end of this chapter provides links to more information on specific types of stereotyped operations, including the **Finder**, **SpecificFinder**, and **IdEnumerator** methods discussed here.

.NET CONNECTIVITY ASSEMBLIES

When you create a new connection for a BDC model in SharePoint Designer 2010, you've probably noticed that you're presented with three options for the type of connection— Microsoft SQL Server®, Windows® Communication Foundation (WCF) service, or Microsoft .NET type. This last option, the .NET type, is designed to allow you to use a .NET connectivity assembly (variously referred to as a .NET shim, a BCS shim, or a shim assembly) to drive your BDC model. Creating a .NET connectivity assembly allows you to write custom code to define the stereotyped operations for your BDC model. For example, you could create a **Finder** method, using the recommended method signature for that operation, and include custom logic that queries and concatenates data from multiple entities.

A .NET connectivity assembly maps to the external system level (**LobSystem** in the BDC schema) of the BDC model. Because of this, the .NET connectivity assembly must provide classes and methods for all the entities in your model—you can't mix and match with other connection types. Typical scenarios in which you should consider using a .NET connectivity assembly include the following:

- You want to aggregate data from multiple services and expose a single data model to SharePoint.

- You want to access data that is not accessible through a SQL Server database connection or a WCF Web service.

- You want to convert proprietary data types returned by an external system into .NET data types that are understood by the BDC runtime.

- You want to "flatten" complex data entities into fields that are compatible with the user interface (UI) components provided by the BCS.

Visual Studio provides tools for modeling and building .NET connectivity assemblies. Where possible, you should aim to make your .NET connectivity assembly methods conform to the recommended signatures for stereotyped operations, because this will enable you to maximize functionality without writing custom code. For more details on creating .NET connectivity assemblies and where to find the recommended signatures for stereotyped operations, see the Further Information section at the end of this chapter.

CONSTRAINTS AND RELATIONSHIPS

A Business Data Connectivity (BDC) model can include *associations* between external content types (ECTs). An association is a relationship that allows the BDC runtime to navigate between external content types. You can create two different types of associations between external content types:

- **Foreign key association**. This type of association maps a field in one ECT (the foreign key) to an identifier in another ECT.
- **Foreign key-less association**. This type of association uses custom logic to relate one ECT to another ECT.

For example, suppose you create an ECT named Customers, with an identifier of *CustomerID*. You also create an ECT named Orders, which includes a *CustomerID* field. You create a foreign key association from the Orders ECT to the Customers ECT, as shown in Figure 5. Note that the field types must be the same on both sides of the association.

FIGURE 5
Foreign key association between external content types

This association allows you to create user interfaces using built-in BCS components. For example, you can create a profile page for a customer that automatically shows all of their orders in a Business Data Related List Web Part. The association would also allow you to use external item picker controls to select a customer when you create an order.

Note: *Associations in a BDC model do not enforce referential integrity. For example, the cascade delete and restrict delete functionality found in regular SharePoint list relationships do not apply to BDC associations. However, the underlying database or service may enforce referential integrity.*

Just like the stereotyped operations that define an ECT, associations are created as methods in the BDC model. Each association includes an input parameter, which must be an identifier on the destination ECT, and a set of return parameters. In the previous example, *CustomerID* is the input parameter and *OrderID* and *Amount* are likely choices for return parameters. The association method could be expressed as "Get me all the orders where the *CustomerID* is equal to the specified value." Associations are best thought of as navigational relationships between entities. The BCS will not perform any kind of join across a relationship.

SharePoint Designer enables you to interactively create the following types of associations:

- **One-to-one foreign key associations**. One item in the destination table relates to one item in the source table. For example, you could use a one-to-one association to model the relationship between an employee and a department.
- **One-to-many foreign key associations**. One item in the destination table relates to many items in the source table. For example, you could use a one-to-many association to model the relationship between a customer and his orders.

- **Self-referential foreign key associations**. One item in the source table relates to other items in the source table. For example, you could use a self-referential association to model relationships between people.

All of these associations are expressed declaratively as non-static methods in the BDC model. However, in the following cases, you will need to edit the BDC model XML directly:

- **Foreign key-less associations**. This refers to any association (one-to-one, one-to-many, or many-to-many) that cannot be modeled directly by a foreign key relationship.
- **Multiple ECT associations**. This refers to any association that returns fields from more than one ECT.

In each of these cases, it's worth using SharePoint Designer to take the model as far as you can before you export the .bdcm file and manually edit the XML. Foreign key-less associations always require custom logic to define the relationship between the ECTs. This custom logic could be a stored procedure in a database, a Web service, or a method in a .NET connectivity assembly. Typical scenarios in which you might require a foreign key-less association include when you need to navigate between entities that are related by an intermediate table. The following are some examples:

- You use an intermediate table to model a many-to-many relationship. For example, you might have a many-to-many relationship between parts and machines—a machine contains many parts, and a part is found in many machines.
- A customer is related to an order, and an order is related to a line item. You want to show the customer in a line item view.

For example, Figure 6 illustrates a foreign key-less association between OrderLines and Customers. The foreign key-less association would use a stored procedure to navigate back to Customers through the Orders table.

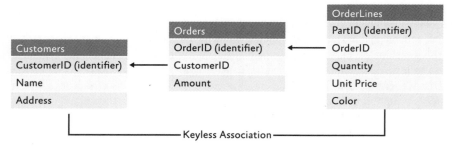

FIGURE 6
Foreign key-less association between external content types

Note that you can only create associations between entities in the same BDC model. Later in this chapter, you will see how associations are actually defined within the model.

BDC Models and Common Scenarios

Depending on your requirements, there are three basic approaches you can take to creating a Business Data Connectivity (BDC) model for an external system:

- You can create a purely declarative BDC model.
- You can create a declarative BDC model and create additional database stored procedures or additional Web service logic to support foreign key-less associations or type flattening.
- You can create a .NET connectivity assembly to connect to the external system and perform data operations, and then build your BDC model around the .NET connectivity assembly.

The following table lists which of these approaches is typically used in various common scenarios.

Note: *The table does not prescribe specific approaches to specific scenarios. Your own application scenarios may merit a different approach.*

Scenario	Declarative BDC model	Declarative BDC model with additional stored procedures or service logic	.NET connectivity assembly
Single entity	✔		
One-to-one relationships	✔		
One-to-many relationships	✔		
Many-to-many relationships		✔	
Non-integer-based foreign key relationships	✔		
Complex data types*	✔		✔
Blob storage	✔		
Unsupported data types			✔
Proprietary protocol for accessing external system			✔
Aggregating data into a single entity from multiple data sources			✔

*Complex data types are limited to read operations in Business Data Web Parts.

Modifying Identifier Fields

If you want to allow the user to modify the identifier field for a BDC entity instance, you must add a **PreUpdaterField="true"** attribute value to the type descriptor for the relevant parameter in the **Update** method. For example, if you were using SKU as your identifier field, and you allowed the user to change the SKU when updating a part, you must set this field to **true**. You must add this attribute by manually editing the BDC model XML. After making this change, you will not be able to edit your model in SharePoint Designer 2010.

The External Data Models reference implementation in the Developing Applications for SharePoint 2010 online guidance provides practical examples of these scenarios. It also enables you to explore a realistic declarative BDC model to get a feel for how the pieces fit together. For more information, refer to the *See It in Action* section at the end of this chapter.

Implementing Advanced BDC Models

Now that you understand the basics of how BDC models are created, it's worth taking a look at some of the more complex issues you may encounter when you build your own models. First, if you want to build foreign key-less associations between your entities, you will need to manually edit the BDC model XML to define the relationship. Second, if your external data source uses complex data types, you may need to manipulate the structure of the data in your BDC model in order to use certain BCS components, such as Business Data Web Parts or external lists.

Understanding Associations in External Data

It can be instructive to take a look at how associations are represented in the underlying BDC model. In most cases, you can use the tooling in SharePoint Designer to build a foreign key association. However, if you want to specify a foreign key-less association, you must manually define the logic that traverses the related entities. To start with, let's briefly review how operations are defined within BDC entities.

- Each **Entity** element includes various **Method** elements. A **Method** is an abstract description of a particular function of the underlying data source. This could be a Transact-SQL statement, a stored procedure, a Web service method, or some other command.

- Each **Method** element includes one or more **MethodInstance** elements. A **Method Instance** is the executable part of a **Method** and conforms to the signature of a stereotyped operation. In other words, when you invoke an operation on an ECT, you are actually invoking a **MethodInstance**. Effectively, the **MethodInstance** tells the BDC runtime how to use the **Method**.

In the BDC model, associations are defined within **Method** elements. The association is actually a type of method instance, so the **Association** element takes the place of a **MethodInstance** element.

Note: *For a good overview of the BDC model schema, see BDC Model Infrastructure at http://msdn.microsoft.com/en-us/library/ee556378.aspx.*

For example, SharePoint Designer created the following association method, which represents a foreign key association between an **InventoryLocations** entity and a **Parts** entity. Notice the automatically generated Transact-SQL in the **RdbCommandText** property. Defined on the **InventoryLocations** entity, the association method allows you to navigate from a specific **Parts** instance to the related **InventoryLocations** instance by providing a **PartSKU** parameter.

XML
```xml
<Method IsStatic="false" Name="InventoryLocationsNavigate Association">
  <Properties>
    <Property Name="BackEndObject" Type="System.String">InventoryLocations
    </Property>
    <Property Name="BackEndObjectType" Type="System.String">SqlServerTable
    </Property>
    <Property Name="RdbCommandText" Type="System.String">
      SELECT [ID] , [PartSKU] , [BinNumber] , [Quantity]
      FROM [dbo].[InventoryLocations]
      WHERE [PartSKU] = @PartSKU
    </Property>
    <Property Name="RdbCommandType" Type="System.Data.CommandType, System.Data,
      Version=2.0.0.0, Culture=neutral, PublicKeyToken=b77a5c561934e089">Text
    </Property>
    ...
```

The **Method** element also defines every parameter, but these have been omitted for brevity. Within the **Method** element, the **Association** element—the *method instance*—defines the specific logic that is actually invoked to traverse the association. Note that the element has a **Type** attribute value of **AssociationNavigator**. This is the standard stereotyped operation for methods that navigate an association. Also note the **Source Entity** and **DestinationEntity** elements that actually define the association. A single method definition could contain multiple associations, each defining a relationship between **InventoryLocations** and another entity (providing that all the associations are based on the **PartSKU** field).

XML
```xml
...
<MethodInstances>
  <Association Name="InventoryLocationsNavigate Association"
               Type="AssociationNavigator"
               ReturnParameterName="InventoryLocationsNavigate Association"
               DefaultDisplayName="InventoryLocations Navigate Association">
    <Properties>
      <Property Name="ForeignFieldMappings"
```

```
                     Type="System.String">
&lt;?xml version="1.0" encoding="utf-16"?&gt;
&lt;ForeignFieldMappings xmlns:xsi="http://www.w3.org/2001/XMLSchema-instance"
xmlns:xsd="http://www.w3.org/2001/XMLSchema"&gt;
&lt;ForeignFieldMappingsList&gt;
&lt;ForeignFieldMapping ForeignIdentifierName="SKU" ForeignIdentifierEntityName="
Parts" ForeignIdentifierEntityNamespace="DataModels.ExternalData.PartsManagement"
FieldName="PartSKU" /&gt;
&lt;/ForeignFieldMappingsList&gt;
&lt;/ForeignFieldMappings&gt;
        </Property>
      </Properties>
      <SourceEntity Namespace="DataModels.ExternalData.PartsManagement"
                    Name="Parts" />
      <DestinationEntity Namespace="DataModels.ExternalData.PartsManagement"
                         Name="InventoryLocations" />
    </Association>
  </MethodInstances>
</Method>
```

Note: *The* **Association** *class derives from the* **MethodInstance** *class. In terms of the object model, an* **Association** *is one specific type of* **MethodInstance**.

The encoded XML within the **ForeignFieldMappings** element can be hard to read. Essentially, this identifies the foreign key—in other words, the field in the **Parts** entity that provides the **PartSKU** parameter. Decoded and simplified, the field value resembles the following.

XML
```
<ForeignFieldMappings>
  <ForeignFieldMappingsList>
    <ForeignFieldMapping ForeignIdentifierName="SKU"
                         ForeignIdentifierEntityName="Parts"
                         ForeignIdentifierEntityNamespace=
                             "DataModels.ExternalData.PartsManagement"
                         FieldName="PartSKU" />
  </ForeignFieldMappingsList>
</ForeignFieldMappings>
```

Compare this association to a manually-defined foreign key-less association. The following association method defines an association between a **Machines** entity and a **Parts** entity. Because this is a many-to-many relationship, you need to specify a stored procedure to navigate the association. In this case, the **RdbCommandText** property identifies the stored procedure to call.

XML

```xml
<Method IsStatic="false" Name="GetPartsByMachineID">
  <Properties>
    <Property Name="BackEndObject" Type="System.String">GetPartsByMachineID
    </Property>
    <Property Name="BackEndObjectType" Type="System.String">SqlServerRoutine
    </Property>
    <Property Name="RdbCommandText" Type="System.String">
     [dbo].[GetPartsByMachineID]
    </Property>
    <Property Name="RdbCommandType" Type="System.Data.CommandType, System.Data,
     Version=2.0.0.0, Culture=neutral, PublicKeyToken=b77a5c561934e089">
     StoredProcedure
    </Property>
    ...
```

Again, the method definition also defines each parameter, but these have been omitted for brevity. Because the relationship is not based on a foreign key, the method instance definition does not need to identify foreign key mappings. Instead, it simply specifies the **SourceEntity** and the **DestinationEntity**.

XML

```xml
  ...
  <MethodInstances>
    <Association Name="GetPartsByMachineID"
                 Type="AssociationNavigator"
                 ReturnParameterName="GetPartsByMachineID"
                  DefaultDisplayName="Parts Read With Sproc">
      <SourceEntity Namespace="DataModels.ExternalData.PartsManagement"
                    Name="Machines" />
      <DestinationEntity Namespace="DataModels.ExternalData.PartsManagement"
                         Name="Parts" />
    </Association>
  </MethodInstances>
</Method>
```

MODELING COMPLEX TYPES IN EXTERNAL DATA

When your external system contains tabular data structures, it's straightforward to build a representative BDC model. SharePoint Designer 2010 will discover the data structures for you, and tabular entities map well to SharePoint lists. However, advanced scenarios require more complex handling. How do you create a BDC model that aggregates data from multiple sources? How do you create your data entities when your external system contains complex, nested data structures? Let's look at some of the options that can help you address these issues.

In an XML data structure, a complex type refers to an element that has child elements. A complex type that contains only one level of descendants can be represented as a tabular data structure. However, if a complex type contains more than one level of descendants—in other words, the parent node has grandchildren as well as children—the type can no longer be represented as a table or a list. In this situation, you must take additional action if you want to use built-in data constructs, such as external lists and Business Data Web Parts, to provide an interface for your external data. Flattening describes the process whereby a complex, nested type is converted into a flat two-dimensional structure that can be managed more easily by the out-of-the-box BCS components.

In general, there are two approaches you can use to manage nested complex types in SharePoint data models:

- You can flatten the nested complex types into one or more simple types.
- You can build a custom user interface that is able to represent the complex structure, such as through the use of custom fields or custom Web Parts.

If you choose to flatten the nested complex types, there are various options available to you. Consider the following example of a **Customer** entity, returned by a Web service, which includes a nested **Address** element.

```XML
<Customer>
  <Name>Contoso</Name>
  <Address>
    <Street>1 Microsoft Way</Street>
    <City>Redmond</City>
    <StateProvince>WA</StateProvince>
    <PostalCode>98052</PostalCode>
  </Address>
</Customer>
```

One approach would be to modify the Web service to return a flattened data structure that maps well to external lists and Business Data Web Parts:

```XML
<Customer>
  <Name>Contoso</Name>
  <AddressStreet>1 Microsoft Way</AddressStreet>
  <AddressCity>Redmond</AddressCity>
  <AddressStateProvince>WA</AddressStateProvince>
  <AddressPostalCode>98052</AddressPostalCode>
</Customer>
```

Although this approach certainly solves the problem, in many cases you will not want, or will not be able, to modify the Web service. An alternative approach is to include a format string in the BDC model, so that the data entity is displayed as a flattened structure. In this case, the customer address is flattened and displayed as a single string.

```
XML
<TypeDescriptor TypeName="CustomerAddress" IsCollection="false"
Name="CustomerAddresses" >
   <TypeDescriptors>
      <Properties>
         <Property Name="ComplexFormatting" Type="System.String" />
      </Properties>
      <TypeDescriptor TypeName="CustomerAddress" Name="CustomerAddress" >
         <Properties>
            <Property Name="FormatString"
                      Type="System.String">{0}, {1}, {2} {3}</Property>
         </Properties>
         <TypeDescriptors>
            <TypeDescriptor TypeName="System.String" Name="Street"/>
            <TypeDescriptor TypeName="System.String" Name="City" />
            <TypeDescriptor TypeName="System.String" Name="StateProvince" />
            <TypeDescriptor TypeName="System.String" Name="PostalCode" />
         </TypeDescriptors>
      </TypeDescriptor>
   </TypeDescriptors>
</TypeDescriptor>
```

In this example, the format string tells the BDC runtime how to render the address entity as a single string, in the order that the child elements are listed in the **TypeDescriptors** collection. If you apply the sample data to this BDC model, the address is formatted on a single line as 1 Microsoft Way, Redmond, WA 98052. You can programmatically retrieve the formatted data by using the **EntityInstance.GetFormatted("FieldName")** method. However, this approach has several limitations. First, the approach is only viable if the data entity can be represented effectively as a single string. Second, this formatting only handles the display of data. If you need to update the external data, you must add programming logic or custom forms to parse the new values and update the data source. Unfortunately, you can only use format strings with Business Data Web Parts. This approach will not work with external lists.

A third option is to use a custom renderer. A custom renderer is a .NET class containing a static method that takes in an array of objects and returns a string. The runtime calls this renderer to format the objects into a string. To use this approach, in the **TypeDescriptor** element you would use the **RendererDefinition** attribute to identify the method, class, and assembly of the custom renderer. Using a custom renderer is an expensive operation because the renderer must be called on a per-item basis; because of this, you should generally only use a custom renderer when no other options are available. Just like format strings, custom renderers can only be used with Business Data Web Parts and will not work with external lists.

Another option is to create a custom field type. A custom field type defines a data type for a SharePoint list column, and provides a useful way of storing complex list data in a manageable way. You can also create custom field controls that interpret the data in the custom field type and render it in a user-friendly way. For example, you could create a custom field type that stores nested address data, together with a custom field control that displays the data in a flattened, list-friendly format. Custom field controls typically define two interfaces—one that presents the data, and one that allows the user to edit the data—so that the control works in both list view forms and list edit forms. In the edit view, you can provide a user interface that allows the user to provide the field data in its nested format, thereby preserving the integrity of the underlying data. Custom field types and field controls offer the most flexible approach to working with complex data, and you can build in sophisticated behavior such as sorting and filtering. However, creating field types and field controls involves creating several classes and definition files, which makes them somewhat complicated to implement.

Finally, you can use a .NET connectivity assembly to manage the conversion between complex types and flat types. This is a powerful approach, because you can specify exactly how your data is flattened and unflattened for each stereotyped operation. The .NET connectivity assembly bridges the gap between the external system and the BDC model—the external system sees nested complex types, while the BDC model sees flattened data structures.

Working with Database Views

In some scenarios, you may want to model external content types on composite views of entities in your external system. For example, you might create an external content type from a database view or a specialized service method instead of simply replicating database tables or other external entities. This approach is useful for read operations in which you need to aggregate fields from multiple external tables or entities, especially when you are working with large amounts of data. If you don't use a database view, you would need to traverse individual entity associations in order to generate the composite view you require. This increases the load on the BDC runtime and can lead to a poor user experience.

The drawback of binding external content types to database views is that **create**, **update**, and **delete** operations become more complicated, because updating a view inevitably involves performing operations on more than one table. There are two approaches you can use to enable updates to database views:

- You can create an *INSTEAD OF trigger* on the SQL Server database to drive update operations. An INSTEAD OF trigger defines the Transact-SQL commands that should be executed when a client attempts a particular update operation. For example, you might define an INSTEAD OF INSERT routine that is executed when a client attempts an INSERT operation.

- You can develop stored procedures on the SQL Server database to perform the update operations and map the relevant stereotyped operations for your external content type to these stored procedures.

Unless you are expert in creating Transact-SQL routines, using triggers can be somewhat cumbersome and complex. You may find that creating stored procedures offers a more palatable approach.

You might think that binding external content types to database views is more trouble than it's worth; especially if you must create stored procedures to support update operations. However, if you took the alternative approach of modeling database tables directly, one update to your user interface view would require updates to multiple external content types in the BDC model. To accomplish these updates in a single operation, you would need to write code using the BDC object model. By putting the multiple update logic in a stored procedure on the database, you reduce the load on the BDC runtime. From an efficiency perspective, the stored procedure approach requires only a single round trip to the database server, because the database view represents a single entity to the BDC runtime. In contrast, managing updates to multiple entities through the BDC object model requires multiple round trips to the database server; therefore, it is a more expensive operation.

Performance and Security Considerations

In SharePoint 2010, BDC models are able to retrieve and manipulate data in many external systems. Many of these systems may perform business-critical functions and contain sensitive information. As such, it's important to manage your BDC models carefully to ensure that you do not jeopardize the performance or the security of the back-end systems to which you connect.

FILTERS AND THROTTLING IN THE BDC

The Business Data Connectivity (BDC) runtime includes configurable filtering and throttling functionality. Administrators can use this functionality to control both the load that BDC operations put on SharePoint and the load that the operations put on the external systems that you connect to. Filters constrain the result set by restricting the scope of the query, such as by including wildcard queries or paging sets. Throttling prevents BDC operations from using excessive system resources by terminating requests that exceed the resource thresholds set by the administrator. Figure 7 illustrates the filtering and throttling process.

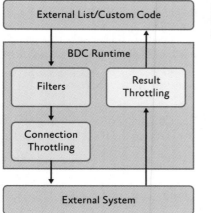

FIGURE 7
Filtering and throttling in the BDC runtime

Filters encompass a wide range of information that the BDC can pass to the external system in order to constrain the result set. The types of filters you can use depend on the types of filters that are supported by the external system. The BDC allows you to use two key types of filters: *system filters* and *user filters*. System filters provide context information to the external system. For example, system filters can include a **UserContext** value that securely provides the identity of the caller to the external system and an **ActivityId** value that represents the current operation context for diagnostic purposes. Conversely, user filters enable end users or application logic to refine a query. For example, user filters can include **Wildcard** and **Comparison** filters for pattern matching and a **PageNumber** value to support data retrieval on a page-by-page basis.

Conceptually, throttling in the BDC is similar to the query throttling for regular lists found in SharePoint 2010. The BDC runtime throttles external data requests based on various criteria, including maximum acceptable response times, maximum permissible response sizes in data rows or bytes, and the total number of concurrent connections to databases or services. Each throttling rule can be associated with one of four scopes: Web services, WCF services, databases, or global. The default threshold values are as follows:

- 2,000 rows for a database query.
- 3,000,000 bytes for a WCF service or Web service response.
- 180-second response time for a WCF service or a database request.
- 200 total connections across databases, Web services, and WCF services.

The throttling criteria that are available to the administrator depend on the scope of the rule. The following table shows the criteria that apply to each of the four possible scopes.

	Global	Database	Web service	WCF service
Items		✔		
Size			✔	✔
Connections	✔			
Timeout		✔		✔

SECURITY AND IDENTITY

Business Connectivity Services in SharePoint 2010 supports two different security modes for accessing services and databases—*PassThrough authentication* and *RevertToSelf authentication*:

- **PassThrough authentication**. This uses the credentials of the logged-on user to authenticate to the Web service or the database.
- **RevertToSelf authentication**. This uses the credentials of the process running the application to authenticate to the Web service or the database. This is known as a *trusted subsystem* model.

By default, RevertToSelf authentication is disabled because it poses a potential security risk and is not permitted in hosting environments. If you enable RevertToSelf authentication in the BCS, a malicious developer or designer could point the service endpoint back to SharePoint and use the elevated privileges of the application pool account to circumvent security restrictions.

The Secure Store Service (SSS) is a BCS component that is licensed with SharePoint Server 2010. The SSS provides additional options for authenticating to external services and databases. The SSS maps SharePoint user identities to other external credentials and supports claims-based approaches to authentication. The SSS offers an impersonation model that provides a trusted subsystem approach in a safer way than RevertToSelf authentication, because the SSS does not use the application pool account to access the external service.

Meeting security requirements can become more complex when you use the BCD through the runtime APIs or through external lists. The user security token is not available in every context. Without the security token, PassThrough security will not work. Additionally, you will be unable to use the SSS to map the identity of the user to external credentials. The following are two common scenarios in which the user security token is unavailable:

- **Sandboxed solutions**. In the sandbox environment, the **SPUser** object is available, but the security tokens are stripped from the user context.
- **Workflows**. Because a workflow runs asynchronously, the security tokens for the user will not be available. You can create an **SPUser** context by using impersonation in a workflow, but this will not create an identity token for the impersonated account.

In these situations, you need to work around the lack of an identity token and use a trusted subsystem model where all users will use the same account to access the services or database. In sandboxed solutions, external data is accessed through an external list. As described in Chapter Four, "Hybrid Approaches to Execution," the user code proxy service (SPUCWorkerProcessProxy.exe) enables the external list to send and receive external data through the BCS. As a result, a common approach to authentication is to use the SSS to map the credentials of the managed account that runs the user code proxy service to the credentials that provide access to the external system. A similar approach can be used for workflow, although the workflow scenario is a little more complicated. Workflow can run in the context of several processes, including the application pool identity of the Web application hosting the application (W3wp.exe), the timer job identity (Owstimer.exe), or the user code proxy service (SPUCWorkerProcessProxy.exe). Typically, a workflow runs in the context of the content Web application when it is initiated (although under heavy load it may instead be started by the timer service) and in the OWSTimer process if it is triggered by a timed event, such as a timeout or a timer job. It can also run in the sandbox proxy process if the workflow is triggered by an action that is initiated by sandboxed code, such as programmatically adding an item to a list. In order to use BCS in a workflow you will need to map each of the managed accounts for these three processes to the single account used to impersonate to the service or database. You can also use RevertToSelf under these circumstances as long as you are aware of and accept the risks described previously. If you use RevertToSelf, then the service or database must accept the credentials of the three managed accounts. As described in Chapter 4, "Hybrid Approaches to Execution," you must also configure user permissions on individual ECTs.

Where Should I Build My Data Store?

As you've seen over the last two chapters, SharePoint 2010 provides a wide range of functionality to help you build data models with SharePoint lists and external data. You should also now be familiar with some of the key advantages, issues, and limitations of each approach. So how do these advantages, issues, and limitations affect your solution design? Choosing where to store your data is a fairly fundamental design decision. At a high level, you have two choices: you can store your data in the SharePoint content database, or you can use an external data source and connect to it through BCS.

In some cases, the decision is easy. For example, SharePoint has an extensive functionality set devoted to document management, so it makes sense to store documents in the SharePoint content database. Likewise, if your application consumes data from line-of-business applications or other existing repositories of any kind, there are very few circumstances in which there will be benefit in replicating large amounts of data to the SharePoint content database. In most cases, you will want to access existing data where it resides, through the BCS.

There are two high-level scenarios in which the choice may be less clear.

- You are building a new data-driven application with no legacy code or preexisting data (a green field development scenario). In this case, you could either use list-based SharePoint data structures as a data store or you could develop an external data source such as a relational database and connect to it through the BCS. The factors that drive your decision are likely to include the ease of implementing the data model, the performance of the application, and the ease of programming against the data model.

- You are porting an existing data-driven application to SharePoint (a quasi-brown field development scenario). In this case, you can continue to use the existing data store and connect through the BCS or you can implement a SharePoint list-based data model and migrate your data to the SharePoint content database. Your decision may be influenced by any design constraints in the existing data model. Note that this option only applies to complete migration scenarios. In other words, if you move the data to SharePoint, you can destroy the existing data store and there are no ongoing synchronization costs.

This comparison focuses on a choice between implementing a data model in a SharePoint list and using an external database with the BCS. Of course, there are other data modeling options. You could implement a model that uses a combination of external database tables and SharePoint lists—for example, if you want to extend the data model provided by an existing database, you could continue to use the external database tables and develop SharePoint lists to extend the model. In support of this scenario, SharePoint 2010 allows you to look up data in an external list from a SharePoint list. However, you cannot look up data in a SharePoint list from an external list, because the external list represents external data that is unaware of the SharePoint implementation. For more complex business logic requirements, you should also consider building a service tier between an external database and your SharePoint application. In this case, you would build your BDC model entities against service methods instead of against database tables. However, these scenarios are beyond the scope of this chapter.

In most cases, experience shows that implementing a data model using SharePoint lists can reduce development time, providing that the capabilities of SharePoint lists meet the needs of your data model and fulfill any non-functional requirements. The following table describes the development complexity and other issues for various data modeling scenarios when you use SharePoint lists or an external database with the BCS.

Note: *In the following table, an entity can be considered to represent a SharePoint list or a table in a relational database.*

Modeling scenario	SharePoint lists	External database with BCS
One-to-one relationships	Straightforward	Straightforward
One-to-many relationships	Straightforward	Straightforward
Many-to-many relationships	Straightforward	Complex Requires mtanual customization of the BDC model Default external list forms do not support all **create**, **update**, and **delete** operations Picker controls do not work for all **create**, **update**, and **delete** operations
Relationships with non-integer-based primary keys	Not applicable You cannot specify the field on which to build a list relationship. In a SharePoint list, the built-in ID field is effectively always the primary key	Complex Requires manual customization of the BDC model
Event handling on item added, updated, or deleted	Straightforward	Limited You can use stored procedure triggers for events within the database, but any SharePoint logic will remain unaware of the event
Alerts	Straightforward	Not supported
RSS feeds	Straightforward	Not supported
Workflow for item added, updated, or deleted	Straightforward	Not supported

Transactions	Not supported	Moderate to complex
		Requires additional entity classes to model the aggregated entities for update
		Requires stored procedures to manage the transaction
		A Web service layer or a .NET connectivity assembly could be used instead of stored procedures
Aggregate calculations	Straightforward but inefficient	Moderate to complex
	You can aggregate data using LINQ to SharePoint, but the resulting query will retrieve all items and the aggregation will be performed as a post-query operation on the client	Requires additional entity classes to represent aggregated data
Right outer joins and cross joins	Not supported	Moderate
		Requires additional entity classes to model composite entities
Distinct queries	Not supported	Straightforward
Item-level security	Moderate	Not supported
Field-level security	Not supported	Not supported
Storing binary large object (BLOB) data	Straightforward	Straightforward
		Use the Business Data Item Web Part with StreamAccessors
Nested queries	Not supported	Straightforward to moderate, depending on whether you need to create additional entity classes
Complex business intelligence requirements	Limited support using the Chart Web Part, Excel Services, and Performance Point	Full database capabilities
Simple user input validation	Straightforward	Not supported
		Requires custom user interface development or a .NET connectivity assembly
Complex user input validation	Moderate	Not supported
		Requires custom user interface development or a .NET connectivity assembly

Compatibility with sandbox	Straightforward	Depends on security requirements
		No security: Straightforward
		Trusted subsystem model: Moderate (requires access to the Secure Store Service, which is not available in SharePoint Foundation 2010)
		Other security models: Complex (requires ability to install full-trust proxies)
		Requires access to Central Administration or Tenant Administration Web sites to install external content types

Conclusion

This chapter provided insights into the external data capabilities of SharePoint 2010, together with the key issues you should consider when you work with these capabilities. The following aspects of external data in SharePoint 2010 were discussed:

- **Business Connectivity Services (BCS) architecture**. Remember, the BCS is the collection of features and components in SharePoint 2010 that enables you to connect to, retrieve, manipulate, and present external data in SharePoint sites and applications. The core functionality of the BCS is provided by the Business Data Connectivity (BDC) service application.

- **Business Data Connectivity (BDC) models**. You learned that a BDC model contains the metadata that describes an external data source. The BDC model tells the BDC service application how to connect to the data source and how to perform stereotyped operations, such as create, read, update, and delete. A BDC model consists of a declarative XML file (the .bdcm file) and can also include a .NET connectivity assembly for more sophisticated operations.

- **Associations and complex types**. You can use the interactive tooling in SharePoint Designer 2010 to build many straightforward BDC models. However, certain tasks, such as modeling foreign key-less associations and flattening complex data types, require you to manually edit the model XML and as such require a deeper understanding of the BDC model schema.

- **Managing BDC models**. BDC models and the functionality of the BCS allow you to access and manipulate a wide range of external data sources. These data sources may be critical to the functioning of your organization and will often contain sensitive data. It's important to manage your BDC models carefully so as not to jeopardize the performance or security of your back-end systems.

See It in Action: *The External Data Models Reference Implementation in the Developing Applications for SharePoint 2010 online guidance is a fully documented, downloadable solution that illustrates many key aspects of working with external data in SharePoint 2010. For example, the reference implementation illustrates how you can:*

- *Create BDC models for Microsoft SQL Server databases and external services.*
- *Customize BDC models to support many-to-many relationships and non-integer primary keys.*
- *Use stored procedures and other custom logic to navigate foreign key-less relationships in a BDC model.*
- *Create .NET connectivity assemblies to flatten complex data from an external service.*
- *Use external lists and built-in business data Web Parts to interact with BDC models.*
- *Develop custom code to interact with external data by using the BDC object model.*
- *You can deploy the reference implementation to a SharePoint 2010 test environment and explore the source code at your leisure in Visual Studio 2010.*
- *For more information, see Reference Implementation: External Data Models at http://msdn.microsoft.com/en-us/library/ff798509.aspx.*

FURTHER INFORMATION

The following resources should prove helpful to you. You can find them in the book's bibliography online at http://msdn.microsoft.com/gg213840.aspx along with more links.

- "Service applications and service management"
- "Mechanics of Using Business Connectivity Services"
- "Designing a Business Data Connectivity Model"

3   Accessing Data in SharePoint 2010

Microsoft® SharePoint® 2010 introduces several new ways in which you can programmatically interact with your data. Most notably, the introduction of *LINQ to SharePoint* allows you to build complex list queries with the user-friendly language integrated query (LINQ) syntax instead of constructing queries with the somewhat cumbersome collaborative application markup language (CAML). Both LINQ to SharePoint and CAML now support **join** predicates in queries, which moves the SharePoint list-based data model a step closer to the power and flexibility of a relational database. One of the major evolutions in the latest version of SharePoint is the blurring of the distinction, from the user's perspective, between internal and external data. The introduction of external lists in SharePoint 2010 means that you can use many of the same techniques to query data, regardless of whether that data resides in a SharePoint content database or an external system.

The introduction of new options for data access brings new challenges and best practices for developers. This chapter provides an overview of each approach to server-side data access and provides guidance on the benefits and potential pitfalls of each approach.

> **Note:** *Client data access techniques, such as the new client object model and REST services, are not covered in this chapter. These techniques cover a large area f functionality and merit a chapter of their own. For more information, see Chapter Nine, "Data Access for Client Applications."*

What Are the Key Approaches to Data Access?

SharePoint 2010 offers three key approaches that you can use to query data: CAML queries, LINQ to SharePoint, and the BCS object model.

- **CAML queries**. The **SPQuery** and **SPSiteDataQuery** classes allow you to construct and submit CAML queries to perform data operations. CAML suffers from a number of shortcomings, including quirky syntax, lack of tooling support, and difficult debugging. However, CAML remains the core engine for data operations and is still the most appropriate choice in some scenarios. The CAML schema has been expanded in SharePoint 2010 to include support for join predicates. You can also use the **SPQuery** class to query external lists. Note that the results returned by CAML queries are non-typed items.

- **LINQ to SharePoint**. SharePoint 2010 allows you to use LINQ queries to perform data operations on SharePoint lists, including support for join predicates. LINQ to SharePoint operates against strongly typed entities that represent the items in your lists, and SharePoint 2010 includes a command-line tool named *SPMetal* that you can use to generate these entities. Internally, the LINQ to SharePoint provider generates the underlying CAML queries that perform the data operations.

- **The Business Connectivity Services (BCS) object model**. SharePoint 2010 includes new BCS APIs that enable you to interact with external data. The BDC Object Model allows you to programmatically navigate the data entities and associations in your Business Data Connectivity (BDC) models and to invoke the stereotyped operations defined on these entities.

The following table provides a summary of the different scenarios in which you can use each of these approaches to data access.

Scenario	LINQ to SharePoint	SPQuery	SPSite DataQuery	BDC object model
Querying SharePoint list data within a site	✔	✔		
Using joins on SharePoint lists within a site	✔	✔		
Using joins on SharePoint list data across sites within a site collection	✔	✔		
Aggregating list data across multiple sites within a site collection			✔	
Querying external list data within a site		✔		✔
Navigating associations between entities in a BDC model (external data)				✔
Accessing binary streams from external data				✔
Accessing external data from a sandboxed application (requires the use of external lists)		✔		
Querying external data that returns complex types				✔
Querying external data that uses a non-integer, or 64-bit integer, **ID** field				✔

Navigating bidirectional associations between entities in a BDC model (external data)				✔
Locating an entity by specifying a field other than the **ID** field (external data)				✔
Querying entities that include fields that do not map to an **SPFieldType** (external data)				✔
Perform bulk operations on external data				✔

In the remainder of this chapter, we take a closer look at each of these approaches in turn.

Using Query Classes

Before the advent of LINQ to SharePoint, the **SPQuery** and **SPSiteDataQuery** classes were the predominant approaches to performing data operations on SharePoint lists. There are still many scenarios in which these classes provide the most effective approach—and, in some cases, the only viable approach—to data access.

Both the **SPQuery** class and the **SPSiteDataQuery** class allow you to construct a query using collaborative application markup language (CAML). You can then use the **SPList** object model to execute your query against one or more SharePoint lists. This topic explains when you should use each class and describes the considerations that should guide your implementations.

Using SPQuery

The **SPQuery** class is used to retrieve data from a specific list. In most cases, you should use LINQ to SharePoint, instead of the **SPQuery** class, to perform data operations on lists. However, there are still some circumstances in which **SPQuery** is the most appropriate option—or the only option—for data access. Most notably, using the **SPQuery** class is the only supported server object model approach for programmatically working with data in external lists.

In SharePoint 2010, the **SPQuery** class has been extended to allow you to specify joins and projected fields. The high-level process for using the **SPQuery** class is as follows:

• Create an **SPQuery** instance.

• Set properties on the **SPQuery** instance to specify the CAML query, along with various additional query parameters as required.

• Call the **GetItems** method on an **SPList** instance, passing in the **SPQuery** instance as a parameter.

The following code example illustrates this process.

```C#
SPListItemCollection results;

var query = new SPQuery
{
  Query = "[Your CAML query statement]",
  ViewFields = "[Your CAML FieldRef elements]",
  Joins = "[Your CAML Joins element]",
  ProjectedFields = "[Your CAML ProjectsFields element]"
};

results = SPContext.Current.Web.Lists["ListInstance"].GetItems(query);
```

This chapter does not provide guidance on CAML syntax or instructions on how to configure **SPQuery** instances because these are well covered by the product documentation. However, the following are brief summaries of the key properties of interest:

- The **Query** property specifies the CAML query that you want to execute against the list instance.
- The **ViewFields** property specifies the columns that you want your queries to return as CAML **FieldRef** elements.
- The **Joins** property specifies the join predicates for your query as a CAML **Joins** element.
- The **ProjectedFields** property defines fields from foreign joined lists as a CAML **ProjectedFields** element. This allows you to reference these fields in your **ViewFields** property and in your query statement.

The following code example illustrates these options. Note that the **ContentTypeId** value has been shortened for readability.

```C#
var query = new SPQuery
{
  Query = "
    <Query>
      <Where>
        <And>
          <BeginsWith>
            <FieldRef Name="ContentTypeId" />
              <Value Type=»ContentTypeId»>0x0100...</Value>
          </BeginsWith>
          <Eq>
            <FieldRef Name=»SponsorTitle» />
            <Value Type=»Lookup»>David Pelton</Value>
          </Eq>
        </And>
```

```
        </Where>
      </Query>»,

  ViewFields = «
    <FieldRef Name=»Title» />
    <FieldRef Name=»SponsorTitle» />
    <FieldRef Name=»ProjectsLookupProject_x0020_Manager» />»,

  Joins = «
    <Joins>
      <Join Type=»LEFT» ListAlias=»ProjectsLookup»>
      <!--List Name: Projects-->
        <Eq>
          <FieldRef Name=»ProjectsLookup» RefType=»ID» />
          <FieldRef List=»ProjectsLookup» Name=»ID» />
        </Eq>
      </Join>
      <Join Type=»LEFT» ListAlias=»Sponsor»>
      <!--List Name: Sponsors-->
        <Eq>
          <FieldRef Name=»Sponsor» RefType=»ID» />
          <FieldRef List=»Sponsor» Name=»ID» />
        </Eq>
      </Join>
    </Joins>»,

  ProjectedFields = «
    <ProjectedFields>
      <Field Name=»SponsorTitle» Type=»Lookup» List=»Sponsor» ShowField=»Title» />
      <Field Name=»ProjectsLookupProject_x0020_Manager» Type=»Lookup»
            List=»ProjectsLookup» ShowField=»Project_x0020_Manager» />
    </ProjectedFields>»
};
```

Using SPQuery with Regular SharePoint Lists

You should consider using the **SPQuery** class, instead of LINQ to SharePoint, in the following scenarios:

- **When a lookup column in a list refers to a list in another site within the site collection**. In this situation, **SPQuery** allows you to use a join predicate that spans both sites. Although you can use LINQ to SharePoint to query across sites with some additional configuration, the process required to generate entity classes is more complex. By default, LINQ to SharePoint returns only the **ID** field from the target list, in which case, you would need to run additional queries to retrieve relevant field values from the target list.

- **When performance is paramount**. Using LINQ to SharePoint incurs some additional overhead, because the LINQ query must be dynamically converted to CAML at run time. If you are running a time-sensitive operation and performance is critical, you may want to consider creating the CAML yourself and using **SPQuery** to execute the query directly. Generally speaking, this approach is only required in extreme cases.

> **Note:** *In the RTM version of SharePoint 2010, LINQ to SharePoint does not support anonymous access. However, the August 2010 cumulative update for SharePoint 2010 addresses this limitation.*

Using SPQuery with External Lists

Using the **SPQuery** class is the only supported way to query external lists. Using this approach, you can query an external list in exactly the same way that you would query a regular SharePoint list. However, there are some additional considerations when you access data from an external list:

- You cannot join across external lists, even if you have defined entity associations in the BDC model.
- You can specify authorization rules by assigning permissions to the external content type. Most Web services and databases will also implement authentication and authorization. You will need to implement a security scheme either by using the Secure Store Service or by configuring your own security mechanisms.
- Throttling mechanisms and limits differ from those that apply to regular SharePoint lists. When you query an external list, the throttling settings for the BDC runtime apply.

If you want to access external data from a sandboxed application, without using a full-trust proxy, you must use an external list. Using the BDC Object Model or directly accessing external systems is prohibited in the sandbox environment. As a result, using the **SPQuery** class and the **SPList** object model with external lists is the only option for external data access if you want your solution to run in the sandbox.

> **Note:** *For security reasons, the identity token for the current user is removed from the sandbox worker process. If you need to access external lists from within the sandbox environment, you must use the Secure Store Service to map the managed account that runs the User Code Proxy Service to the credentials required by the external system. For more information, see Chapter Four, "Hybrid Approaches to Execution Models."*

Using SPSiteDataQuery

The **SPSiteDataQuery** class is used to query data from multiple lists across different sites in a site collection. **SPSiteDataQuery** is commonly used in list aggregation scenarios, where list data from team sites or other subsites is collated and presented in a single interface. Unlike the **SPQuery** class, you cannot use join predicates or projected fields with the **SPSiteDataQuery** class. An **SPSiteDataQuery** instance will only aggregate data from SharePoint lists and will ignore data from external lists.

The high-level process for using the **SPSiteDataQuery** class is as follows:

* Create an **SPSiteDataQuery** instance.

* Set properties on the **SPSiteDataQuery** instance to specify the lists or list types to include in the query, the individual sites to include in the query, and the CAML query itself.

* Call the **GetSiteData** method on an **SPWeb** instance, passing in the **SPSiteData Query** instance as a parameter. The **GetSiteData** method returns a **DataTable**.

The following code example illustrates this. In this example, statements of work (SOWs) are stored in document libraries across a site collection. The query retrieves the *SOW Status* and *Estimate Value* fields for every statement of work in the site collection, and orders the results by the *Estimate Value* field.

C#

```csharp
SPSiteDataQuery query = new SPSiteDataQuery();
query.Lists = "<Lists BaseType='1' />";
query.ViewFields = "<FieldRef Name='SOWStatus' />" +
                   "<FieldRef Name='EstimateValue' />";
query.Query = "<OrderBy>
                 <FieldRef Name='EstimateValue' />
               </OrderBy>";
query.Webs = "<Webs Scope='SiteCollection' />";

SPWeb web = SPContext.Current.Web;
DataTable results = web.GetSiteData(query);
```

In terms of efficiency, the **SPSiteDataQuery** class provides an optimal approach to data access in the following scenarios:

* When you need to query multiple lists within the same site collection for the same content

* When you need to query across two or more lists that are not related by lookup columns

You should avoid using LINQ to SharePoint to aggregate list data across sites. LINQ to SharePoint is designed to aggregate data across list relationships defined by lookup columns. Attempting cross-site operations in LINQ to SharePoint typically requires a post-query join operation in memory, which is a resource- intensive process. In contrast, the **SPSiteDataQuery** class is optimized for querying list data across multiple sites in a site collection and across multiple lists within a single site.

Note: *The **SPSiteDataQuery** class is available in SharePoint Foundation 2010. SharePoint Server 2010 includes additional built-in components that are appropriate for certain list aggregation scenarios. These components include the Content Query Web Part and the Portal Site Map Navigation Provider.*

Note: *Because of a bug in SharePoint 2010, an* **SPException** *(hr=0x80004005) is thrown if you execute an* **SPSiteDataQuery** *on a site that contains an external list with a column named* **Id***. This may be fixed in a future service pack or cumulative update.*

Using LINQ to SharePoint

The LINQ to SharePoint provider is a new feature in SharePoint 2010 that allows you to use a strongly typed entity model and the LINQ query syntax to query SharePoint list data. Essentially, LINQ to SharePoint hides the complexity of developing CAML queries from developers, which can reduce development time and make code more readable. The LINQ to SharePoint provider converts the LINQ expressions into CAML queries at run time.

Using LINQ to SharePoint in your own solutions consists of three main steps:

- **Generate the entity classes**. Before you can start writing LINQ queries against your SharePoint lists, you must create or generate the strongly typed entity classes that represent your list data and lookup column relationships.

- **Develop the solution**. After you add the entity classes to your Microsoft Visual Studio® 2010 project, you can write LINQ queries against the strongly typed entities that represent your data model.

- **Run the solution**. At run time, the LINQ to SharePoint provider dynamically converts your LINQ expressions into CAML queries, executes the CAML, and then maps the returned items to your strongly typed data entities.

THE LINQ TO SHAREPOINT PROCESS

Although you can manually develop your entity classes, in most cases, you will want to use the *SPMetal* command line tool. This is included in SharePoint Foundation 2010 and can be found in the BIN folder in the SharePoint root. The SPMetal tool targets an individual SharePoint site and, by default, generates the following code resources:

- **A data context class that derives from DataContext**. This is the top-level entity class. It represents the content of your site and provides methods that allow you to retrieve list entities. The data context class uses the **EntityList<TEntity>** class to represent the lists in your site, where **TEntity** is a class that represents a content type.

- **Classes that represent content types**. These are marked with the **ContentType Attribute**. Content type classes are generated for implicit content types as well as content types that are explicitly defined on the site. For example, if a user adds a column to an existing list, the user is creating an implicit content type and a representative class will be generated.

- **Classes and properties that represent relationships between lists**. SPMetal can detect relationships based on lookup columns. Within the entity class that represents a content type, SPMetal uses the **EntityRef<TEntity>** class to represent the singleton side of a one-to-many relationship and the **EntitySet<TEntity>** class to represent the "many" side of one-to-many or many-to-many relationships (known as a reverse lookup). Properties that are mapped to a field in a related list are decorated with the **AssociationAttribute**.

Note: *You can configure the SPMetal tool to generate entity classes for specific lists, instead of for all the content in your site, by creating a parameters file. For links to more information, see the Further Information section at the end of this chapter.*

After the entity classes are generated, you can write LINQ queries against strongly typed entities instead of creating CAML queries. Under the covers, the LINQ to SharePoint provider converts your LINQ queries into CAML at run time and executes the CAML against your SharePoint lists. To illustrate how you can use the LINQ syntax to query your entity classes, consider a SharePoint site for a manufacturing team that includes a list named *Priority Projects*. This list contains various columns, such as *Title* and *Executive Sponsor*, together with a lookup column that links each list item to a central *Projects* list. Suppose you want to retrieve all the priority projects that were sponsored by David Pelton. In each case, you want to retrieve the *Title* and *Executive Sponsor* fields from the *Priority Projects* list together with the *Leader* field from the related item in the *Projects* list. Your code would resemble the following:

C#
```
using (ManufacturingSiteDataContext context = new
          ManufacturingSiteDataContext(SPContext.Current.Web.Url))
{
  string sponsor = "David Pelton";

  var results = from projectItem in context.PriorityProjects
                where projectItem.ExecutiveSponsor == sponsor
                select projectItem;

  foreach (var proj in results)
  {
      output.AppendFormat("Title: {0}  Sponsor: {1}  Leader: {2} \n",
      proj.Title, proj.ExecutiveSponsor, proj.Project.Leader);
  }
}
```

All the entity classes in this example were generated by the **SPMetal** tool. The example illustrates the following key points:

- The query uses a data context class. The **ManufacturingSiteDataContext** class inherits from the **DataContext** class and includes strongly typed properties for each list on the manufacturing site, such as the *Priority Projects* list.

- The content type class that represents the entities within the list includes strongly typed properties for each column value, such as **Title** and **ExecutiveSponsor**.

- The entity classes understand the relationships defined by lookup columns—the **Project.Leader** property retrieves a **Leader** field value from a related **Project** entity.

Note that you should always dispose of the data context instance after use. The **Data Context** base class implements the **IDisposable** interface, and thereby ensures that the data context instance is released when execution passes beyond the scope of the **using** statement.

The product documentation for SharePoint 2010 provides comprehensive information on the basics of how to use LINQ to SharePoint, and you can find links to relevant material in the Further Information section at the end of this chapter. In this section, we focus on the capabilities, key issues, and limitations of LINQ to SharePoint as a data access strategy, to help you to evaluate whether LINQ to SharePoint is the right approach for you in particular application scenarios.

How Are LINQ to SharePoint Queries Executed?

LINQ to SharePoint uses deferred loading—commonly known as lazy loading—of result sets to improve query efficiency. If you create a query that returns a collection of entities, the query won't actually execute until you commence an action that uses the result set—such as iterating over the results or converting the result set to an array. In the preceding code example, the LINQ query is only converted to CAML and executed when the **foreach** statement starts enumerating the result set.

LINQ to SharePoint also uses the deferred loading approach for related entities. Any related entities are only loaded when the entity is actually accessed, in order to reduce unnecessary calls to the content database. In the preceding code example, the **Project** entity is only loaded when the **foreach** statement reads the **Project.Leader** property.

When a query is executed in the context of an HTTP request, LINQ to SharePoint uses the **SPContext.Current** property to load the data context. This makes the process of loading the data context relatively efficient. However, if you use a LINQ query outside the context of an HTTP request, such as in a command line application or a Windows® PowerShell ™ script, the LINQ to SharePoint provider must construct context objects, such as the **SPWeb** and the **SPSite**, in order to build the data context instance. In this case, the process becomes more resource intensive. Any **create**, **update**, or **delete** operations within your LINQ queries are automatically batched by the data context instance and applied when the **DataContext.SubmitChanges** method is called by your code.

Generating Entities for Content Types

The SPMetal command line tool generates entity classes for the content types defined in a SharePoint site. Content types have various characteristics that can make this process difficult to understand:

- Content types support inheritance.
- Content types can be defined at the site level or at the list level. When a content type is added to a list, SharePoint creates a local copy of the content type, which can be modified.
- A list can have multiple content types associated with it.

SPMetal uses the following rules when it generates content types:

- An entity class is generated for every content type on the site (**SPWeb**).

- If a content type inherits from another content type, the entity class that represents the child content type will inherit from the entity class that represents the parent content type. For example, in the sandbox reference implementation, the **SOW** (statement of work) content type inherits from the built-in **Document** content type, which in turn inherits from the built-in **Item** content type. SPMetal generates entity classes for **SOW**, **Document**, and **Item**, and builds an inheritance relationship between the classes.

- If a list content type has been modified from the corresponding site content type, SPMetal will generate a new entity class for the list content type. If the list content type is identical to the corresponding site content type, SPMetal will simply use the entity class for the site content type instead. Entities created from list content types are named by preceding the content type name with the list name. For example, if you add a StartDate column to the **SOW** content type in the Estimates list, an entity class named **EstimatesSOW** will be generated to represent the list content type. Conversely, if you have not modified the **SOW** content type in the Estimates list, an entity class named **SOW** will be generated to represent the site content type.

- If a column is removed from a list content type, the corresponding property is made virtual in the entity class that represents the site content type. The entity class that represents the list content type overrides this method and will throw an **Invalid OperationException** if you attempt to access the property. For example, if you remove the VendorID column from the **SOW** content type in the Estimates list, the **VendorID** property is made virtual in the **SOW** entity class, and the **Estimates SOW** entity will throw an exception if you attempt to access the property.

- If a list contains a single content type, the **EntityList<TEntity>** class that represents that list in the data context class will use that content type entity as its type parameter. For example, if the Estimates list contained only documents based on the **SOW** content type, the list would be represented by an **EntityList<SOW>** instance.

- If a list contains more than one content type, the **EntityList<TEntity>** class that represents that list will use the closest matching base content type as its type parameter. For example, the Estimates list actually contains the **SOW** content type and the **Estimate** content type, which both inherit from the built-in **Document** content type. In this case, the list is represented by an **EntityList<Document>** instance. Because **SOW** entities and **Estimate** entities both inherit from the **Document** entity, the list can contain entities of both types.

Modeling Associations in Entity Classes

When you use the SPMetal command-line tool to generate entity classes, it automatically detects relationships between lists based on lookup columns, and it adds properties to the entity classes to enable you to navigate these relationships. Consider an inventory management site that contains a *Parts* list and an *Inventory Location* list. The *Inventory Location* list includes a lookup column named *Part* that retrieves values from the *Parts* list. When you generate the corresponding entity classes, the **InventoryLocation** class includes a **Part** property that allows you to navigate to the associated entity instance in the *Parts* list.

```
C#
private Microsoft.SharePoint.Linq.EntityRef<Part> _part;

[Microsoft.SharePoint.Linq.AssociationAttribute(Name="PartLookup",
  Storage="_part",
  MultivalueType=Microsoft.SharePoint.Linq.AssociationType.Single,
  List="Parts")]
public Part Part
{
  get { return this._part.GetEntity(); }
  set { this._part.SetEntity(value); }
}
```

> **Note:** *These examples are taken from the SharePoint List Data Models Reference Implementation in the Developing Applications for SharePoint 2010 online guidance. The* **InventoryLocation** *class also includes event handlers that ensure the* **Part** *reference remains up to date if the associated entity instance is changed.*

The SPMetal tool also adds properties to the Parts list that enable you to navigate to the Inventory Locations list. This is known as a *reverse lookup association*. The **Parts** class includes an **InventoryLocation** property that returns the set of inventory locations that are associated with a specific part—in other words, each **InventoryLocation** instance that links to the specified part through its **Part** lookup column.

```
C#
private Microsoft.SharePoint.Linq.EntitySet<InventoryLocation> _inventoryLocation;

[Microsoft.SharePoint.Linq.AssociationAttribute(Name="PartLookup",
  Storage="_inventoryLocation", ReadOnly=true,
  MultivalueType=Microsoft.SharePoint.Linq.AssociationType.Backward,
  List="Inventory Locations")]
public Microsoft.SharePoint.Linq.EntitySet<InventoryLocation> InventoryLocation
{
  get { return this._inventoryLocation; }
  set { this._inventoryLocation.Assign(value); }
}
```

Note: *The* **Part** *class also includes event handlers that ensure that the* **Inventory Location** *references remain up to date if the associated entity instance is changed.*

However, there is a limitation in the way the current version of SPMetal builds reverse lookups:

- If a site lookup column is used by one list, SPMetal will generate a reverse lookup association for the relationship.
- If a site lookup column is used by more than one list, SPMetal will not generate reverse lookup associations for any of the relationships based on that lookup column.

In many scenarios, you will want to use a lookup column in more than one list. For example, in the reference implementation, there are three lists that use lookup columns to retrieve values from the Parts list. In some cases, depending on how you intend to query your data, you may not require reverse lookup associations. However, if you do need to traverse the relationship in the reverse direction, your LINQ to SharePoint queries will be far less efficient if you proceed without a reverse lookup association in place. Consider the relationship between Parts and Inventory Locations. If you need to find all the inventory locations associated with a specified part, you would first need to retrieve the part, and then query the inventory location entity for all locations where the lookup column for the part equaled the ID value for the Part item. In this case, the reverse lookup association simplifies the LINQ expressions and reduces the processing overhead.

There are various approaches you can use to work around this limitation of SPMetal, each of which has drawbacks:

1. Create a new site column for each list that requires a lookup column for a particular list. This results in multiple site columns that retrieve information from the same list—the columns are duplicates in everything but name. This has several negative consequences:
   - If a developer uses a site lookup column that is already in use, reverse lookups will not be generated for that column the next time you use SPMetal, and some existing code will break.
   - Site administrators will need to manage multiple site columns for the same value, which will be confusing. This drawback can be mitigated by hiding the duplicate lookup fields.
   - The site columns are not really reusable, which is the main purpose of using site columns in the first place.

2. Create lookup columns at the list level. This eliminates the problems associated with duplicate site columns. This has the following negative consequences:
   - Your content types will no longer represent your data model, because the lookup columns are now pushed into individual lists. This makes information management more challenging. It also reduces the effectiveness of search and queries that retrieve items from different lists, because the information from the lookup column is not included in the content type.

3. Create duplicate site columns and use them in content types or list definitions to generate the entity classes with SPMetal, as in option 1. After you generate the entity classes, delete the duplicate site lookup columns and manually edit the entity classes to use a single lookup column. This keeps your data model clean because you do not need to maintain duplicate site columns, and it avoids the problems associated with option 2 because the lookup column is included in the relevant content types. This is the preferred approach in most scenarios. However, it has the following negative consequences:

   • Extra effort is required to create the duplicate site columns, create the content type definitions, remove the duplicate site columns, and edit the entity classes.

   • Manual editing of the entity classes can be error prone and difficult to debug. However, the edit should only involve straightforward renaming of properties.

4. Avoid using reverse lookup associations in cases where more than one list or content type uses a particular site lookup column. Although this approach is simple, you will need to use more complex and less efficient LINQ queries if you need to navigate the association in the reverse direction without reverse lookup properties.

QUERY EFFICIENCY WITH LINQ TO SHAREPOINT

Although LINQ to SharePoint makes it quick and easy to query SharePoint lists, you still need to consider whether your LINQ expressions will translate into efficient CAML queries. If your LINQ code translates into efficient CAML queries, the performance overhead of the LINQ to SharePoint provider can be considered negligible in all but the most extreme cases—in fact, you may actually see better performance with LINQ to SharePoint because it can be difficult to manually create efficient CAML queries. This section describes how nuances in your LINQ expressions can have substantial effects on the efficiency of the generated queries.

In some cases, LINQ to SharePoint prevents you from executing queries that contain certain inefficiencies. The LINQ to SharePoint provider is not always able to convert a LINQ expression into a single CAML query; for example, if you use a join predicate to query across two lists that are not connected by a lookup column, the LINQ to SharePoint provider would actually need to submit two queries in order to return a result set. In cases like this where LINQ to SharePoint cannot perform an operation using a single CAML query, the runtime will throw a **NotSupportedException**. In other cases, the LINQ to SharePoint provider cannot translate the entire LINQ code into an efficient CAML query. In these cases the provider will first execute a CAML query to retrieve items from the list and then perform a **LINQ to Objects** query on the list item collection results to satisfy the portions of the LINQ query that could not be translated to CAML.

As an example, suppose you want to review orders for every customer. You might use the following LINQ expression.

C#
```
dataContext.Customers.Select(c=>c.Orders).ToArray();
```

In this example, the LINQ to SharePoint provider would need to submit an additional query for every customer in order to retrieve their orders. As a result, the runtime would throw an exception. Similarly, suppose you want to aggregate data from two different lists of customers. You might use the following LINQ expression.

C#
```
dataContext.Customers.Union(dataContext.MoreCustomers).ToArray();
```

In this case, the LINQ to SharePoint provider would need to submit two queries—one for each list. Again, the runtime would throw an exception. The remainder of this section describes ways in which you can perform this type of query and other common operations without compromising efficiency.

Reviewing the CAML Output
In many cases, it can be useful to review the CAML output that is generated by your LINQ queries. The **DataContext** class includes a **Log** property that exposes a **TextWriter** object. You can use this property to log the generated CAML query to a text file or to the user interface. For example, the following code shows how you can modify the previous example to view the generated CAML query. In this example, the CAML query is appended to the query results in a **Literal** control named **displayArea**.

C#
```
using (ManufacturingSiteDataContext context = new
          ManufacturingSiteDataContext(SPContext.Current.Web.Url))
{
  var sb = new StringBuilder();
  var writer = new StringWriter(sb);
  context.Log = writer;

  string sponsor = "David Pelton";
  var results = from projectItem in context.PriorityProjects
                where projectItem.ExecutiveSponsor == sponsor
                select projectItem;

  foreach (var proj in results)
  {
    output.AppendFormat("Title: {0}  Sponsor: {1}  Leader: {2}",
      proj.Title, proj.ExecutiveSponsor, proj.ProjectsLookup.Leader);
  }

  output.Append("\n Query: " + sb.ToString());
  displayArea.Mode = LiteralMode.Encode;
  displayArea.Text = output.ToString();
}
```

After you set the **Log** property to a **TextWriter** implementation, the **DataContext** class will write the CAML query to the underlying stream or string as the LINQ expression is executed. You can then view the CAML query that is generated by the LINQ to Share-Point provider.

```XML
<View>
  <Query>
    <Where>
      <And>
        <BeginsWith>
          <FieldRef Name="ContentTypeId" />
          <Value Type="ContentTypeId">0x0100</Value>
        </BeginsWith>
        <Eq>
          <FieldRef Name="Executive_x0020_Sponsor" />
          <Value Type="Text">David Pelton</Value>
        </Eq>
      </And>
    </Where>
  </Query>
  <ViewFields>
    <FieldRef Name="Executive_x0020_Sponsor" />
    <FieldRef Name="ProjectsLookup" LookupId="TRUE" />
    <FieldRef Name="ID" />
    <FieldRef Name="owshiddenversion" />
    <FieldRef Name="FileDirRef" />
    <FieldRef Name="Title" />
  </ViewFields>
  <RowLimit Paged="TRUE">2147483647</RowLimit>
</View>
```

There are several interesting observations about the automatically generated CAML query:

- Notice the **BeginsWith** element in the **Where** clause. This stipulates that the content type ID of the items returned must begin with **0x0100**. Effectively, this means that the content type of the items returned must be a custom content type that inherits from the built-in **Item** content type—which is true of the **Project** content type. The LINQ to SharePoint provider includes this provision in addition to the **where** clause specified by the LINQ query.

- The CAML query returns a view that contains all the fields in the *Priority Projects* list, including fields that aren't required by the LINQ expression.

- The query returns a lookup field for the *Projects* list, instead of an entity. The **LookupId** attribute indicates that the referenced item in the *Projects* list will be retrieved by its internal ID value.

During the development process, you should take time to examine the CAML that is generated by your LINQ queries in order to proactively identify poorly performing queries. This is especially important when you query lists that you expect to be large in size. For example, you should take care to catch the obviously offending cases in which the LINQ to SharePoint provider is unable to translate some or all of the query into CAML and must resort to LINQ to Objects.

Where Clause Efficiency

When you create a LINQ expression, you typically use operators within a **where** clause to constrain your result set. However, the LINQ to SharePoint provider is unable to translate every LINQ operator into CAML. For example, the **Equals** operator and the **HasValue** operator have no CAML equivalent. The LINQ to SharePoint provider will translate as many **where** clause operators as possible into CAML, and then it will use LINQ to Objects to fulfill the remaining criteria.

The following table shows the operators that are supported by the LINQ to SharePoint provider and their equivalent expressions in CAML.

LINQ Operator	CAML Translation
&&	And
||	Or
==	Eq
>=	Geq
>	Gt
<=	Leq
<	Lt
!=	Neq
== null	IsNull
!= null	IsNotNull
String.Contains	Contains
String.StartsWith	BeginsWith

You should avoid using operators that are not listed in this table in your LINQ to SharePoint queries. Using unsupported operators causes the LINQ to SharePoint provider to return a larger result set and then process the outstanding **where** clauses on the client by using LINQ to Objects. This can create substantial performance overheads. For example, consider the following LINQ expression. The **where** clause includes an **Equals** operator and a **StartsWith** operator.

C#
```
var results = from projectItem in context.PriorityProjects
              where projectItem.ExecutiveSponsor.Equals(sponsor)  &&
                    projectItem.Title.StartsWith("Over")
              select projectItem;
```

The resulting CAML query includes a **Where** clause that reflects the **StartsWith** operator. However, it makes no mention of the unsupported **Equals** operator.

```xml
XML
<View>
  <Query>
    <Where>
      <And>
        <BeginsWith>
          <FieldRef Name="ContentTypeId" />
          <Value Type="ContentTypeId">0x0100</Value>
        </BeginsWith>
        <BeginsWith>
          <FieldRef Name="Title" />
          <Value Type="Text">Over</Value>
        </BeginsWith>
      </And>
    </Where>
  </Query>
  <ViewFields>
    …
  </ViewFields>
  <RowLimit Paged="TRUE">2147483647</RowLimit>
</View>
```

In this case, the LINQ to SharePoint provider would return a results set that includes project items with a **Title** field that begins with "Over," as defined by the CAML query. It would then use LINQ to Objects on the client to query the results set for project items with a matching **ExecutiveSponsor** field, as defined by the unsupported **Equals** operator.

The following XML shows what it looks like if you rewrite the LINQ expression to use the supported == operator instead of the unsupported **Equals** operator.

```xml
XML
var results = from projectItem in context.PriorityProjects
             where projectItem.ExecutiveSponsor == sponsor &&
                   projectItem.Title.StartsWith("Over")
             select projectItem;
```

This time, the resulting CAML query reflects the LINQ expression in its entirety.

```xml
XML
<View>
  <Query>
    <Where>
      <And>
```

```
      <BeginsWith>
       <FieldRef Name="ContentTypeId" />
       <Value Type="ContentTypeId">0x0100</Value>
      </BeginsWith>
      <And>
       <Eq>
         <FieldRef Name="Executive_x0020_Sponsor" />
         <Value Type="Text">David Pelton</Value>
       </Eq>
       <BeginsWith>
         <FieldRef Name="Title" />
         <Value Type="Text">Over</Value>
       </BeginsWith>
      </And>
     </And>
   </Where>
 </Query>
 <ViewFields>
   …
 </ViewFields>
```

In this case, the LINQ to SharePoint provider returns only relevant results to the client; no post-processing steps are required.

Using View Projections

In many cases, you can substantially improve query efficiency by using *view projections*. A view projection queries a specific set of fields from one or more entities. When you want to retrieve a read-only view of a set of data, using a view projection restricts the number of fields returned by the query and ensures that joins are added to the CAML query instead of performed as a post-processing step. You can create a view projection in various ways:

- You can select a single field, such as **projectItem.Title**.
- You can build an anonymous type by selecting a specific set of fields from one or more entities.
- You can instantiate a known type and set the property values in your LINQ expression.

View projections are limited to certain field types. Valid field types for projections are **Text** (single line of text only), **DateTime**, **Counter** (internal IDs), **Number**, and **Content-TypeId**. All remaining field types are not supported; an **InvalidOperationException** will be thrown if a column of that field type is used in the projection.

In the following example, the **new** keyword in the LINQ expression creates an anonymous type that contains fields named **Title**, **ExecutiveSponsor**, and **Leader**.

C#

```
using (ManufacturingSiteDataContext context = new ManufacturingSiteDataContext
  (SPContext.Current.Web.Url))
{
    string sponsor = "David Pelton";

    var results = from projectItem in context.PriorityProjects
                  where projectItem.ExecutiveSponsor == sponsor
                  select new { projectItem.Title,
                               projectItem.ExecutiveSponsor,
                               projectItem.Project.Leader };

    foreach (var proj in results)
    {
        output.AppendFormat("Title: {0}  Sponsor: {1}  Leader: {2}",
                proj.Title, proj.ExecutiveSponsor, proj.Leader);
    }
}
```

In this case, the LINQ to SharePoint provider creates a view that contains only the columns that correspond to the fields in the anonymous type.

```
<View>
  <Query>
    <Where>
      <And>
        <BeginsWith>
          <FieldRef Name="ContentTypeId" />
          <Value Type="ContentTypeId">0x0100</Value>
        </BeginsWith>
        <Eq>
          <FieldRef Name="Executive_x0020_Sponsor" />
          <Value Type="Text">David Pelton</Value>
        </Eq>
      </And>
    </Where>
  </Query>
  <ViewFields>
    <FieldRef Name="Title" />
    <FieldRef Name="Executive_x0020_Sponsor" />
    <FieldRef Name="ProjectLeader" />
  </ViewFields>
  <ProjectedFields>
    <Field Name="ProjectLeader" Type="Lookup" List="Project" ShowField="Leader" />
  </ProjectedFields>
  <Joins>
```

```
    <Join Type="LEFT" ListAlias="Project">
      <!--List Name: Projects-->
      <Eq>
        <FieldRef Name="Project" RefType="ID" />
        <FieldRef List="Project" Name="ID" />
      </Eq>
    </Join>
  </Joins>
  <RowLimit Paged="TRUE">2147483647</RowLimit>
</View>
```

The alternative approach, in which you instantiate a known type and set property values in your LINQ expression, is illustrated by the following example.

C#
```csharp
public class PriorityProjectView
{
  public string Title { get; set; }
  public string ExecutiveSponsor { get; set; }
  public string Leader { get; set; }
}

using (ManufacturingSiteDataContext context = new
         ManufacturingSiteDataContext(SPContext.Current.Web.Url))
{
  IEnumerable<PriorityProjectView> proirityProjects =
      from projectItem in context.PriorityProjects
      where projectItem.ExecutiveSponsor == sponsor
      select new PriorityProjectView
      {
        Title = projectItem.Title,
        ExecutiveSponsor = projectItem.ExecutiveSponsor,
        Leader = projectItem.Project.Leader
      };
}
...
```

Retrieving only the columns that you actually require will clearly improve the efficiency of your queries; in this regard, the use of view projections can provide a significant performance boost. This example also illustrates how the use of view projections forces the LINQ to SharePoint provider to perform the list join within the CAML query instead of retrieving a lookup column and using the deferred loading approach described earlier. The LINQ to SharePoint provider will only generate CAML joins when you use view projections. This is a more efficient approach when you know in advance that you will need to display data from two or more entities, because it reduces the number of round trips to the content database.

Note: *View projections can only be used for* **read** *operations. You must retrieve the full entity instances if you want use LINQ to SharePoint to perform* **create**, **update**, *or* **delete** *operations.*

LINQ to SharePoint can only generate CAML joins from join projections for a limited number of data types. An **InvalidOperationException** will be thrown if the projection contains a disallowed data type. The permitted data types are **Text**, **Number**, **DateTime**, **Count**, and **Content Type ID**. None of the remaining field types can be projected, including Boolean, multi-line text, choice, currency, and calculated fields.

On a final note, for view projections, recall that the LINQ to SharePoint provider will block certain LINQ expressions because they cannot be translated into a single CAML query. For example, the following LINQ expression attempts to retrieve a collection of orders for each customer. However, LINQ to SharePoint is unable to translate the LINQ expression into a single CAML query.

C#
```
dataContext.Customers.Select(c=>c.Orders).ToArray();
```

Suppose you modify the expression to use anonymous types, as shown in the following example.

C#
```
var results = dataContext.Customers.Select(c => new { Description =
            c.Order.Description, CustomerId = c.Order.CustomerId }).ToArray();
```

In this case, the LINQ to SharePoint provider is able to translate the expression into a single CAML query, and the runtime will not throw an exception. As you can see, view projections can provide a valuable resource when you develop LINQ to SharePoint expressions.

Using List Joins across Sites

In many common SharePoint scenarios, a list will include a lookup column that retrieves data from another list in a parent site within the site collection. However, the SPMetal command-line tool generates entity classes for a single site, and LINQ to SharePoint expressions operate within a data context that represents a single site. By default, when a list includes a lookup column that refers to a list on another site, SPMetal will generate an **ID** value for the item in the related list instead of constructing the related entity itself. If you were to write queries against this data model, you would need to retrieve the related entity yourself in a post-processing step. As a result, if you want to use LINQ to SharePoint to query cross-site list relationships effectively, you must perform some additional steps:

1. Temporarily move every list onto a single site before you run the SPMetal tool, so that SPMetal generates a full set of entity classes.

2. When you create a LINQ expression, use the **DataContext.RegisterList** method to inform the runtime of the location of lists that are not on the current site.

Consider the earlier example of a *Priority Projects* list. The list includes a lookup column that retrieves information from a central *Projects* list on a parent site, as shown in Figure 1.

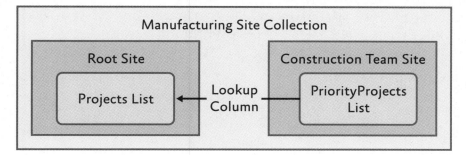

FIGURE 1
Lookup column relationship across sites in a site collection

In order to generate entities for both lists using the SPMetal tool, you should create a copy of the *Priority Projects* list on the root site, as shown in Figure 2.

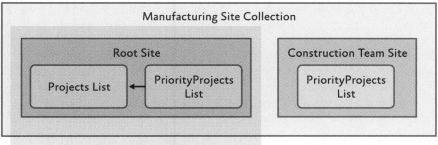

FIGURE 2
Temporary list to build entity classes

SPMetal will now build a full set of entities and entity relationships. After you finish building entity classes, you can remove the duplicate lists from the site. When you run a query in the context of the Construction team site, you must use the **RegisterList** method to tell the runtime where to find the Projects list. The following code example shows this.

C#
```
using (ManufacturingSiteDataContext context = new ManufacturingSiteDataContext
("http://localhost/sites/manufacturing/construction"))
{
```

```
context.RegisterList<Construction.ProjectsItem>("Projects",
  "/sites/Manufacturing", "Projects");

var results = from projectItem in context.PriorityProjects
              select new { projectItem.Title,
                           projectItem.ExecutiveSponsor,
                           projectItem.Project.Leader };

foreach (var item in results)
{
  output.AppendFormat("Title: {0}  Sponsor: {1}  Leader: {2}",
                      item.Title, item.ExecutiveSponsor, item.Leader);
}
}
```

There are various ways in which you could approach setting up your lists for entity generation. In most cases, you will want to generate your entity classes from the site that contains any lists that are referenced by lookup columns, because lookup columns reference a specific list on a specific site. In other words, if a lookup column retrieves data from a list on the root site, you should move all your lists onto the root site and build the entity model from there. If you build an entity model that uses a lookup column to retrieve data from a list on one site and then move that list to another site, you will need to manually update your entity classes.

1.   The key options for building your entity model are as follows:

• Create copies of all your lists on the root site and use SPMetal to build a single, comprehensive entity model from the root site. This approach is recommended for most scenarios, because it is usually the simplest and does not require you to modify the entity classes after creation.

• Use SPMetal with a parameters file to build a specialized entity model for one specific entity relationship. For example, suppose you have a lookup column that retrieves data from a specific team site instead of the root site. In this case, you should consider replicating all related lists on that specific team site and building your entity model from there, in order to avoid having to manually edit the lookup relationship in your entity classes. You might also consider this approach if you have a large number of lists in your site collection, because it may not be worth the extra effort involved in replicating and maintaining every single list on the root site.

• When you have a list on a subsite that includes a lookup column that retrieves values from a list on the root site, you may be tempted to reproduce the root site list on the subsite and generate entity classes from there. However, this approach should generally be avoided. First, you would need to generate temporary lookup columns, because the actual lookup columns you want to use are associated with the specific list instance on the root site. Second, you would need to manually edit the associations in the entity classes in order to use the actual lookup columns instead of the temporary lookup columns.

Finally, remember that the **SPQuery** class supports CAML-based list joins. LINQ to Share-Point is primarily designed to expedite the development process. If the time it takes to set up and maintain copies of lists in order to build a representative entity model outweighs the time savings you derive from writing LINQ expressions instead of CAML queries, you might want to consider whether **SPQuery** is a better choice for your application scenario.

Additional Performance Considerations

LINQ expressions define a generic **IEnumerable<T>** collection of objects. The **Enumerable** class provides a set of extension methods that you can use to query and manipulate this collection. These methods have varying efficiency when you use them in your LINQ to SharePoint expressions. The following table briefly describes some of the performance issues for the operations that have not already been described. Operations that are marked as efficient are translated into CAML and do not require post-processing steps after the list data is retrieved.

Operation	Performance and behavior
Contains	Efficient
OrderBy	Efficient
OrderByDescending	Efficient
ThenBy	Efficient
ThenByDescending	Efficient
GroupBy	Efficient when used in conjunction with **OrderBy**
Sum	Returns all elements that satisfy the **where** clause and then uses LINQ to Objects to compute the sum of the elements
Aggregate	Returns all elements that satisfy the **where** clause and then uses LINQ to Objects to apply an accumulator function to the elements
Average	Returns all elements that satisfy the **where** clause and then uses LINQ to Objects to calculate the average value
Max	Returns all elements that satisfy the **where** clause and uses LINQ to Objects to calculate the maximum value
Min	Returns all elements that satisfy the **where** clause and then uses LINQ to Objects to calculate the minimum value
Skip	Returns all elements that satisfy the **where** clause and then uses LINQ to Objects to perform the **Skip** operation
SkipWhile	Returns all elements that satisfy the **where** clause and then uses LINQ to Objects to perform the **SkipWhile** operation
ElementAt	Unsupported; use the **Take** method instead
ElementAtOrDefault	Unsupported; use the **Take** method instead
Last	Returns all items that satisfy the where clause, and then gets the last
LastOrDefault	Returns all items that satisfy the where clause, and then gets the last or returns default if no such items are found
All	Returns all elements that satisfy the **where** clause, and then uses LINQ to Objects to evaluate the condition

Any	Returns all elements that satisfy the **where** clause, and then uses LINQ to Objects to evaluate the condition
AsQueryable	Efficient
Cast	Efficient
Concat	Efficient
DefaultIfEmpty	Efficient
Distinct	Performed across two collections; returns all elements that satisfy the **where** clause and then uses LINQ to Objects to filter out duplicates
Except	Performed across two collections; returns all elements that satisfy the **where** clause and then uses LINQ to Objects to calculate the set difference
First	Efficient
FirstOrDefault	Efficient
GroupJoin	Efficient
Intersect	Performed across two collections; returns all elements that satisfy the **where** clause and then uses LINQ to Objects to calculate the set intersection
OfType	Efficient
Reverse	Returns all elements that satisfy the **where** clause, and then uses LINQ to Objects to reverse the order of the sequence
SelectMany	Efficient
SequenceEqual	Performed across two collections; returns all elements that satisfy the **where** clause and then uses LINQ to Objects to calculate whether the two sets are equal
Single	Efficient
SingleOrDefault	Efficient
Take	Efficient
TakeWhile	Efficient
Union	Efficient

The Repository Pattern and LINQ to SharePoint

The *repository pattern* is an application design pattern that provides a centralized, isolated data access layer. The repository retrieves and updates data from an underlying data source and maps the data to your entity model. This approach allows you to separate your data access logic from your business logic.

In some ways, the advent of LINQ to SharePoint may appear to obviate the need for repositories. However, there are many good reasons to continue to use the repository pattern with LINQ to SharePoint:

- **Query optimization**. LINQ to SharePoint substantially reduces the effort involved in developing queries, when compared to creating CAML queries directly. However, it is still easy to write LINQ to SharePoint queries that perform poorly, as described earlier in this chapter. Developing your queries in a central repository means that there are fewer queries to optimize and there is one place to look if you do encounter issues.

- **Maintainability**. If you use LINQ to SharePoint directly from your business logic, you will need to update your code in multiple places if your data model changes. The repository pattern decouples the consumer of the data from the provider of the data, which means you can update your queries in response to data model changes without impacting business logic throughout your code.

- **Testability**. The repository provides a substitution point at which you can insert fake objects for unit testing.

- **Flexibility**. The repository pattern promotes layering and decoupling, which leads to more flexible, reusable code.

In practice, you will encounter tradeoffs between the advantages of the repository pattern and the practicalities of implementing a solution. In the reference implementations that accompany the Developing Applications for SharePoint 2010 online guidance, the following practices were established:

- Encapsulate all LINQ to SharePoint queries in a repository. This provides a central point of management for the queries.

- Configure the repository class to return the entity types generated by the SPMetal command-line tool. This avoids the additional overhead of creating custom business entities and mapping them to the SPMetal entity classes, which would be the purist approach to implementing the repository pattern. However, on the negative side, this approach results in a tighter coupling between the data model and the data consumers.

- Add view objects to the repository in order to return composite projections of entities. A view object combines fields from more than one entity, and using view projections can make LINQ to SharePoint queries across multiple entities more efficient, as described earlier in this topic. This approach was used in the reference implementations, even though it deviates from the repository pattern, because the views are relatively simple and the entities that are represented in the views are all owned by the same repository. If the views were more complex, or the entities involved spanned multiple repositories, the developers would have implemented a separate class to manage views to provide a cleaner division of responsibilities.

Using the BDC Object Model

Scenarios for access to external data vary widely in complexity, from simply displaying a list of information from an external source to providing heavily customized interactivity. For many basic scenarios, using the built-in Business Data Web Parts or using the **SPList** API to query external lists provide straightforward and effective approaches to meeting your application requirements. However, for more complex scenarios, you will need to use the BDC object model for full control of how you interact with your external data entities.

The BDC object model is not available in sandboxed solutions. The following table summarizes the scenarios where external lists or Business Data Web Parts may meet your requirements and the scenarios where you must use the BDC object model.

External data scenario	External list	Business Data Web Parts	BCS API
Access two-dimensional (flat) data from a sand-boxed solution	✔		
Access two-dimensional (flat) data from a farm solution	✔	✔	✔
Access data with non-integer identifiers	✔	✔	✔
Navigate one-to-one associations between entities		✔	✔
Navigate one-to-many associations between entities		✔	✔
Navigate many-to-many associations between entities			✔
Read entities with complex types that can be flattened using a format string	✔	✔	✔
Read entities with complex types that cannot be flattened using a format string			✔
Create, update, or delete entities with complex types			✔
Perform paging or chunking of data			✔
Stream binary objects			✔
Access two-dimensional (flat) data from client logic*	✔		✔
Navigate associations between entities from client logic*			✔

*The BDC provides a client API and a server API that offer the same functionality. However, the client API is only available in full .NET applications; it cannot be used from Silverlight or JavaScript.

The BDC runtime API allows you to programmatically navigate a BDC model, and to interact with an external system through the model, without using intermediary components such as external lists or Business Data Web Parts. Figure 3 illustrates the key components of the BDC programming model.

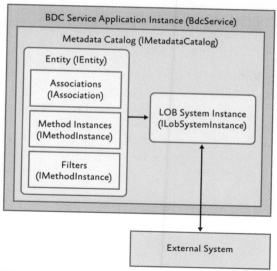

FIGURE 3
Key components of the BDC programming model

Each of the components in the programming model relates to a specific part of the BDC model, which we introduced in the preceding chapter. The *BDC service application instance* (**BdcService** class) represents the service instance that manages the metadata for the external systems you want to access. Remember that the BDC service application instance you use is determined by the service application proxy group associated with the current SharePoint Web application. Each BDC service application instance exposes a *metadata catalog* (**IMetadataCatalog**) that you can use to navigate through the metadata definitions stored by the service.

Within the metadata catalog, the two primary concepts are the *entity* (**IEntity**) and the *LOB system instance* (**ILobSystemInstance**). An entity represents an external content type and defines the stereotyped operations that are used to interact with an external data entity. It can also define associations that allow you to navigate to related entities and filters that enable you to constrain a result set. A *LOB system instance* represents a specific instance, or installation, of the external system that the BDC model represents, and defines the connection and authentication details required to connect to the system.

> **Note:** *"LOB system instance" is a legacy term from Office® SharePoint Server 2007. A LOB system is a line-of-business application, such as customer relationship management (CRM) or enterprise resource planning (ERP) software. Although the term "LOB system instance" is still used within the BDC object model, the broader term "external system" is preferred in other cases.*

Entities, or external content types, are common to all instances of a system. To access data from a specific instance of an external system, you need to use an entity object in conjunction with a LOB system instance object to retrieve an *entity instance* (**IEntityInstance**). The following code example illustrates this.

```
C#
public IEntityInstance GetMachineInstance(int machineId)
{
  const string entityName = "Machines";
  const string systemName = "PartsManagement";
  const string nameSpace = "DataModels.ExternalData.PartsManagement";

  //Get the BDC service application instance.
  BdcService bdcService = SPFarm.Local.Services.GetValue<BdcService>();

  //Get the metadata catalog for the service application.
  IMetadataCatalog catalog =
    bdcService.GetDatabaseBackedMetadataCatalog(SPServiceContext.Current);

  //Get the LOB system instance for the PartsManagement BDC model.
  ILobSystemInstance lobSystemInstance =
    catalog.GetLobSystem(systemName).GetLobSystemInstances()[systemName];

  //Retrieve a machine by ID value.
  Identity identity = new Identity(machineId);
  IEntity entity = catalog.GetEntity(nameSpace, entityName);
  IEntityInstance instance = entity.FindSpecific(identity, lobSystemInstance);

  return instance;
}
```

When a method on an **IEntity** object takes an object of type **ILobSystemInstance** as a parameter—such as the **FindSpecific** method shown here—usually, it is querying the external system for information. The **IEntity** object defines the stereotyped operations that allow you to interact with a particular type of data entity on the external system, while the **ILobSystemInstance** object defines the details required to actually connect to a specific external system instance. Typically, you perform data operations on an **IEntity Instance** object or on a collection of **IEntityInstance** objects. Each **IEntityInstance** object contains a set of fields and values that correspond to the related data item in the external system. These fields can represent simple types or complex types.

This approach to data access is broadly consistent across all BDC object model operations. You first retrieve definitions of entities and associations from the BDC model, and then you use these entities and associations in conjunction with a LOB system instance to retrieve information from the external system. Although this may seem somewhat unnatural at first, it allows you to decouple your applications from the implementation details of the backend service or database.

Note: *It's important to understand the difference between entities and entity instances. The **IEntity** class represents an entity in the BDC model, which corresponds to an external content type. Instances of that entity, which you can think of as list items or* *rows of data, are represented by the **IEntityInstance** class. Methods that query multiple entity instances typically return an **IEntityInstanceEnumerator** object, which represents an enumerable collection of **IEntityInstance** objects.*

When you use the BDC object model to interact with a data store, you are invoking the stereotyped operations that you defined in your BDC model. There are three types of stereotyped operations that are particularly useful for querying data: **Finder** methods, **SpecificFinder** methods, and **AssociationNavigator** methods.

- **Finder** methods. These are methods that return multiple entity instances, typically by applying filtering criteria to the set of entity instances for a particular entity on the BDC.
- **SpecificFinder** methods. These are methods that return a single entity instance, when provided with its identifier.
- **AssociationNavigator** methods. These are methods that return entity instances that are related to a specified entity instance by an association in the BDC model.

When you use the BDC object model to invoke these methods, the approach is broadly similar to that shown in the previous example. In each case, you:

- Retrieve an **IEntity** object from the metadata catalog that represents the entity (external content type) of interest.
- Call a method on the **IEntity** instance to invoke the operation, passing in a **Lob SystemInstance** object and other relevant parameters such as filters or identifier values.

In the sections that follow, we'll look at examples of how to use each of these stereotyped operations.

Note: *The examples that follow are taken from the External Data Models Reference Implementation in the Developing Applications for SharePoint 2010 online guidance. For more information about the reference implementations and the online guidance, see the Further Information section at the end of this chapter.*

Querying Data by Using a Finder Method

A **Finder** method returns all of the entity instances for a specified entity, subject to any filtering criteria. Finder methods typically include one or more *filter descriptors* in the BDC model. When you invoke a Finder method, you can retrieve and use these filters to constrain your result set. Finder methods are often referred to as *Read List* operations. For example, in the **PartsManagement** BDC model, in the **Machines** entity definition, the **Read List** method—a method that conforms to the Finder stereotype—defines the following filter descriptors:

XML
```xml
<FilterDescriptors>
  <FilterDescriptor Type="Wildcard"
                    FilterField="ModelNumber"
                    Name="ModelNumberWildcardFilter">
    <Properties>
      <Property Name="CaseSensitive" Type="System.Boolean">false</Property>
      <Property Name="DontCareValue" Type="System.String"></Property>
      <Property Name="IsDefault" Type="System.Boolean">false</Property>
      <Property Name="UsedForDisambiguation"
                Type="System.Boolean">false</Property>
      <Property Name="UseValueAsDontCare" Type="System.Boolean">true</Property>
    </Properties>
  </FilterDescriptor>
  <FilterDescriptor Type="Limit"
                    FilterField="ID"
                    Name="Filter">
    <Properties>
      <Property Name="CaseSensitive" Type="System.Boolean">false</Property>
      <Property Name="IsDefault" Type="System.Boolean">false</Property>
      <Property Name="UsedForDisambiguation"
                Type="System.Boolean">false</Property>
    </Properties>
  </FilterDescriptor>
</FilterDescriptors>
```

In this case, a wildcard filter has been defined for the **ModelNumber** field on the **Machines** entity. This allows us to search for machines with a model number that contains some specified text. To retrieve the set of machines that match a filter, we call the **Find-Filtered** method on the **IEntity** instance that represents machines, as shown in the following code example.

C#
```csharp
public DataTable GetMachinesByModelNumber(string modelNumber)
{
  //Get the Machines entity (external content type) from the metadata catalog
  IEntity entity = catalog.GetEntity(Constants.BdcEntityNameSpace, "Machines");

  //Get the filters defined on the default Finder method for the entity
  IFilterCollection filters = entity.GetDefaultFinderFilters();

  //Set the Wildcard filter value
  if (!string.IsNullOrEmpty(modelNumber))
  {
```

```
    WildcardFilter filter = (WildcardFilter)filters[0];
    filter.Value = modelNumber;
}


//Return the filtered list of items from the external data source
IEntityInstanceEnumerator enumerator = entity.FindFiltered(filters,
                                                lobSystemInstance);


//Convert the filtered list of items to a DataTable and return it
return entity.Catalog.Helper.CreateDataTable(enumerator);
}
```

Note: *This example uses the* **IMetadataCatalog.Helper.CreateDataTable** *method to return the result set as a* **DataTable** *instance. The* **CreateDataTable** *method is a new BCS method in SharePoint 2010 that allows you to convert a result set from the BDC into a* **DataTable** *object with ease.*

Finder methods typically include the following different types of filter definitions:

- LIMIT filters ensure that the number of results returned by the Read List operation does not exceed the maximum allowed by the BCS. By default, this maximum value is set to 2,000 records. The use of LIMIT filters is highly recommended to prevent performance degradation when you work with large amounts of data.

- WILDCARD filters allow you to filter the results returned by the Read List operation based on partial search matches. The user can constrain the result set by providing a few characters of text, including wildcard characters as required. Including a WILDCARD filter in your Finder methods enables the business data Web Parts to use their built-in search functionality.

- COMPARISON filters allow you to constrain the results returned by the Read List operation to those with field values that exactly match some search text. Comparison filters can be used to evaluate conditions such as equals, not equals, less than, greater than, and so on. Including a COMPARISON filter in your Finder methods also enables exact match and condition-driven filtering in the business data Web Parts.

Filters can also provide contextual information to the external system, such as a trace identifier to use when logging.

QUERYING DATA BY USING A SPECIFICFINDER METHOD

A **SpecificFinder** method returns a single entity instance, where the identifier field value (or values) of the entity instance matches the arguments supplied to the method. Specific-Finder methods are often referred to as *Read Item* operations. To retrieve a machine with a specific identifier, we call the **FindSpecific** method on the **IEntity** instance that represents machines, as shown by the following code example. Note that we must package the identifier value in an **Identity** object before we pass it to the **FindSpecific** method.

```csharp
C#
private IEntityInstance GetBdcEntityInstance(int identifier, string entityName)
{
  //Create an identifier object to store the identifier value
  Identity id = new Identity(identifier);

  //Return the entity on which to execute the SpecificFinder method
  IEntity entity = catalog.GetEntity(Constants.BdcEntityNameSpace, "Machines");

  //Invoke the SpecificFinder method to return the entity instance
  IEntityInstance instance = entity.FindSpecific(id, lobSystemInstance);

return instance;
}
```

QUERYING DATA BY USING AN ASSOCIATIONNAVIGATOR METHOD

At a conceptual level, associations between entities in the BDC model are similar to foreign key constraints in a relational database or lookup columns in regular SharePoint lists. However, they work in a different way. Associations are defined as methods within an entity that allow you to navigate from instances of that entity to instances of a related entity. You cannot create joins across associations in a BDC model. Instead, you must retrieve an entity instance and then use the association method to navigate to the related entity instances.

An **AssociationNavigator** method returns a set of entity instances that are related to a specified entity instance (or instances) through a specified association. To retrieve the set of parts that are associated with a specified machine, we call the **FindAssociated** method on the **IEntity** object that represents machines. The **FindAssociated** method requires four parameters:

- An **EntityInstanceCollection** object. This contains the entity instance, or entity instances, for which you want to find related entity instances. In this case, our **EntityInstanceCollection** contains a single entity instance, which represents a machine with a specified machine ID.

- An **IAssociation** object. This contains the *association navigator* method instance. We retrieve this from the entity definition that represents machines.

- A **LobSystemInstance** object. This represents a specific instance of an external system in the BDC model.

- An **OperationMode** enumeration value. A value of **Online** indicates that data should be retrieved from the external system, while a value of **Offline** indicates that data should be retrieved from the local cache.

This is illustrated by the following code example, which retrieves a set of parts based on a specified machine ID.

```csharp
C#
public DataTable GetPartsByMachineId(int machineId)
{
  //Return the Parts entity - this entity is the destination entity as modeled
  //in the Association method
  IEntity entity = catalog.GetEntity(Constants.BdcEntityNameSpace, "Parts");

  //Return the association defined on the Parts entity which associates the
  //Parts entity with the Machines entity
  IAssociation association =
    (IAssociation)entity.GetMethodInstance("GetPartsByMachineID",
    MethodInstanceType.AssociationNavigator);

  //Return the Machine entity instance for a given Machine ID - this entity is
  //the source entity as modeled in the Association method
  IEntityInstance machineInstance = GetBdcEntityInstance(machineId, "Machines");

  //Create an EntityInstanceCollection to hold the Machine entity instance
  EntityInstanceCollection collection = new EntityInstanceCollection();

  //Add the Machine entity instance to the EntityInstanceCollection
  collection.Add(machineInstance);

  //Execute the association method on the destination entity (Parts) to
  //return all the parts for a given machine
  IEntityInstanceEnumerator associatedInstances =
    entity.FindAssociated(collection, association, lobSystemInstance,
    OperationMode.Online);

  //Convert the associated list of items to a DataTable and return it
  return entity.Catalog.Helper.CreateDataTable(associatedInstances);
}
```

OTHER SCENARIOS THAT REQUIRE THE USE OF THE BDC OBJECT MODEL

In addition to the operations described in this topic, there are several other scenarios for external data access in which you must write custom code using the BDC object model instead of using simpler mechanisms such as external lists or Business Data Web Parts. These include the following:

- You want to perform bulk write-back operations where you write multiple rows of data to the same entity in an external system. For example, you might need to add multiple line items to an order created by a user.

- You want to update multiple entities concurrently. For example, to submit an order, you might need to update order entities, order line item entities, and carrier entities simultaneously.
- You want to use a **GenericInvoker** stereotyped operation. A **GenericInvoker** method is used to invoke logic on the external system, and can call methods with arbitrary parameters and return types.

Conclusion

This chapter examined the key approaches to data access in SharePoint 2010, both for data stored in SharePoint lists and external data accessed through the BCS. The following data access mechanisms were described and compared:

- **Query classes**. You can use the **SPQuery** class and the **SPSiteDataQuery** class to retrieve list data by constructing and submitting CAML queries. The **SPQuery** class is used to retrieve data from a single list, and allows you to use join predicates. You can also use the **SPQuery** class to query external lists. The **SPSiteDataQuery** class is used to retrieve data from multiple lists, and does not support join predicates or external lists. While these classes are used less frequently with the advent of LINQ to SharePoint, there are still many scenarios in which they should be your preferred approach to data access.

- **LINQ to SharePoint**. The LINQ to SharePoint provider enables you to use the LINQ syntax to query list data. In order to use the LINQ to SharePoint provider, you must first generate strongly typed entity classes to represent your SharePoint lists, typically by using the SPMetal command line tool. The LINQ to SharePoint provider dynamically converts your LINQ expressions into CAML queries at run time. It's important to understand the nuances of the LINQ to SharePoint provider to ensure that these dynamically generated CAML queries are efficient. You cannot use LINQ to SharePoint to query external lists.

- **The BDC object model**. The BDC object model enables you to query and manipulate external data directly by interacting with programmatic representations of the entities in your BDC models. The BDC object model is useful for more complex operations, and in scenarios where the SharePoint list object model proves inadequate for your application requirements. To query an external data store through the BDC object model, you first retrieve definitions of entities and associations from the BDC model, and then you use these entities and associations in conjunction with a LOB system instance to retrieve information from the external system.

See It in Action: The Developing Applications for SharePoint 2010 online guidance includes downloadable reference implementations that illustrate all of the data access mechanisms described in this chapter. Many of the code examples in this chapter were taken from these reference implementations. You can find the reference implementations at the following locations:

For Reference Implementation: SharePoint List Data Models, see http://msdn.microsoft.com/en-us/library/ff798373.aspx.

For Reference Implementation: External Data Models, see http://msdn.microsoft.com/en-us/library/ff798509.aspx.

You can deploy each reference implementation to a SharePoint 2010 test environment and explore the source code at your leisure in Visual Studio 2010.

FURTHER INFORMATION

For data topics not covered in this chapter, and for further background information in addition to the documents below, see the book's bibliography online at http://msdn.microsoft.com/gg213840.aspx.

- "Overriding SPMetal Defaults with a Parameters XML File"
- "Managing Data with LINQ to SharePoint"
- "How to: Write to Content Databases Using LINQ to SharePoint"

PART THREE
Client Models

1

Client Application Models in SharePoint 2010

Today, users expect a rich, responsive browser experience. In addition, they expect seamless data access whether they're working in the browser, a Microsoft® Office® application, or a custom solution. Fortunately, Rich Internet application (RIA) technologies such as Ajax and Microsoft Silverlight® provide the responsive experience users want, and Microsoft SharePoint® 2010 introduces native support for RIA technologies along with several new mechanisms for client-side, or remote, data access to meet these needs.

So what do we mean when we speak of a client application? In the context of SharePoint development, we mean any logic that interacts with SharePoint data from an external computer. This includes logic that executes in the browser, such as JavaScript or Silverlight applications, as well as Office applications and stand-alone solutions. This also includes applications that run on mobile devices, but that is beyond the scope of this chapter.

Typically, there are three main reasons for developing client-side logic that interacts with a SharePoint environment:

- You want to provide a richer user experience on a SharePoint Web page.

- You want to perform actions that are unavailable to server-side code running in the sandbox environment, such as accessing information from multiple site collections or retrieving data from an external service.

- You want to access and manipulate SharePoint data from another application, such as an Office client application or a custom solution.

When you design a client application for SharePoint 2010, the factors driving your decisions fall into two broad areas:

- **User experience**. This describes the platform that your users will use to interact with SharePoint and the technologies on which you will build your application. This encompasses a broad range of development scenarios, such as Ajax-enabled Web pages, Silverlight applications, Office client applications, managed .NET applications, and applications that are not running on Microsoft Windows®.

- **Data access**. This is the mechanism by which your application will communicate with the SharePoint server in order to retrieve and manipulate data. SharePoint 2010 provides a comprehensive client-side object model, including APIs for ECMAScript (JavaScript), Silverlight, and managed Microsoft .NET clients. A new

REST interface makes SharePoint data accessible to any application that can send HTTP requests, while a Business Connectivity Services (BCS) client API enables you to interact with your external data models from client applications.

Figure 1 shows some of the options available to you in each of these areas.

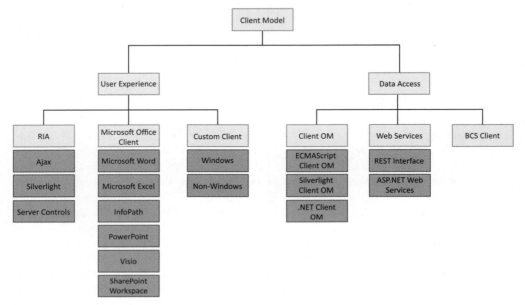

FIGURE 1
Client-side development options for SharePoint 2010

In many cases, a particular approach to user experience will lend itself to a particular data access mechanism. For example, the ECMAScript client object model will clearly lend itself to Ajax clients, the Silverlight client object model is designed for Silverlight clients, and the REST interface will be the best approach for accessing SharePoint data from clients that are not based on Microsoft Windows®. However, there are scenarios in which the choice is not so clear cut. This chapter identifies some of the nuances, advantages, and drawbacks to the different approaches to building a user experience, with a particular focus on RIA technologies. Chapter Nine, "Data Access for Client Applications," provides detailed insights into the use of the client-side object model and the REST interface, and examines how you can optimize the performance of client applications when you use these data access mechanisms.

Building a User Experience

If you've worked with previous releases of SharePoint products and technologies, you're probably familiar with the traditional server-side controls approach to building a Web-based user experience. Typically, your server-side toolbox would include master pages, application pages, themes, cascading style sheets (CSS), Web Parts, delegate controls, navigation controls and providers, and so on. SharePoint uses these resources to construct an ASP.NET page dynamically. This is then converted into HTML, packaged into an HTTP response, and sent to the Web browser on the client.

When you use this approach, all the logic in your application executes on the server. In order to update any of the content on the Web page based upon user interaction that sends data back to the server—to apply a filter or view the details associated with a list item, for example—the browser must send an HTTP POST request to the server. The server processes the request, regenerates the HTML, and sends a new HTTP response to the Web browser on the client, which must render the entire page from scratch. In the context of ASP.NET development, this is known as a *full-page postback*. Figure 2 illustrates this process.

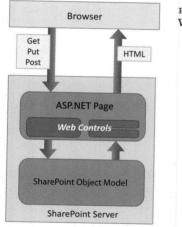

FIGURE 2
Web page with server-side controls

While this technique provides a robust, functional approach to Web application development, it can lead to a frustrating user experience. Interactivity is limited, as users must wait for the page to reload in response to any changes they make in the user interface. As a result, Web developers increasingly rely on RIA technologies, such as Ajax, Silverlight, and Flash, to provide a more engaging user experience. These technologies allow you to execute some logic in the browser, rather than relying entirely on server-side execution.

RIA technologies typically use asynchronous communication to send and receive data from the server without reloading the entire page. With an asynchronous programming model, the request communication is disconnected from the response mechanism. This results in more responsive applications and an increased ability to perform work in the background or in parallel. This results in Web pages with multiple, relatively isolated regions that can be updated independently, and user interfaces that continue to respond to the user while data is being retrieved from the server.

RIA technologies are not mutually exclusive. It's common to see SharePoint Web pages that contain a mixture of server-side controls, Ajax-enabled regions, and Silverlight applications. The next few pages provide an overview of the key approaches to building a client-side user experience for SharePoint applications.

Note: *There is some debate within the technical community as to whether or not Ajax qualifies as an RIA technology. However, in this documentation we view Ajax as an RIA technology, as you can use it to provide a more interactive user experience through client-side logic.*

Ajax User Interface

In the broadest sense of the term, Ajax refers to a set of technologies that allow you to retrieve data asynchronously from the server, and manipulate that data in the client browser, without disrupting the display or behavior of the current Web page. Ajax was originally an acronym for Asynchronous JavaScript and XML, as Ajax applications would traditionally rely on the JavaScript **XMLHttpRequest** API to send asynchronous requests to a Web server and to return the response to the calling script. The script could then use the response to alter the document object model (DOM) of the current page—for example, by updating the values in a table—without refreshing the entire page. However, Ajax has evolved to encompass a broader set of technologies in which scripts running in a browser window can use a variety of asynchronous communication channels to retrieve and manipulate data from a server. Today, the term Ajax has become synonymous with a Web application style in which user interactions are managed predominantly by the browser, rather than the Web server.

The use of Ajax-style technologies in a Web page is rarely an all-or-nothing approach. At one end of the scale, you might use a little bit of JavaScript to display dialog boxes, concatenate strings, or validate user input. You might add Ajax-enabled regions, which make use of partial postbacks to provide users with access to constantly changing data without reloading the entire page. Depending on your requirements and your target audience, you might move to a pure Ajax approach, in which the page is loaded once, all further interactivity takes place on the client, and all further client-server communication takes place asynchronously in the background. However, you will still need to design a server-side page to host your Ajax components, you'll typically still require Web Parts to host the Ajax-enabled content, and the browser will still need to retrieve your page from the server at least once. Your Web page will typically use a combination of full-page postbacks and asynchronous communication to communicate with the server, depending on the extent to which you implement Ajax features in your user interface. This is illustrated by Figure 3.

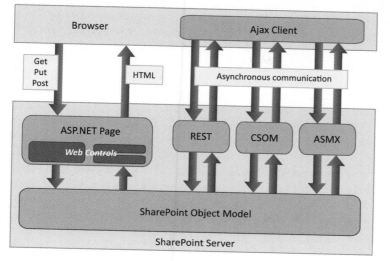

FIGURE 3
Web page with Ajax components

> **Note:** *The client-side asynchronous data access mechanisms shown in the illustration include the client-side object model (CSOM), the REST interface, and the ASP.NET (ASMX) Web services. These are described in more detail in the next chapter.*

Ajax functionality is supported by virtually all Web browsers, with some minor differences in how scripting logic is interpreted. Popular JavaScript frameworks such as jQuery help to manage the complexity of variations between browsers, and improved debugging support for JavaScript has made Ajax more accessible. The Ajax approach delivers a more responsive user experience for several reasons:

- It only loads part of the page at a time. This reduces the amount of data that is passed between the client and server, and largely eliminates entire page refreshes. Only data is sent between the server and the client on asynchronous requests; no HTML markup is included.

- It handles more events on the client without requiring a postback to the server.

- It caches information on the client between user interactions. This is more efficient than the full-page postback approach in which state information is typically passed between the client and the server on every request.

SharePoint 2010 makes extensive use of Ajax principles in the out-of-the-box user interface, and client-side APIs in the 2010 release make it easier for you to use Ajax approaches when you develop SharePoint applications.

SILVERLIGHT USER INTERFACE
Silverlight is a development platform that enables you to create rich, engaging applications that run in Web browsers and on other devices. Silverlight developers use a specialized, lightweight version of the Microsoft .NET Framework to create applications. Along-

side the benefits of a familiar .NET development experience, Silverlight offers capabilities in areas such as graphics, animation, and multimedia that go beyond what you can achieve with Ajax.

Silverlight applications can run on a variety of platforms—in fact the latest release, Silverlight 4.0, allows you to build applications that can be taken offline and started from the desktop. However, in this documentation we focus on the use of Silverlight as an RIA technology. In the case of Web pages, compiled Silverlight applications (XAP, pronounced "zap," files) are hosted within HTML object elements, which can either be embedded in the page or generated dynamically through JavaScript. In the case of a SharePoint Web page, Silverlight applications are typically hosted within a Web Part. SharePoint 2010 includes a Silverlight Web Part that is specifically designed for hosting XAPs within a Share-Point page. Just like Web pages that contain Ajax-enabled components, the browser must use a traditional synchronous page load at least once in order to render the page and download associated resources, such as the Silverlight XAP and any JavaScript files. The Silverlight application can then use a variety of data access mechanisms to communicate asynchronously with the SharePoint server. This is illustrated by Figure 4.

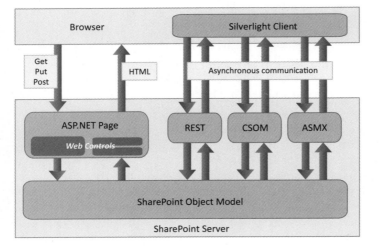

FIGURE 4
Web page with Silverlight components

Silverlight applications can also interact directly with Ajax elements on a page. It's increasingly common to use a combination of Silverlight applications, Ajax elements, and traditional server-side controls together to provide a full range of functionality for SharePoint users.

Note: *SharePoint 2010 includes a new class named* **SilverlightWebPart**. *It provides a Web Part that simplifies the hosting of Silverlight applications within SharePoint Web pages.*

MICROSOFT OFFICE CLIENTS AND MANAGED CODE CLIENTS

Managed code clients are typically stand-alone applications that use the full capabilities of the .NET Framework. Managed code clients include Microsoft Office clients, rich stand-alone clients built on Windows Presentation Foundation (WPF) and Windows Forms applications, and administrative applications built as console applications or Windows PowerShell™ extensions. A Silverlight application in offline mode could also be considered a rich client application. Rich clients usually provide a full UI and often integrate data and functionality from multiple sources into one composite application. These applications can use the SharePoint client APIs synchronously or asynchronously, in order to access and manipulate data on the SharePoint server. This is illustrated by Figure 5.

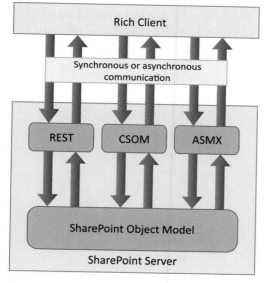

FIGURE 5
Rich client application

Microsoft Office client applications, such as Microsoft Word, Microsoft Excel®, Microsoft Access®, and SharePoint Workspace, have their own development framework in Visual Studio® Tools for Office (VSTO) as well as more advanced out-of-the-box integration with SharePoint. Microsoft Office client applications can also use the Business Connectivity Services (BCS) client object model, which installs with Office and is licensed with SharePoint Enterprise.

This capability enables Microsoft Office clients to connect directly to external services through a Business Data Connectivity (BDC) model defined on the SharePoint server. Portions of the BDC model can be deployed to the client as part of an application, and the client application uses the model to connect directly to external services through the client BCS runtime. The client application can also use the Secure Store Service on the SharePoint server to authenticate to the external services that it accesses. The BCS client includes offline caching capabilities and an API for developers. The API is accessible outside of Microsoft Office when the Office client is installed. However, its use is not supported outside the context of a Microsoft Office client.

Development for Office clients is a specialized area that differs substantially from other approaches to client-side development for SharePoint. For this reason, this book does not cover Microsoft Office client development in any detail.

Reach Considerations for RIA Technologies

When you design and build a user experience, you need to think about whether all your end users have an environment that supports your chosen approach. Users in a tightly controlled environment may not be able to download or use the plug-ins required to support technologies such as Silverlight or Flash. Older Web browsers, or browsers with high security settings, may prevent Web pages from executing script. Older Web browsers, in particular, may provide a more idiosyncratic interpretation of cascading style sheet (CSS) files and non-standardized HTML constructs. Essentially, Web UI technologies present a tradeoff between reach and capability, as illustrated by Figure 6.

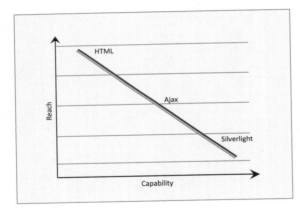

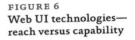

FIGURE 6
**Web UI technologies—
reach versus capability**

Clearly, plain HTML has the broadest reach of all Web UI technologies. As such, the use of traditional server-side controls, which render Web content as HTML, will have the most pervasive reach of all our approaches to user experience. Ajax-style programming has also gained broad acceptance, especially as browser implementations of JavaScript and CSS become increasingly consistent. Popular JavaScript libraries, such as the open source jQuery library, can provide a level of abstraction that isolates browser idiosyncrasies from user code. Just like plain HTML, JavaScript is interpreted by the Web browser and does not require the user to download and install any additional plug-ins.

Like other similar multimedia technologies, users must install a plug-in—the Silverlight runtime—in order to view Silverlight content. The installed base of Silverlight has grown quickly, so you can increasingly depend on it already being installed on client machines. However, as described previously, users in some environments may be unable or unwilling to download and install a plug-in in order to view your content. A common solution is to provide alternative HTML content, within the object tag that hosts the Silverlight control, for users who have not installed the Silverlight runtime. This content can either point users to the download location for the Silverlight plug-in, or provide a plain HTML alternative rendering of the Silverlight content. If your applications increasingly rely on multimedia content, or you need to perform complex logic with large datasets, you may find that Silverlight is the right solution.

Performance Considerations for RIA Technologies

Performance is an important consideration when you design a Web-based UI, as users quickly lose patience with Web pages that are slow to load or slow to update. Each approach to user experience has benefits and drawbacks for particular aspects of performance. However, there are also various strategies—such as caching, delayed loading, predictive loading, and "minifying" (more on this later)—that you can use to mitigate some of the potential performance issues associated with each technology. The sections that follow examine these aspects of UI design in more detail.

INITIAL LOAD TIME

In classic thin-client approaches, where all the logic executes on the server and the browser simply renders HTML, there is little difference between initial load time and subsequent load times. Since HTTP is a stateless protocol, each request to the server results in a response that includes the entire page. The biggest issue that hampers initial load time concerns resources such as CSS files, images, and JavaScript files that must be downloaded by the browser. These resources are typically cached by the browser on initial load and do not need to be reloaded for subsequent responses.

In terms of browser loading and rendering, Ajax clients are broadly similar to thin clients, although they typically contain significantly more JavaScript that will slow the initial load time if not already cached by the browser. Common JavaScript libraries that are used by many applications, such as jQuery, are typically downloaded and cached once by the browser and do not need to be reloaded for different applications. Ajax clients will often retrieve data related to a page on first load, which can also impact initial load times. However, to some degree this is the price you pay for the additional functionality that Ajax provides, and subsequent user interactions will be significantly faster than those of a traditional thin client. A typical Ajax client has substantially more functionality on a single page than a traditional server-driven Web page, and it therefore requires less frequent page loads.

You can improve the initial load times for Ajax clients through careful management of your JavaScript resources. First of all, you need to decide whether to use inline script (JavaScript functions embedded into the HTML of your Web page) or include a separate JavaScript file with your application. In most non-trivial solutions, you will want to include a JavaScript file. However, if you have a small amount of JavaScript—say less than 10KB—and you're not reusing JavaScript functions across controls or Web Parts, it may be preferable to use the inline scripting approach, especially if the JavaScript file will not be cached.

Another important consideration is the number of JavaScript files in your application. Browsers can only open a limited number of connections to the Web server at any one time. Historically, this limit was two connections, as mandated by the HTTP 1.1 specification, although more recent browser versions have relaxed this behavior and now support up to eight connections. However, a rich Web page includes many resources, such as images, that require a download connection. When the connection limit to a domain is reached, resources will begin downloading sequentially. Having many JavaScript files will result in more concurrent connections, and potentially sequential downloads if a connection limit is reached, both of which can impact performance. By consolidating JavaScript functions that are frequently used together into a single file, you can minimize the impact of this limitation on your page load times. You can also reduce JavaScript load times by "minifying" your JavaScript files. Minifying is a process that compresses JavaScript files by removing all unnecessary characters, such as white space, without altering the functionality of the file. You can also minify CSS files. There are various open source tools available that you can use to minify JavaScript files, such as the Microsoft Ajax Minifier. You can dynamically minify and combine scripts in an HTTP handler and cache the results, or you can perform similar actions as part of a build process. If you use reusable JavaScript libraries in your Ajax clients, be sure to reference the minified versions of the libraries in your production code.

Silverlight applications are compiled into a XAP file that includes .NET Framework and custom assemblies as well as other resources, such as XAML files and images. This file must be downloaded to the browser, parsed by the Silverlight runtime, and loaded into memory. Not surprisingly, the load time corresponds to the size of the XAP file. While XAP files can be cached like other Web resources, there is still a performance penalty on page load as the XAP file still needs to be parsed. As a result, initial load times are typically higher for Silverlight clients than for other client approaches. As with JavaScript, there are techniques you can use to minimize the initial load time for Silverlight clients. For example, you can split a solution into multiple XAP files, and you can delay the loading of some of the resources and assemblies.

Caching JavaScript Files and Silverlight XAP Files

One of the easiest ways to reduce the initial load time for Ajax and Silverlight clients is to enable caching of the related JavaScript and XAP files, both on the client browser and on the SharePoint Web front-end server. There are two main options for caching in a SharePoint environment.

- **Put the JavaScript or XAP files in a subfolder of the layouts folder in the SharePoint root**. SharePoint Web front-end servers cache the contents of the layouts folder to reduce the time required to retrieve the content in response to client requests. When Internet Information Services (IIS) creates the _layouts virtual directory, it applies an expiration policy to the content within the folder. This means that client browsers can also cache content from the layouts folder. However, you cannot deploy files to the layouts folder—or any other folder on the server file system—from a sandboxed solution.

  Note: *By default, IIS specifies that content in the _layouts virtual directory will expire after 365 days. This is configurable, but we do not recommend that you change this value. The preferred approach to retrieve JavaScript or XAP files that are subject to frequent change is to add query strings to the URLs you use to retrieve* *the files. Although the query strings themselves are ignored, adding a new query string to each request will prevent the browser from matching the requested URL to the cached resources. As a result, the browser will download the latest files from the server.*

- **Put the JavaScript or XAP files in a SharePoint library, and enable binary large object (BLOB) caching**. BLOB caching instructs SharePoint to cache BLOB content, such as JavaScript and XAP files, on the SharePoint Web front-end servers. It also enables client browsers to cache the content. If BLOB caching is not enabled, the HTTP header that returns the JavaScript or XAP resources to the client will instruct the browser not to cache the files. It does this by including a **cache-control: private** directive and by setting an expiration time in the past. As a result, neither the client browser nor the Web front-end server will cache the content, which instead will be retrieved from the content database on every request. BLOB caching is a SharePoint Server 2010 feature and must be enabled in the configuration files for the SharePoint Web applications, so to some degree you are at the mercy of the farm administrator.

If you are creating a sandboxed solution, you must deploy your resources to a SharePoint library as you do not have access to the file system on the server. You may also have to manage without BLOB caching, depending on administrative policy and whether you are able to request changes.

> **Note:** *Consider deploying JavaScript and XAP files to the master page gallery for Internet-facing sites. The master page gallery is preconfigured to allow access by anonymous users. By deploying resources to this location, you avoid the need to manage permissions on a custom library containing your JavaScript and XAP files.*

You should aim to package, consolidate, and divide your JavaScript and XAP files to maximize the sharing of resources across controls, applications, and pages. That way, when one page has caused the browser to download and cache a particular resource, other pages can benefit from the cached content until it reaches its expiration time. In the case of Ajax clients, you can maximize browser caching of resources by referencing JavaScript library files in a central location. For example, large cloud providers, such as the Microsoft Ajax Content Delivery Network (CDN), host many publicly available JavaScript libraries. By referencing the libraries in these locations, you increase the chance that the file will already be cached on the browser from its use in other applications.

When you work with Silverlight, you can use application library caching to improve load times on pages hosting multiple Silverlight applications and for subsequent visits to your Web page. When you enable application library caching for a Silverlight project in Visual Studio, library assemblies (such as System.Xml.Linq.dll) are packaged separately from your application assemblies, which are included in the XAP file. Each library is packaged as a zip file—for example System.Xml.Linq.zip—in the output directory of your project. This approach allows client browsers to cache system libraries separately from your XAP files. As library assemblies such as these are often used by multiple Silverlight controls, application library caching can substantially reduce total download sizes. For example, in the Client reference implementation in the Developing Applications for

SharePoint 2010 online guidance, removing the shared resources (including the SharePoint libraries) reduced the size of the XAP file by over 97 percent, from 500KB to 11KB. Visual Studio determines whether or not to separate out an individual assembly based on an external mapping file, which is unique to a particular assembly. The SharePoint client assemblies—Microsoft.SharePoint.Client.Silverlight.dll and Microsoft.SharePoint.Client.Silverlight.Runtime.dll—do not have an external mapping file. In order to separate these assemblies from your XAP file, you need to add an external mapping file for each assembly to the ClientBin folder within the SharePoint root folder on your server file system. The naming convention for the external mapping file is the assembly name with an .extmap.xml extension, such as Microsoft.SharePoint.Client.Silverlight.extmap.xml. The following example shows the external mapping file that instructs the compiler to separate out Microsoft.SharePoint.Client.Silverlight.dll into a zip file if application library caching is configured for a project that uses the assembly.

```XML
<?xml version="1.0"?>
<manifest xmlns:xsi="http://www.w3.org/2001/XMLSchema-instance"
          xmlns:xsd="http://www.w3.org/2001/XMLSchema">
  <assembly>
    <name>Microsoft.SharePoint.Client.Silverlight</name>
    <version>14.0.4762.1000</version>
    <publickeytoken>71e9bce111e9429c</publickeytoken>
    <relpath>Microsoft.SharePoint.Client.Silverlight.dll</relpath>
    <extension downloadUri="Microsoft.SharePoint.Client.Silverlight.zip" />
  </assembly>
</manifest>
```

A similar file is also then defined for Microsoft.SharePoint.Client.Silverlight.Runtime.dll.

To use application library caching for a SharePoint Silverlight client, you would do the following:

1. Configure your Silverlight project to use application library caching. To do this, select **Reduce XAP size by using application library caching** on the properties page of your project.

2. Rebuild the application.

Once you rebuild your solution, you will see zip files in the output directory for each system assembly. If you also added the external mapping files for the SharePoint client assemblies, you will see a zip file for those assemblies. You should also notice that the size of your XAP file has been reduced substantially. The application manifest embedded in the XAP file instructs the Silverlight runtime to download these assemblies separately. For example, the following code shows the application manifest for a Silverlight application after rebuilding the solution with application library caching turned on. Each **Extension Part** element specifies a compressed assembly that should be downloaded when required.

XML

```xml
<Deployment xmlns="http://schemas.microsoft.com/client/2007/deployment"
  xmlns:x="http://schemas.microsoft.com/winfx/2006/xaml"
  EntryPointAssembly="Client.CSOM.Silverlight"
  EntryPointType="Client.CSOM.Silverlight.App"
  RuntimeVersion="4.0.50401.0">
  <Deployment.Parts>
    <AssemblyPart x:Name="Client.CSOM.Silverlight"
                  Source="Client.CSOM.Silverlight.dll" />
  </Deployment.Parts>
  <Deployment.ExternalParts>
    <ExtensionPart Source="Microsoft.SharePoint.Client.Silverlight.zip" />
    <ExtensionPart Source="Microsoft.SharePoint.Client.Silverlight.Runtime.zip" />
    <ExtensionPart Source="System.ComponentModel.DataAnnotations.zip" />
    <ExtensionPart Source="System.Data.Services.Client.zip" />
    <ExtensionPart Source="System.Windows.Controls.Data.zip" />
    <ExtensionPart Source="System.Windows.Controls.Data.Input.zip" />
    <ExtensionPart Source="System.Windows.Data.zip" />
    <ExtensionPart Source="System.Xml.Linq.zip" />
  </Deployment.ExternalParts>
</Deployment>
```

Once this is completed, you will need to deploy these zip files alongside the XAP file to your SharePoint environment. The zip files and the XAP file must be in the same location, regardless of whether that location is a physical folder on the server or a document library. If you deploy all of the Silverlight applications in your site collection to the same library, then you only need to include a single zip file for a particular assembly—even though multiple Silverlight applications use the assembly. If BLOB caching is enabled, each zip file will only be downloaded once. This significantly reduces download times and bandwidth utilization.

An alternative to deploying the zip files alongside the XAP files is to deploy the zip files to one central location. In this case, you must define the URL of this location in the external mapping file for each assembly, as illustrated by the following example. The extension element indicates the location of the zip file.

XML

```xml
<?xml version="1.0"?>
<manifest xmlns:xsi="http://www.w3.org/2001/XMLSchema-instance"
          xmlns:xsd="http://www.w3.org/2001/XMLSchema">
  <assembly>
    <name>Microsoft.SharePoint.Client.Silverlight</name>
    <version>14.0.4762.1000</version>
    <publickeytoken>71e9bce111e9429c</publickeytoken>
    <relpath>Microsoft.SharePoint.Client.Silverlight.dll</relpath>
    <extension downloadUri=
    "http://contoso/XAP/Microsoft.SharePoint.Client.Silverlight.zip" />
```

```
    </assembly>
</manifest>
```

As a result, the application manifest will include a reference to the full URL from which to download the zip file, as illustrated by the following code example. As you can see, the assembly is now referenced by a fully qualified URL.

XML

```
<Deployment xmlns="http://schemas.microsoft.com/client/2007/deployment"
xmlns:x="http://schemas.microsoft.com/winfx/2006/xaml"
EntryPointAssembly="Client.CSOM.Silverlight" EntryPointType=
    "Client.CSOM.Silverlight.App" RuntimeVersion="4.0.50401.0">
  <Deployment.Parts>
    <AssemblyPart x:Name="Client.CSOM.Silverlight" Source=
    "Client.CSOM.Silverlight.dll" />
  </Deployment.Parts>
  <Deployment.ExternalParts>
    <ExtensionPart Source=
      "http://contoso/_layouts/XAP/Microsoft.SharePoint.Client.Silverlight.zip" />
    <ExtensionPart Source="Microsoft.SharePoint.Client.Silverlight.Runtime.zip" />
    <ExtensionPart Source="System.ComponentModel.DataAnnotations.zip" />
    <ExtensionPart Source="System.Data.Services.Client.zip" />
    <ExtensionPart Source="System.Windows.Controls.Data.zip" />
    <ExtensionPart Source="System.Windows.Controls.Data.Input.zip" />
    <ExtensionPart Source="System.Windows.Data.zip" />
    <ExtensionPart Source="System.Xml.Linq.zip" />
  </Deployment.ExternalParts>
</Deployment>
```

One of the drawbacks of this approach is that you must modify the external mapping files for the system assemblies, which by default are located at C:\Program Files (x86)\ Microsoft SDKs\Silverlight\v4.0\Libraries\Client. Since these URLs are embedded in the application manifest files, you will likely need to rebuild your Silverlight applications for production environments. As such you would need to implement a policy for building XAPs for specific environments, or configure development and test environments to mimic production URLs. The advantage of this approach is that you can define a single download location for your entire organization. As a result, the assemblies are cached by browsers for all of the Silverlight applications built with application library caching within your organization.

Maximizing Responsiveness

Ajax and Silverlight clients offer many inherent benefits over traditional thin clients in the area of responsiveness. A thorough understanding of these benefits can help you take maximum advantage and provide a slick, responsive user experience.

Asynchronous Execution Model

Ajax and Silverlight clients typically have a higher initial load cost compared to traditional thin client approaches. However, in most cases you will more than compensate for that load cost through enhanced UI responsiveness. Since the UI is controlled from the client, in many cases the client can react locally to user interaction without communicating with the server. When the client needs to send or retrieve information from the server, the communication takes place asynchronously and the UI remains responsive. The ability to build more capable UIs that run on the client also means that you can include more functionality on a single page. This compensates for the slower initial page load time, as pages typically need to be loaded far less frequently.

Local Processing Power

In almost all Web UI models, the operations that take the most time are those that require communication with the server. Both Ajax and Silverlight allow you to take advantage of client-side processing, which reduces the number of round-trips to the server. When communication with the server is required, the data exchange is restricted to only what is necessary for the operation. This contrasts with the traditional server controls approach, in which every request from the client results in the server building and resending the entire page—even if many areas of the page remain unchanged. This increases the load on the server, increases the volume of network traffic—the average page size is several orders of magnitude larger than the average asynchronous data request—and results in a somewhat disjointed user experience.

If your application requires substantial computation on the client, such as calculations or the processing of many rows of data, Silverlight will generally outperform Ajax approaches. This is because in these circumstances JavaScript incurs a certain amount of interpretation overhead due to the untyped nature of the language.

Client-side Data Caching

RIA clients such as Ajax and Silverlight can maintain state information on the client. This contrasts with traditional thin client approaches, where state must be maintained on the server and tracked through cookies or posted back and forth with every request through view state. Data retrieved from the server can be retained in memory and reused across different operations. For example, suppose a manager must approve 20 orders once a day. With a thin client (server control) model, the manager navigates into an order, reviews the line items, and approves the order. Each time the manager approves an order, he or she is redirected back to the order list. The remaining orders are reloaded on the server, which rebuilds the page and sends it back to the browser. With an RIA approach, the orders are retrieved once and stored on the client. As the manager navigates into each order, the line item details are retrieved asynchronously from the server, and approvals are sent asynchronously back to the server. In this case the orders have only been retrieved once, and the client is far more responsive since it can cache the information in memory and avoid unnecessary round-trips to the server.

Predictive Loading

Predictive loading approaches anticipate the actions of a user to make the client seem even more responsive. Building on the previous example, you could assume that managers will work through approvals in the order in which they are listed in the UI. The client might then anticipate that the order which appears after the order being currently viewed will be viewed next. The client could retrieve the details of the next order in advance, in order to avoid any delay in retrieving the information from the server. However, if the manager chooses to view a different order next, he will incur the usual delay while the data is retrieved asynchronously from the server. The disadvantage of this approach is that you are performing additional server-side processing that may not be used. Consequently you should use this approach when you can predict the actions of the user with a fairly high degree of accuracy.

Security Considerations for RIA Technologies

In traditional, server control-based user interfaces for SharePoint applications, security concerns were largely managed for you by the server environment. Authentication was managed by IIS (for Windows credentials) or by an ASP.NET authentication provider (for forms-based authentication). The SharePoint environment would then apply authorization rules to the authenticated credentials for each server resource. When you move to a client-based, RIA user interface, there are some additional aspects to managing security that you will need to consider.

AUTHENTICATION

Each of the client-side programming models provided by SharePoint 2010 is underpinned by a secure Web service.

- The JavaScript, Silverlight, and managed client object models use the client.svc Windows Communication Foundation (WCF) service under the covers.

- The REST interface is provided by the listdata.svc WCF service.

- Backward-compatible client-side access to various resources is provided by ASP. NET (ASMX) Web services.

When you develop Ajax and Silverlight clients that run within a SharePoint Web page, the client-side object model and the REST interface will by default inherit the security credentials that were used to authenticate the browser session. In this way, Ajax and Silverlight will support any mechanism with which you can authenticate a browser session, including Windows authentication, forms-based authentication, and claims-based authentication.

When you use the managed client API for stand-alone clients, you can specify the authentication mode and other security details through the **ClientContext** instance. For example, the following code example configures the **ClientContext** instance to use forms-based authentication and specifies a user name and password.

```csharp
C#
ClientContext context = new ClientContext("http://contoso/sites/manufacturing");
context.AuthenticationMode = ClientAuthenticationMode.FormsAuthentication;
context.FormsAuthenticationLoginInfo =
    new FormsAuthenticationLoginInfo(myUsername, myPassword);
```

When you access SharePoint ASP.NET Web services that are secured with forms-based authentication from a Silverlight client, you must call the Authentication Web service and provide your credentials. The Authentication Web service returns a cookie, which you can supply to the other SharePoint Web services in order to authenticate your requests. You can also use claims-based approaches to authentication from a stand-alone client, although this is more complex and is beyond the scope of our guidance.

CROSS-DOMAIN DATA ACCESS AND CLIENT ACCESS POLICY

Both Ajax and Silverlight clients are subject to certain restrictions and caveats when it comes to accessing data from a different domain. Cross-site scripting (XSS) attacks were once one of the most prevalent threats to Web applications, so modern browsers now prevent scripts from making calls across domain boundaries. As a result, Ajax clients have traditionally been unable to access resources on a different domain. Developers often worked around this limitation by including a proxy on the Web server that retrieves data from external services. However, emerging standards allow script calls across domain boundaries if those calls are explicitly permitted by the server hosting the Web page. This is based on the W3C draft specification *Cross-Origin Resource Sharing* (CORS). The most recent versions of the major browsers support CORS, although not in entirely consistent ways. Implementing CORS, however, is beyond the scope of this book.

In the case of Silverlight clients for SharePoint 2010, there are two key cross-domain data access scenarios that you need to consider:

1. When a Silverlight application on a SharePoint page needs to access data from an external (non-SharePoint) service on another domain.

2. When a Silverlight application on a Web page (SharePoint or non-SharePoint) needs to access data from a SharePoint Web application on another domain.

Note: *Silverlight considers different ports, different protocols, and different sub-domains to represent different domains. For example, https://services.contoso.com, http://services. constoso.com, http://www.constoso.com, and http://services.contoso.com:8080 are all considered different domains.*

In the first scenario, the fact that the Silverlight application is hosted on a SharePoint page is irrelevant. Silverlight looks for a client access policy file (clientaccesspolicy.xml) on the external domain to determine whether it is allowed cross-domain access to resources on that domain. The client access policy should be located at the root of the site you are attempting to access on the external domain. This scenario is illustrated in Figure 7.

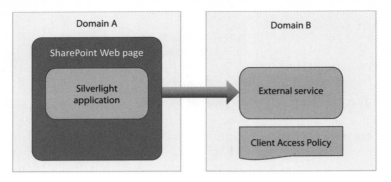

FIGURE 7
Cross-domain access to non-SharePoint resources

Essentially, the service owner modifies the client access policy to specify which domains are allowed cross-domain access to which resources. For example, the following client access policy file grants access to callers from the **http://www.contoso.com** domain. The caller is only permitted to access resources in the **Vendor** subfolder of the site.

```XML
<?xml version="1.0" encoding="utf-8" ?>
<access-policy>
  <cross-domain-access>
    <policy>
      <allow-from http-request-headers="SOAPAction">
        <domain uri="http://www.contoso.com"/>
      </allow-from>
      <grant-to>
        <resource include-subpaths="true" path="/Vendor/"/>
      </grant-to>
    </policy>
  </cross-domain-access>
</access-policy>
```

Silverlight can also use an Adobe Flash cross-domain policy file (crossdomain.xml) if the client access policy is not present.

In the second scenario, a Silverlight application needs to access SharePoint data on a different domain. This could be a Silverlight application running in a standard Web page, running as a stand-alone application, or running in a SharePoint Web page from a different Web application. In this case you need to take a different approach, as modifying the client access policy in a SharePoint environment is not supported. Instead, SharePoint 2010 provides a framework named Silverlight Cross-Domain Data Access, or Silverlight CDA, that allows farm administrators to manage access to resources by clients on other domains. This scenario is illustrated in Figure 8.

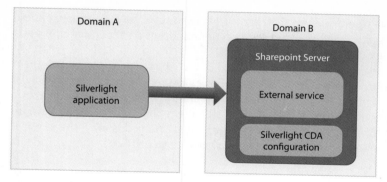

FIGURE 8
Cross-domain access to SharePoint resources

Configuring Silverlight CDA is beyond the scope of this guidance. The Further Information section at the end of this chapter provides links to resources on this and many other topics that we've touched upon here.

Overcoming Sandbox Restrictions

As you know, SharePoint 2010 restricts the functionality of solutions that are deployed to the sandbox environment within a site collection. One way to address the limitations of sandboxed solutions is to implement the restricted functionality in your client-side logic. Sandboxed solutions can include both Ajax and Silverlight components that run in the client browser. Scenarios in which you might choose to implement functionality in client logic include the following:

- When you need to access data from an external service. The sandbox environment does not permit server-side code to call external services. However, an Ajax component or a Silverlight application can call an external service and retrieve data directly from the client.

- When you need to access data across site collection boundaries. The sandbox environment does not allow you to access data from outside the site collection in which the solution is running. However, an Ajax component or a Silverlight application can use the client data access mechanisms to access data from any site collection where the user has sufficient permissions.

- When you need to access more advanced capabilities, such as the user profile service, that are not available with the sandbox environment. In this scenario you can use the SharePoint ASP.NET Web Services to access these capabilities.

When you access SharePoint data, each client-side data access mechanism is secured by the SharePoint environment. As such, users can only access resources on which they have the necessary permissions, thus security is maintained. A more important consideration is the processing load that you place on the client. The sandbox environment prevents you from performing expensive, process-intensive operations in server-side code in order to maintain the performance of the server as a whole, so circumventing these safeguards by moving process-intensive operations to the client is likely to result in a poor user experience. For example, aggregation across site collection boundaries is an expensive operation and should be used judiciously from client-side code.

In more complex scenarios, you can use Ajax and Silverlight to build composite client UIs that bridge SharePoint data and external data. For example, you might retrieve a list of statements of work from a SharePoint document library. When the user selects a statement of work in the user interface, an Ajax or Silverlight client can then retrieve information for that vendor from a vendor management system. In this way, the client is bridging the SharePoint environment and the external service to provide a composite data application.

Clearly, when you bridge services in this way you need to consider how to authenticate to each service. The Client reference implementation in the Developing Applications for SharePoint 2010 online guidance demonstrates how to bridge services using Windows authentication. The use of other authentication techniques, such as claims-based authentication, is beyond the scope of this book.

Conclusion

This chapter examined the key technologies and approaches that you can use to build a user experience for SharePoint 2010 clients. The following areas were discussed:

- **Key approaches**. In previous versions of SharePoint, the predominant approach to building a user experience was to create page layouts and Web Parts with server controls. SharePoint 2010 makes it easier to use other options, including Ajax functionality, Silverlight applications, and Office clients.

- **Reach considerations**. When selecting a technology on which to build a user experience, it's important to consider whether your target audience is able or willing to use it. Generally speaking, there is a trade-off between reach and capabilities. Pure HTML has universal reach but limited capabilities. Ajax brings richer functionality but may not be supported by every browser. Finally, client platforms that require browser plug-ins, such as Silverlight or Flash, provide the broadest set of capabilities but will only work if the user installs the plug-in.

- **Performance considerations**. Pages that contain Ajax or Silverlight functionality will typically have a higher initial load time than traditional thin client approaches. However, the asynchronous communication model ensures that the page remains more responsive through subsequent user interactions. Caching strategies, together with more advanced techniques such as predictive loading of resources, can provide further performance improvements.

- **Security considerations**. All of the SharePoint client-side APIs are underpinned by secure Web services. When you add Ajax and Silverlight components to a Web page hosted by SharePoint, the Ajax or Silverlight client inherits the credentials that were used to authenticate the browser session. In this way, Ajax and Silverlight can use any authentication mechanism that is supported by the SharePoint environment. In order for a Silverlight application to access services on a different domain, the external domain must include a client access policy file at the root of the Web site. Cross-domain access from JavaScript is more complex but is possible under some circumstances.

- **Overcoming sandbox restrictions**. The sandbox environment in SharePoint 2010 enables users with sufficient permissions to deploy solutions to a site collection, without access to the server environment or the prior permission of the IT team. In turn, SharePoint restricts the permissions and capabilities of sandboxed solutions. However, since you can deploy Ajax and Silverlight components within a sandboxed solution, you can use client-side logic to execute functionality that would not be permitted to run on the server. This can include retrieving data from other site collections, accessing external services, and many other scenarios.

See It in Action: The Client Reference Implementation in the Developing Applications for SharePoint 2010 online guidance is a fully-documented, downloadable solution that illustrates various approaches to building a user experience for SharePoint clients, together with different techniques for client-side data access. You can deploy the reference implementation to a SharePoint 2010 test environment and explore the source code at your leisure in Visual Studio 2010.

For more information, see Reference Implementation: Client at http://msdn.microsoft.com/en-us/library/ff798454.aspx.

FURTHER INFORMATION

Building user experiences for SharePoint could constitute a whole book in itself. This guidance focuses primarily on rich Internet applications (RIAs) and the underlying data access mechanisms that support these approaches. However, the book's online bibliography will be helpful in locating additional background information. It can be found at http://msdn.microsoft.com/gg213840.aspx. Some documents to get you started include those listed below.

- "Understanding Business Connectivity Services"
- "Microsoft Business Connectivity Services Model"
- "Business Connectivity Services: How-tos and Walkthroughs"
- "Business Connectivity Services: Sample XML and Code Examples"

2   Data Access for Client Applications

In the previous version of Microsoft® SharePoint®, your options for accessing data from client applications were largely limited to the SharePoint ASP.NET Web services. The lack of a strongly typed object model and the need to construct complex Collaborative Application Markup Language (CAML) queries in order to perform simple data operations made the development of SharePoint client applications challenging and somewhat limited. SharePoint 2010 introduces several new data access mechanisms that make it easier to build rich Internet applications (RIAs) that consume and manipulate data stored in SharePoint. There are now three principal approaches to accessing SharePoint data from client applications:

- **The client-side object model**. The client-side object model (CSOM) consists of three separate APIs that provide a subset of the server-side object model for use in client applications. The ECMAScript object model is designed for use by JavaScript or JScript that runs in a Web page, the Microsoft Silverlight® client object model provides similar support for Silverlight applications, and the Microsoft .NET managed client object model is designed for use in .NET client applications such as Windows® Presentation Foundation (WPF) solutions.

- **The SharePoint Foundation REST interface**. The SharePoint Foundation Representational State Transfer (REST) interface uses Windows Communication Foundation (WCF) Data Services (formerly ADO.NET Data Services) to expose SharePoint lists and list items as addressable resources that can be accessed through HTTP requests. In keeping with the standard for RESTful Web services, the REST interface maps read, create, update, and delete operations to GET, POST, PUT, and DELETE HTTP verbs, respectively. The REST interface can be used by any application that can send and retrieve HTTP requests and responses.

- **The ASP.NET Web Services**. SharePoint 2010 continues to expose the ASMX Web services that were available in SharePoint 2007. Although these are likely to be less widely used with the advent of the **client-side object model (CSOM)** and the REST interface, there are still some scenarios in which these Web services provide the only mechanism for client-side data access. For future compatibility, use CSOM and REST where possible.

In addition to these options, you can develop custom WCF services to expose SharePoint functionality that is unavailable through the existing access mechanisms. The product documentation for SharePoint 2010 includes extensive details about each of these approaches, together with examples and walkthroughs describing approaches to common client-side data access requirements. This chapter focuses on the merits and performance implications of each approach for different real-world scenarios, and it presents some guidance about how to maximize the efficiency of your data access operations in each case.

Before you start, you need a broad awareness of the capabilities of each approach. The following table shows what you can do in terms of data access with the CSOM, the REST interface, and the ASP.NET Web services.

	CSOM	REST interface	Web services
List queries	✔	✔	✔
List join queries	✔	✔ *	
External list queries	✔		
View projections	✔	✔	✔
Request batching	✔	✔	
Synchronous operations	✔ (except ECMA)		✔
Asynchronous operations	✔	✔	✔
SharePoint Foundation object model access	✔		✔
Access to SharePoint Server functionality (beyond SharePoint Foundation)			✔
Support non-Windows clients	✔ (ECMA only)	✔	✔
Support strongly-typed LINQ queries	✔ (objects only, no list queries)	✔ (with proxy, lists only)	

*The REST interface will perform implicit list joins, but only to satisfy **where** clause evaluation.*

In this chapter, we focus on the capabilities, performance, and limitations of using the CSOM and the REST interface to access SharePoint data. Because the ASP.NET Web services exposed by SharePoint 2010 work in the same way as the previous release, they are not covered in detail here. Generally speaking, you should prefer the use of the CSOM or the REST interface over the ASP.NET Web services when they meet your needs. However, the Web services expose some advanced data, such as organization profiles, published links, search data, social data, and user profiles, which is unavailable through the CSOM or the REST interface.

Note: *The code examples used in this chapter are taken from the Client Reference Implementation in the Developing Applications for SharePoint 2010 online guidance. The Client reference implementation is a downloadable solution that illustrates many key facets of working with SharePoint data from client platforms. For more details, see the Further Information section at the end of this chapter.*

Using the Client-Side Object Model

The client-side object model (CSOM) provides client-side applications with access to a subset of the SharePoint Foundation server object model, including core objects such as site collections, sites, lists, and list items. As described above, the CSOM actually consists of three distinct APIs—the ECMAScript object model, the Silverlight client object model, and the .NET managed client object model—that target distinct client platforms. The ECMAScript object model and the Silverlight client object model provide a smaller subset of functionality. This is designed to enhance the user experience, because it minimize the time it takes Silverlight applications or JavaScript functions running in a Web page to load the files required for operation. The .NET managed client object model provides a larger subset of functionality for standalone client applications. However, these APIs provide a broadly similar developer experience and work in a similar way.

Of the three principal approaches to client-side data access, using the CSOM APIs is the only approach that provides the kind of hierarchical, strongly-typed representation of SharePoint objects, such as sites and Webs, that compares to server-side development. The CSOM is the only approach for any client-side data access scenarios beyond list queries. The CSOM allows you to query SharePoint lists by creating CAML queries. This is the most efficient way to query lists, although it requires that developers revert to creating CAML queries. Specific cases where you should favor the use of the CSOM include the following:

* You need to perform advanced list operations, such as complicated joins or paging. You can also perform joins through REST requests, although this is subject to various limitations.
* You need to manipulate SharePoint objects, such as sites or Webs.
* You need client-side access to other areas of SharePoint functionality, such as security.

Query Efficiency and the Client Object Model

Although the CSOM APIs mirror the server APIs in terms of functionality, the way CSOM actually works necessitates some changes to the way in which you approach your development tasks. The CSOM uses a set of specialized Windows Communication Foundation (WCF) services to communicate with the SharePoint server. Each API is optimized to work efficiently with remote clients and with the asynchronous loading model used by the Ajax and Silverlight frameworks. This section looks at how these efficiency mechanisms work and how you can use them to best effect in your client-side SharePoint applications.

Request Batching

All the CSOM APIs include a class named **ClientContext** that manages the interaction between client-side application code and the SharePoint server. Before you perform any operations in client-side code, you must instantiate a **ClientContext** object with the URL of a SharePoint site, as shown by the following code example.

C#

```csharp
ClientContext clientContext = new ClientContext(webUrl);
```

The **clientContext** instance provides programmatic access to the objects within your site, such as the current **Web** object, the parent **Site** object, and a **Lists** collection. Communication with the server occurs when you call the **ExecuteQuery** method, or the **ExecuteQueryAsync** method, on the **ClientContext** instance. The following code example illustrates this process. Notice that the class names in the CSOM differ from their server-side counterparts in that they no longer have the "SP" prefix, like **SPList** or **SPWeb**—instead, they are simply **List** and **Web**.

C#

```csharp
private void GetParts(string searchSku)
{
  Parts.Clear();
  List partsList = clientContext.Web.Lists.GetByTitle("Parts");
  List inventoryLocationsList =
    clientContext.Web.Lists.GetByTitle("Inventory Locations");

  CamlQuery camlQueryPartsList = new CamlQuery();
  camlQueryPartsList.ViewXml =
    @"<View>
        <Query>
          <Where>
            <BeginsWith>
              <FieldRef Name='SKU' />
              <Value Type='Text'>" + searchSku + @"</Value>
            </BeginsWith>
          </Where>
        </Query>
      </View>";

  CamlQuery camlQueryInvLocationList = new CamlQuery();
  camlQueryInvLocationList.ViewXml =
    @"<View>
        <Query>
          <Where>
            <BeginsWith>
              <FieldRef Name='PartLookupSKU' />
```

```
          <Value Type='Lookup'>" + searchSku + @"</Value>
        </BeginsWith>
      </Where>
      <OrderBy Override='TRUE'>
        <FieldRef Name='PartLookupSKU' />
      </OrderBy>
    </Query>
    <ViewFields>
      <FieldRef Name='PartLookup' LookupId='TRUE' />
      <FieldRef Name='PartLookupSKU' />
      <FieldRef Name='PartLookupTitle' />
      <FieldRef Name='PartLookupDescription' />
      <FieldRef Name='BinNumber' />
      <FieldRef Name='Quantity' />
    </ViewFields>
    <ProjectedFields>
      <Field Name='PartLookupSKU' Type='Lookup' List='PartLookup'
          ShowField='SKU' />
      <Field Name='PartLookupTitle' Type='Lookup' List='PartLookup'
          ShowField='Title' />
      <Field Name='PartLookupDescription' Type='Lookup' List='PartLookup'
          ShowField='PartsDescription' />
    </ProjectedFields>
    <Joins>
      <Join Type='LEFT' ListAlias='PartLookup'>
      <!--List Name: Parts-->
        <Eq>
          <FieldRef Name='PartLookup' RefType='ID' />
          <FieldRef List='PartLookup' Name='ID' />
        </Eq>
      </Join>
    </Joins>
  </View>";

partListItems = partsList.GetItems(camlQueryPartsList);
inventoryLocationListItems =
  inventoryLocationsList.GetItems(camlQueryInvLocationList);

clientContext.Load(partListItems);
clientContext.Load(inventoryLocationListItems);
clientContext.ExecuteQueryAsync(onQuerySucceeded, onQueryFailed);
}
```

Essentially, the code in this example performs four key steps that are common to many client-side data operations:

1. The client-side code uses the **ClientContext** class to define a series of operations to execute against a SharePoint site. In this example, the operations are the following:

    a. Retrieve the Parts list.

    b. Retrieve the Inventory Locations list.

    c. Build a query for the Parts list.

    d. Build a query for the Inventory Locations list.

    e. Execute the query against the Parts list.

    f. Execute the query against the Inventory Locations list.

    g. Load the Parts query results (which causes them to be returned to the client).

    h. Load the Inventory Locations query results.

2. The client code calls the **ClientContext.ExecuteQueryAsync** method. This instructs the CSOM to send a request containing all operations to the server.

3. The SharePoint server executes the series of operations in order and returns the results to the client.

4. The CSOM notifies the client-side code of the results by invoking the callback method associated with the **onQuerySucceed** delegate.

Figure 1 illustrates this process.

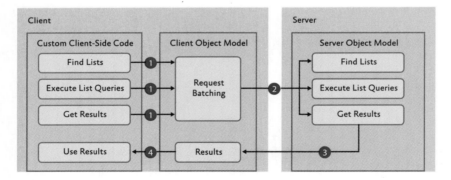

FIGURE 1
Client object model request batching

This request batching process helps to improve performance and reduce network traffic in two ways. First, fewer Web service calls occur between the client and the SharePoint server, which reduces the "chattiness" of the client-server interface. For example, you can perform two list queries in a single request. Second, as a set of operations occur on the server in a single request, the data being acted on doesn't need to be moved between the client and the server for the intermediate operations—only the list of operations and the final result set are passed between the client and the server.

Request batching requires a different mindset when you create queries from client-side code. First, be aware that you do not have access to any results until you call **Execute QueryAsync** (or **ExecuteQuery**) and receive the call back with the results. If you need to implement conditional logic in the client-side code that can't be expressed in the command list that you send to the server, you will need to execute more than one query batch. Second, you should aim to group your operations to minimize the number of service calls. This means you may need to think about how you sequence your logic in order to take full advantage of request batching.

List Queries with CAML

As you can see from the preceding code example, the CSOM supports querying list data using CAML. The CSOM allows you to submit any CAML queries that you could use with the **SPQuery** class, including the use of join statements and view projections. In fact, the CSOM is the only client-side data access mechanism that supports the use of joins with view projections that execute as a single list query (although the REST interface does provide partial support for joins, when you specify implicit joins as part of the filter criteria).

The ability to use join statements and view projections in list queries leads to more efficient queries and reduces the number of queries required. The following example includes a CAML query that uses list joins and view projections. The query performs a left join between the Part Suppliers list and the Suppliers list. These lists are related by lookup columns, as shown by Figure 2.

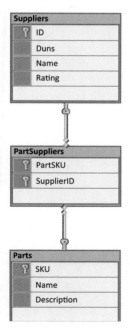

FIGURE 2
Entity-relationship diagram for parts and suppliers

The query then uses a view projection to select the supplier name, DUNS, and rating that match a specified part SKU from the join table.

```csharp
private void GetPartSuppliers()
{
  if (currentItem != null)
  {
    List partSuppliersList = clientContext.Web.Lists.GetByTitle("Part Suppliers");
    CamlQuery camlQuery = new CamlQuery();
    camlQuery.ViewXml =
      @"<View>
          <Query>
            <Where>
              <Eq>
                <FieldRef Name='PartLookup' LookupId='TRUE' />
                <Value Type='Lookup'>" + currentItem.Part.Id + @"</Value>
              </Eq>
            </Where>
          </Query>
          <ViewFields>
            <FieldRef Name='SupplierLookupTitle' />
            <FieldRef Name='SupplierLookupDUNS' />
            <FieldRef Name='SupplierLookupRating' />
          </ViewFields>
          <ProjectedFields>
            <Field Name='SupplierLookupTitle' Type='Lookup'
                   List='SupplierLookup' ShowField='Title' />
            <Field Name='SupplierLookupDUNS' Type='Lookup'
                   List='SupplierLookup' ShowField='DUNS' />
            <Field Name='SupplierLookupRating' Type='Lookup'
                   List='SupplierLookup' ShowField='Rating' />
          </ProjectedFields>
          <Joins>
            <Join Type='LEFT' ListAlias='SupplierLookup'>
            <!--List Name: Suppliers-->
              <Eq>
                <FieldRef Name='SupplierLookup' RefType='ID' />
                <FieldRef List='SupplierLookup' Name='ID' />
              </Eq>
            </Join>
          </Joins>
        </View>";
```

```
    partSuppliersListItems = partSuppliersList.GetItems(camlQuery);
    clientContext.Load(partSuppliersListItems);

    //Get Supplier Data
    clientContext.ExecuteQueryAsync(onPartSupplierQuerySucceeded, onQueryFailed);
  }
}
```

In this example, the use of a list join improves the efficiency of the query and reduces network traffic. Without the list join, you would need to issue more queries and perform the join logic in your application code. The use of a view projection reduces the amount of data returned by the query, because it returns only a subset of field values that are relevant to your requirements. In the case of client-side data access, the benefits of this approach are even more pronounced. The ability to join lists in client-side data queries reduces the load on the server, reduces the number of round trips required between the client and server, and reduces the overall amount of data transmitted between the client and server.

The CSOM does not provide a mechanism for querying data across multiple lists that are not associated by a lookup field. In other words, there is no client-side functional equivalent of the **SPSiteDataQuery** class. If you need to perform a cross-list query from client-side code, consider creating a list view on the server that performs the list aggregation. You can then query the aggregated data from your client-side code.

Using LINQ for Objects

When you use the CSOM, you can write LINQ queries against client-side objects, such as lists and Webs, and then use the **ClientContext** class to submit these queries to the server. It's important to understand that when you take this approach, you are using *LINQ to Objects* to query SharePoint objects, not *LINQ to SharePoint*. This means that your LINQ expressions are not converted to CAML and you will not see the performance benefits that are associated with CAML conversion. The LINQ to SharePoint provider is not supported by any of the client-side data access mechanisms.

Submitting a LINQ to Objects expression to the server reduces network traffic between the client and the server and alleviates some of the processing burden on the client platform. This is because you use the LINQ expression to narrow down the objects returned through server-side processing, instead of retrieving all objects in a collection, such as all Webs on a site and iterating through the collection on the client. LINQ to Objects makes it easy to specify fairly complex criteria with which to narrow down your result set. For example, you could use the following code to retrieve all non-hidden lists that have been created since March 20, 2010.

```C#
private IEnumerable<List> newLists;

var dt = new DateTime(2010, 3, 20);
var query = from list
            in clientContext.Web.Lists
            where list.Created > dt && list.Hidden == false
            select list;

newLists = clientContext.LoadQuery(query);
clientContext.ExecuteQueryAsync(onNewListQueryComplete, onNewListQueryFail);
```

In-Place Load and Queryable Load

The client object model provides two different mechanisms for data retrieval—*in-place load* and *queryable load*.

- **In-place load**. This loads an entire collection into the client context. To perform an in-place load, you use the **ClientContext.Load** method.
- **Queryable load**. This returns an enumerable collection of results. To perform a queryable load, you use the **ClientContext.LoadQuery** method.

For example, the following code uses an in-place load to load the collection of lists in the context site into the client context object.

```C#
clientContext.Load(clientContext.Web.Lists);
clientContext.ExecuteQueryAsync(onQuerySucceeded, onQueryFailed);
```

After executing the query, you can access the list collection through the **clientContext.Web.Lists** property. When you perform an in-place load, the client context manages object identity for you. If you modify a setting, such as the title of a list, and then you perform a second query that loads the same list, the client context understands that the returned items refer to the same list and it preserves the changes.

The following code uses an equivalent queryable load to load the collection of lists in the context site.

```C#
private IEnumerable<List> allLists;

var query = from list in clientContext.WebLists
            select list;

this.allLists = clientContext.LoadQuery(query);
clientContext.ExecuteQueryAsync(onQuerySucceeded, on QueryFailed);
```

When you use a queryable load, you are not loading items into the client context. Instead, you are loading items into a results array—in this case, the **allLists** field. In this instance, object identity is not managed by the client context. If you were to repeat the query, the client context would simply repopulate the **allLists** field from server-side data and would overwrite any changes you had made on the client in the meantime.

In terms of performance, there are no advantages or disadvantages to either approach. Because you can only use an in-place load to load one collection of objects at a time, there are circumstances in which you may want to use a queryable load to simultaneously load an alternative view of the data on your site. For example, suppose you would like to add the completion date for every project within your organization into all the calendars on your SharePoint site. The projects are distributed across several custom lists. In this scenario, you would use the in-place load for the collection of calendar lists, because these are the objects that you want to update. You would use the queryable load for the collection of project lists, because these will not be updated.

SYNCHRONOUS AND ASYNCHRONOUS OPERATIONS

As described earlier in this topic, the CSOM batches your client-side operations and sends them to the server for execution. The CSOM provides both a synchronous model and an asynchronous model for invoking this server-side execution. If you use the .NET managed client API or the Silverlight client API, you can use either approach. If you use the ECMAScript API, you must use the asynchronous approach. This prevents service calls from causing the Web browser to block user interaction for the duration of the call.

For example, suppose you are using the .NET managed client API or the Silverlight client API to retrieve data from the server:

- If you call the **ClientContext.ExecuteQuery** method, your operation will be invoked synchronously. The thread that executes your code will wait for the server to respond before continuing.

- If you call the **ClientContext.ExecuteQueryAsync** method, your operation will be invoked asynchronously. In this case, you specify callback methods to handle the server response, and the current thread remains unblocked.

Although the Silverlight client API supports the synchronous **ExecuteQuery** method, in most cases you will want to use **ExecuteQueryAsync** to submit your operation set. The following example illustrates how you can use the **ExecuteQueryAsync** method with the Silverlight client API. The **PartSearchButton_Click** method executes when the user clicks a button in the Silverlight application.

C#

```csharp
private void PartSearchButton_Click(object sender, RoutedEventArgs e)
{
    bindingViewsModels.Clear();
    List partsList = clientContext.Web.Lists.GetByTitle("Parts");
```

```
CamlQuery camlQueryPartsList = new CamlQuery();
camlQueryPartsList.ViewXml = @"
  <View>
    <Query>
      <Where>
        <BeginsWith>
          <FieldRef Name='SKU' />
          <Value Type='Text'>" + PartSkuTextBox.Text + @"</Value>
        </BeginsWith>
      </Where>
    </Query>
  </View>";

partListItems = partsList.GetItems(camlQueryPartsList);
clientContext.Load(partListItems);
clientContext.ExecuteQueryAsync(onQuerySucceeded, onQueryFailed);
}
```

The **ExecuteQueryAsync** method accepts two arguments—a delegate for a method that is called if the server-side operation succeeds and a delegate for a method that is called if the server-side operation fails. If the operation is successful, the **onQuery Succeeded** method is called.

```
C#
private void onQuerySucceeded(object sender, ClientRequestSucceededEventArgs args)
{
  this.Dispatcher.BeginInvoke(DisplayParts);
}
```

As you can see, this method also makes an asynchronous method call. The **Dispatcher.BeginInvoke** method invokes the **DisplayParts** method on the user interface (UI) thread. This is a mandatory approach when you work with Silverlight, because you must use the UI thread to execute logic that updates the UI. The **DisplayParts** method simply binds the query results to the appropriate UI controls. Figure 3 illustrates how this process works at a high level.

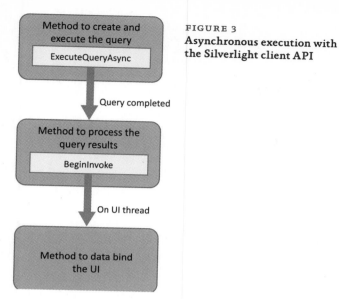

FIGURE 3
Asynchronous execution with the Silverlight client API

In the previous example, what would happen if you called **ExecuteQuery** instead of **ExecuteQueryAsync**? Silverlight would throw an **InvalidOperationException** with the following message:

> The method or property that is called may block the UI thread and it is not allowed. Please use background thread to invoke the method or property, for example, using **System.Threading.ThreadPool.QueueUserWorkItem** method to invoke the method or property.

In other words, Silverlight will not allow you to block the UI thread. To avoid this exception, you would need to execute the query on a background thread, as shown in the following code example.

```C#
private void PartSearchButton_Click(object sender, RoutedEventArgs e)
{
  bindingViewsModels.Clear();
  List partsList = clientContext.Web.Lists.GetByTitle("Parts");
  List inventoryLocationsList =
    clientContext.Web.Lists.GetByTitle("Inventory Locations");

  CamlQuery camlQueryPartsList = new CamlQuery();
  camlQueryPartsList.ViewXml = @"
    <View>
      <Query>
        <Where>
          <BeginsWith>
```

```
            <FieldRef Name='SKU' />
            <Value Type='Text'>" + PartSkuTextBox.Text + @"</Value>
        </BeginsWith>
      </Where>
    </Query>
  </View>";

 partListItems = partsList.GetItems(camlQueryPartsList);
 clientContext.Load(partListItems);
 System.Threading.ThreadPool.QueueUserWorkItem(
   new WaitCallback(ThreadCallback), clientContext);
}

private void ThreadCallback(object s)
{
  var context = (ClientContext)s;
  context.ExecuteQuery();
  this.Dispatcher.BeginInvoke(DisplayParts);
}
```

In other words, if you don't use the **ExecuteQueryAsync** method, you must manually implement the asynchronous logic. Both methods are functionally correct. However, the **ExecuteQueryAsync** method makes your code easier to understand and is preferred from a stylistic perspective. The **ExecuteQuery** method is useful in applications where a synchronous execution model is appropriate, such as a command-line application or a Windows® PowerShell™ extension.

ACCESSING BINARY DATA

In some cases, you may want to either upload or download binary files, such as images or documents, from your RIA or managed client. You can use the CSOM to access binary data such as documents; however, there are varying levels of support, depending on the CSOM API that you use.

The managed version of the CSOM supports both binary file upload and download using **File.OpenBinaryDirect** and **File.SaveBinaryDirect**. The following example shows how to retrieve and save a picture using these APIs from a WPF client. In this case, the method **DisplayPix** retrieves all the items in the Pix picture library and displays them to a WPF control in the call to **AddPix**. The **SavePix** method saves the supplied file stream as an image to the Pix library, using the file name for the title.

```
C#
private void DisplayPix()
{
  List pixList = clientContext.Web.Lists.GetByTitle("Pix");

  CamlQuery camlQuery = new CamlQuery();
  camlQuery.ViewXml = "<View/>";
```

```
pictureItems = pixList.GetItems(camlQuery);

clientContext.Load(pictureItems);
clientContext.ExecuteQuery();

foreach (ListItem pictureItem in pictureItems)
{
  string fileRef = pictureItem["FileRef"].ToString();
  FileInformation fileInfo = File.OpenBinaryDirect(clientContext, fileRef);
  AddPix(fileInfo.Stream);
}
}

private void SavePix(string filename, Stream stream)
{
  string url = "/sites/sharepointlist/Pix/" + filename;
  File.SaveBinaryDirect(clientContext, url, stream, true);
}
```

The Silverlight CSOM supports opening binary files from SharePoint with **File.Open BinaryDirect** using the same syntax as the managed CSOM, but does not support saving binary files. The ECMAScript CSOM does not support either saving or reading binary files from SharePoint.

Using the REST Interface

The SharePoint 2010 REST interface is a WCF Data Service that allows you to use construct HTTP requests to query SharePoint list data. Like all RESTful Web services, the SharePoint REST interface maps HTTP verbs to data operations, as shown in the following table.

HTTP verb	Data operation
GET	Retrieve
POST	Create
PUT	Update (update all fields and use default values for any undefined fields)
DELETE	Delete
MERGE	Update (update only the fields that are specified and changed from current version)

Note: *In practice, many firewalls and other network intermediaries block HTTP verbs other than GET and POST. To work around this issue, WCF Data Services (and the OData standard) support a technique known as verb tunneling. In this technique, PUT, DELETE, and MERGE requests are submitted as a POST request, and an X-HTTP-Method header specifies the actual verb that the recipient should apply to the request.*

A RESTful service models data entities, in this case SharePoint lists, as HTTP resources that can be addressed by a URL. You can append query strings to the URLs in order to specify filter criteria or query logic. The following examples show some URLs that correspond to simple REST operations.

```
http://localhost/_vti_bin/listdata.svc/Parts
```

This returns the contents of the Parts list in XML format as an Atom feed.

```
http://localhost/_vti_bin/listdata.svc/Parts(3)
```

This returns the Parts list item with an ID value of 3 as an Atom feed.

```
http://localhost/_vti_bin/listdata.svc/Parts?$orderby=Name
```

This returns the Parts list as an Atom feed, ordered by the Name field.

However, you don't need to manually construct HTTP requests in order to use the SharePoint REST interface. When you use Microsoft Visual Studio® 2010 to create a SharePoint client application, Visual Studio will generate a WCF Data Services Framework service proxy when you add a reference to the service. The service proxy provides strongly typed entity classes and enables you to use LINQ expressions to build queries. Behind the scenes, the service proxy manages the details of building and submitting requests to the service.

The SharePoint REST interface is based on the REST-based Open Data protocol (OData) for Web-based data services, which extends the Atom and AtomPub syndication formats to exchange XML data over HTTP. Because OData is a platform-independent open standard, the SharePoint REST interface is a great way to access SharePoint list data from platforms on which the CSOM may be unavailable to you, such as from non-Windows–based operating systems. However, the REST interface only provides access to list data—if you need to manipulate other data on your SharePoint site, you will need to use the CSOM. The REST implementation can also return the output in JavaScript Object Notation (JSON) format as an alternative to an ATOM feed. JSON is a compact representation of the returned results that can be easily parsed by JavaScript clients.

USING THE SERVICE PROXY

The WCF Data Services service proxy for the SharePoint REST interface includes classes that provide strongly typed representations of the lists and content types in your SharePoint site. At the top level in the service proxy object model, a data context class that inherits from **DataServiceContext** provides the starting point for all your service calls. In this way, it performs a role similar to that of the data context class that you use with the LINQ to SharePoint provider. When you want to perform a data operation using the REST interface, your first step is always to instantiate the data context class to the WCF service endpoint for your SharePoint site. For example, in the Client reference implementation, the data context class is named **PartsDataContext**.

C#
```
PartsDataContext context = new PartsDataContext(
  new Uri("http://localhost/sites/sharepointlist/_vti_bin/listdata.svc""));
```

The data context class allows you to specify contextual information for the operations, such as user credentials, and it provides methods that you can use to build and execute REST queries. Your code runs in a browser—using either JavaScript or Silverlight—the calls to SharePoint will use the security context already established by the browser session. You can use the LINQ query syntax to build query expressions. For example, the following method retrieves parts that start with the SKU search string.

C#
```
var partsQuery = (DataServiceQuery<PartsItem>)
      context.Parts.Where(p => p.SKU.StartsWith(SearchSku))
        .Select(p => new PartsItem { Title = p.Title,
                                     SKU = p.SKU,
                                     Id = p.Id,
                                     Description = p.Description
                                   });

// Execute query
partsQuery.BeginExecute(DisplayParts, partsQuery);
```

The preceding example demonstrates various key points of submitting queries to the REST interface by using the service proxy:

- It creates a LINQ expression from the data context object.

- The LINQ expression returns a query in the form of a **DataServiceQuery<TElement>** instance. This is a WCF Data Services class that represents a query request to a service, where the query returns a collection of **TElement** instances. The **DataServiceQuery<TElement>** class implements the **IQueryable** interface, which allows you to use the LINQ extension methods provided by the **Queryable** class to query the result set. In this case, **TElement** is **PartsItem**.

- The **DataServiceQuery.BeginExecute** method is used to send the query to the REST service asynchronously, passing in the callback delegate and the query object as arguments. The results of the query in **partsQuery** are not available until the callback delegate, **DisplayParts**, is invoked.

- The proxy generates a REST statement from the LINQ expression and submits it to the REST service, as shown here.

```
http://contoso/sites/sharepointlist/_vti_bin/listdata.svc/Parts()
  ?$filter=startswith(SKU,'sku')
    &$select=Title,SKU,Id,Description
```

Note: *You can also use the **CreateQuery** method to create the query object explicitly from the data context. In the previous example, where a LINQ statement was specified without calling **CreateQuery**, the WCF Data Services proxy created the query object implicitly when the results of the LINQ statement were cast to a **DataServiceQuery<PartsItem>** instance. For example, the following statement is functionally equivalent to the previous code example:*

context.CreateQuery<PartsItem>("Parts").Where(p => p.SKU. StartsWith(SearchSku)).Select(p => new PartsItem { Title = p.Title, SKU = p.SKU, Id = p.Id, Description = p.Description });

In general, the implicit approach is preferred for readability and simplicity.

The callback method iterates through the query results and adds each item to the Parts observable collection. The Parts collection is bound to a UI control that renders the results in a grid. Because this is a Silverlight application, you must use the **Dispatcher. BeginInvoke** method to execute the data binding logic asynchronously on the UI thread.

```C#
Dispatcher.BeginInvoke(
  () =>
  {
    Parts.Clear();
    DataServiceQuery<PartsItem> query =
      (DataServiceQuery<PartsItem>) result.AsyncState;

    var partResults = query.EndExecute(result);

    foreach (var part in partResults)
    {
      Parts.Add(part);
    }
});
```

Although the queries themselves will vary, the pattern of use remains broadly the same for all REST interface queries.

How Does the REST Interface Work?

When you create a WCF Data Services service proxy for the REST interface, you can use it to send a query to the REST interface in one of three ways:

- You can use the data context class to create a **DataServiceQuery<TElement>** instance, as seen in the preceding code examples. When you use this approach, you submit a LINQ expression to the service proxy. The service proxy converts the LINQ expression into a URL-based REST request and submits it to the REST interface.

- You can use view projection, in which case the **DataServiceQuery<TElement>** is created implicitly. This approach is described in more detail in the next section.
- You can use the data context class to submit a URL-based REST request directly, as shown by the following code example.

C#
```
context.Execute<PartsItem>(new
  uri("http://contoso/_vti_bin/listdata.svc/Parts()
      ?$filter=startswith(SKU,'Sku2')
      &$select=Title,SKU,Id,Description"));
```

The LINQ expression used on the client is specific to the WCF Data Services proxy, which converts the LINQ expression into a REST statement. On the SharePoint server, the REST service implementation translates the REST statement into a LINQ to Share-Point expression. This translation process is not visible to the developer. The important thing to note is that the LINQ expressions you submit to the service proxy on the client are completely independent of the LINQ to SharePoint expressions that the REST service implementation generates in order to fulfill the request. The LINQ to SharePoint provider converts the server-generated LINQ expressions into CAML, and then it executes the CAML queries against your SharePoint lists. The REST interface returns the results to the service proxy in JSON format or as an Atom feed, using the OData protocol. The service proxy then converts the response into strongly typed entity instances and returns the results to the caller. Figure 4 illustrates this process.

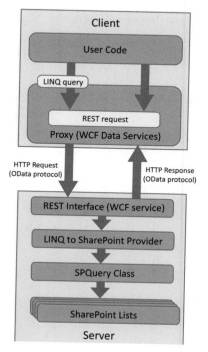

FIGURE 4
The SharePoint REST interface

It can be instructive to see how LINQ expressions are translated into REST queries, and how these REST queries translate into the HTTP requests and responses that are exchanged between the client and the server. Using the preceding LINQ expression as an example, the process is as follows:

1. The proxy forms a REST query from the LINQ expression.

```
http://localhost/sites/sharepointlist/_vti_bin/listdata.svc/Parts()
   ?$filter=startswith(SKU,'sku')
     &$select=Title,SKU,Id,Description
```

2. The proxy submits the REST query to the server as an HTTP GET request.

```
HTTP Request
GET http://localhost/sites/sharepointlist/_vti_bin/listdata.svc/Parts()
?$filter=startswith(SKU,'sku1')&$select=Title,SKU,Id,Description HTTP/1.1
Accept: application/atom+xml,application/xml
Accept-Language: en-US
Referer: file:///C:/spg3/Trunk/Source/Client/Client.REST/Client.REST.
   Silverlight/Bin/Debug/Client.REST.Silverlight.xap
Accept-Encoding: identity
DataServiceVersion: 2.0;NetFx
MaxDataServiceVersion: 2.0;NetFx
User-Agent: Mozilla/4.0 (compatible; MSIE 8.0; Windows NT 6.1; WOW64;
Trident/4.0; SLCC2; .NET CLR 2.0.50727; .NET CLR 3.5.30729;
   .NET CLR 3.0.30729; Media Center PC 6.0; InfoPath.3; MS-RTC LM 8;
   .NET4.0C; .NET4.0E)
Host: contoso
Connection: Keep-Alive
```

3. The server responds with an OData-formatted result set. (The HTTP headers have been omitted for brevity.)

```
HTTP Response
<?xml version="1.0" encoding="utf-8" standalone="yes"?>
<feed xml:base="http://contoso/sites/sharepointlist/_vti_bin/listdata.svc/"
      xmlns:d="http://schemas.microsoft.com/ado/2007/08/dataservices"
      xmlns:m=
        "http://schemas.microsoft.com/ado/2007/08/dataservices/metadata"
      xmlns="http://www.w3.org/2005/Atom">
  <title type="text">Parts</title>
  <id>http://contoso/sites/sharepointlist/_vti_bin/listdata.svc/Parts</id>
  <updated>2010-05-30T14:20:47Z</updated>
  <link rel="self" title="Parts" href="Parts" />
  <entry m:ETag="W/&quot;2&quot;">
    <id>http://contoso/sites/sharepointlist/_vti_bin/listdata.svc/Parts(2)
    </id>
```

```
<title type="text">SHAFT - PUMP 1</title>
<updated>2010-05-21T14:06:12-04:00</updated>
<author>
  <name />
</author>
<link rel="edit" title="PartsItem" href="Parts(2)" />
<category term="Microsoft.SharePoint.DataService.PartsItem"
scheme="http://schemas.microsoft.com/ado/2007/08/dataservices/scheme" />
<content type="application/xml">
  <m:properties>
    <d:Title>SHAFT - PUMP 1</d:Title>
    <d:SKU>SKU1</d:SKU>
    <d:Description m:null="true" />
    <d:Id m:type="Edm.Int32">2</d:Id>
  </m:properties>
</content>
</entry>
</feed>
```

4. The WCF Data Services proxy invokes the **DisplayParts** delegate and provides the results from the request as a strongly-typed collection of **PartsItem** instances.

QUERY EFFICIENCY WITH THE REST INTERFACE

In order to understand the performance implications of using the REST interface, you need to understand what happens when you request data from the service:

1. You submit a LINQ expression to the service proxy.

2. The service proxy converts your LINQ expression into a URL-based REST request, and then submits the request to the REST interface on the server.

3. The REST interface converts the REST request into a LINQ to SharePoint expression.

4. The LINQ to SharePoint provider converts the LINQ expression into a CAML query.

You have some control over whether the REST interface generates LINQ expressions with efficient syntax. You can gain an insight into the performance of REST-based queries by understanding how some specific REST constructs are implemented by the service.

Joins

The REST interface does not support explicit list joins. You can use the **Expand** method to navigate from one entity to a related entity. Although this appears similar to a join, it actually results in the execution of additional list queries on the server. If required, the REST provider performs an implicit join to satisfy the **where** clause. However, for each item in the result set, the **Expand** method causes an additional list query on the server to retrieve the related entity instance that corresponds to the value in a lookup column. For example, consider the following query that retrieves a list of inventory locations ordered by **Part.SKU**.

```C#
var query = (DataServiceQuery<InventoryLocationsItem>)
            context.InventoryLocations
                    .Expand("Part")
                    .Where(p => p.Part.SKU.StartsWith(SearchSku))
                    .OrderBy(p => p.Part.SKU);
```

The **Expand** method in our LINQ query is translated to an $expand="Part" query string in the REST request URL, as shown here.

```
http://contoso/sites/sharepointlist/_vti_bin/listdata.svc/InventoryLocations()
  ?$filter=startswith(Part/SKU,'sku')
    &$orderby=Part/SKU
      &$expand=Part
```

In this case, the following actions take place in order to execute the query on the server:

1. A list join is performed between the Inventory Locations list and the Parts list, in order to satisfy the **where** clause match on the part SKU. From the REST statement, the implicit join occurs because **Part/SKU** in the **startswith** statement follows a lookup field relationship.

2. The inventory location items are ordered by part SKU.

3. For each inventory item in the result set, a query is executed on the server to retrieve the related part to satisfy the **expand** clause.

4. The results are formatted using the OData protocol and returned to the caller.

As you can see, this operation is going to be less efficient than submitting a CAML query with a join predicate where all values can be retrieved in a single list query. However, the CSOM is the only data access mechanism that supports explicit joins. The CSOM allows you to submit a CAML query that specifies a list join and a view projection directly from your client-side logic.

Projections

The REST interface supports view projections. As described in *Chapter 7 – Data Access in SharePoint 2010*, view projections improve query efficiency by limiting the field values returned to only those fields that are of interest. For example, the following query uses a view projection to select parts, based on a partial part SKU match.

```C#
context.Parts.Where(p => p.SKU.StartsWith(SearchSku))
            .Select(p => new PartsItem {  Title = p.Title,
                                          SKU = p.SKU,
```

```
                                        Id = p.Id,
                                        Description = p.Description
                                });
```

The service proxy translates this query into the following REST request URL, and then it parses the response feed into a collection of **PartsItem** instances.

```
http://contoso/_vti_bin/listdata.svc/Parts()
  ?$filter=startswith(SKU,'SKU2')
    &$select=Title,SKU,Id,Description
```

You can also perform query projections explicitly on the query object. This can be useful as a concise way to query multiple related entities.

```
C#
var query = (DataServiceQuery<InventoryLocationsItem>)context.
    CreateQuery<InventoryLocationsItem>("InventoryLocations")
      .Expand("Part")
      .AddQueryOption("$select",
                          "BinNumber,Quantity,Title,Id,PartId,Part/SKU,Part/Title")
      .Where(p => p.Part.SKU.StartsWith(SearchSku)).OrderBy(p => p.Part.SKU);
```

In this case, only the **BinNumber**, **Quantity**, **Title**, **ID**, and **PartId** values are retrieved from each inventory location item, and only **SKU** and **Title** are retrieved from each part item. If you use view projections, you need to be aware that the result set will include null values for the fields that you have omitted. For example, if you attempt to access **inventoryItem.Part.Description** from a returned result, the value will always be null because your query excluded the **Part.Description** property. The expression results in the following REST query.

```
http://contoso/sites/sharepointlist/_vti_bin/listdata.svc/InventoryLocations()
  ?$filter=startswith(Part/SKU,'sku')
    &$orderby=Part/SKU
      &$expand=Part
        &$select=BinNumber,Quantity,Title,Id,PartId,Part/SKU,Part/Title
```

In addition to projecting fields from related entities onto a target entity—such as projecting Part fields onto an Inventory Location entity, as illustrated in the preceding example—you can also create a new view entity that combines the fields of interest. The following query populates a **PartInvView** instance that contains fields from the Inventory Locations list and the Parts list.

```
C#
var query =
  (DataServiceQuery<PartInvView>)context.InventoryLocations
    .Where(p => p.Part.SKU.StartsWith(SearchSku))
    .OrderBy(p => p.Part.SKU)
    .Select((i) => new PartInvView
      {
```

```
        BinNumber = i.BinNumber,
        Quantity=i.Quantity,
        InvTitle=i.Title,
        InvId=i.Id,
        PartId=i.PartId,
        SKU=i.Part.SKU,
        PartTitle=i.Part.Title
    });
```

This projection produces the same REST query as the previous example. The only difference is that the service proxy will use the results to populate a collection of **Part InvView** instances, instead of a collection of **InventoryLocationsItem** instances.

```
http://contoso/sites/sharepointlist/_vti_bin/listdata.svc/InventoryLocations()
  ?$filter=startswith(Part/SKU,'sku')
    &$orderby=Part/SKU
      &$expand=Part
        &$select=BinNumber,Quantity,Title,Id,PartId,Part/SKU,Part/Title
```

You should consider using view projections whenever you are retrieving lists of items, in order to reduce network traffic and improve query efficiency.

CONCURRENCY MANAGEMENT

By default, the REST implementation supports *optimistic concurrency*. This means that no locks are placed on the underlying database tables between the time you read an item and the time you write an update to the item. This is a standard approach to service development that prevents clients from controlling precious database resources and impacting other clients. To detect whether an underlying entity has changed between a read operation and an update operation, the REST interface records information about the version of the entity you originally retrieved. If this version information is found to have changed when you perform the update operation, the REST interface will return the following error.

XML
```
<?xml version="1.0" encoding="utf-8" standalone="yes"?>
<error xmlns="http://schemas.microsoft.com/ado/2007/08/dataservices/metadata">
  <code></code>
  <message xml:lang="en-US">
    Since entity type 'Microsoft.SharePoint.DataService.PartsItem' has one or
    more ETag properties, If-Match HTTP header must be specified for DELETE/PUT
    operations on this type.
  </message>
</error>
```

The OData standard used by the REST interface uses ETags to perform this concurrency control. ETags are a mechanism defined by the HTTP protocol for efficient cache control between a client browser and a Web server. An ETag consists of a unique value that the Web server specifies to identify a particular version of a resource. When you update an entity, the service proxy will automatically add an ETag to the HTTP request. The ETag value matches the value provided by the service when you retrieved the data that you want to update. However, if the server-side data changes between the point at which you retrieve it and the point at which you persist an update, the ETag values will not match, and the server will detect a conflict. In this case, you receive the error described earlier. This error may also occur within your code if you have more than one data context retrieving the same entity, or if you create a new data context to save an item that was previously retrieved. If you want to persist your changes regardless of whether the underlying entity has changed, you can use the following code to force the service to apply your updates.

C#
```
context.MergeOption = MergeOption.OverwriteChanges;
context.AttachTo("Parts", currentItem, "*");
```

The **DataServiceContext.AttachTo** method instructs the context object to track the object that you intend to update. By specifying an ETag value of *, you are telling the service to overwrite the object, regardless of the ETag value.

PUT AND MERGE Operations

The WCF Data Services proxy uses two different HTTP verbs for different update operations:

- A PUT request is used to update an entire entity. If no values are specified for fields in the entity, the fields will be set to default values.
- A MERGE request is used to update only those field values that have changed. Any fields that are not specified by the operation will remain set to their current value.

Because the service proxy and the **DataServiceContext** class manage the creation of HTTP requests, you generally do not need to worry about these details when you use the REST interface from managed code. However, when you use JavaScript, you must manually create the HTTP requests and, as such, you need to understand this distinction. The next section provides more details about using the REST interface from JavaScript.

USING THE REST INTERFACE FROM JAVASCRIPT

Using the REST interface from JavaScript requires some extra work, because you can't generate a service proxy to build requests and handle responses. In order to use the REST interface to create entities from JavaScript, you must perform the following actions:

- Create an HTTP request using the POST verb.
- Use the service URL of the list to which you want to add an entity as the target for the POST.
- Set the content type to **application/json**.
- Serialize the JSON objects that represent your new list items as a string, and add this value to the request body.

This is illustrated by the following code, which creates a new inventory location item.

```JavaScript
var url =
 'http://localhost/sites/sharepointlist/_vti_bin/listdata.svc/InventoryLocations';
var inventoryLocation = {};

// Insert a new Part location.
inventoryLocation.PartId = $('#hidPartId').val();
inventoryLocation.BinNumber = $('#binText').val();
inventoryLocation.Quantity = $('#quantityText').val();

var body = Sys.Serialization.JavaScriptSerializer.serialize(inventoryLocation);

$.ajax({
        type: 'POST',
        url: url,
        contentType: 'application/json',
        processData: false,
        data: body,
        success: function ()
        {
          alert('Inventory Location Saved.');
        }
      });
```

Updating an existing entity is a little more complex. If you've worked with REST services before, you might be tempted to use an HTTP PUT operation to update the entity. However, this approach can be problematic. Even if you load the entire entity, keep the entity in memory, and use the entity in a PUT operation, you may still experience problems with field values. Experience with this approach has shown issues with date and time conversion and the population of lookup fields. This is because the OData protocol assumes that a PUT operation will update the entire entity, and any fields that are not explicitly specified are reset to their default values, most of which are a null value. A better approach is to use the HTTP MERGE operation, which updates only the fields that have changed. This approach also improves performance, because you don't need to initially retrieve a full representation of the entity just to send it back to the server to update it.

To use this approach to update an existing entity, you must perform the following actions:

- Create an HTTP request using the POST verb.
- Add an **X-HTTP-Method** header with a value of **MERGE**.
- Use the service URL of the list item you want to update as the target for the POST—for example, **_vti_bin/listdata.svc/InventoryLocations(XXX)**, where XXX is the ID of the list item.
- Add an **If-Match** header with a value of the entity's original ETag.

This is illustrated by the following code, which updates an existing inventory location item.

```csharp
var locationId = $('#hidLocationId').val();
var url =
'http://localhost/sites/sharepointlist/_vti_bin/listdata.svc/InventoryLocations';
var beforeSendFunction;
var inventoryLocationModifications = {};

// Update the existing Part location.
url = url + "(" + locationId + ")";
beforeSendFunction = function (xhr)
{
  xhr.setRequestHeader("If-Match", inventoryLocation.__metadata.ETag);
  // Using MERGE so that the entire entity doesn't need to be sent over the wire.
  xhr.setRequestHeader("X-HTTP-Method", 'MERGE');
}

inventoryLocationModifications.BinNumber = $('#binText').val();
inventoryLocationModifications.Quantity = $('#quantityText').val();

var body = Sys.Serialization.JavaScriptSerializer.serialize
  (inventoryLocationModifications);

$.ajax({
        type: 'POST',
        url: url,
        contentType: 'application/json',
        processData: false,
        beforeSend: beforeSendFunction,
        data: body,
        success: function ()
        {
          alert('Inventory Location Saved.');
        }
     });
```

BATCHING

The OData protocol used by WCF Data Services supports the batching of multiple REST queries into a single HTTP request. Using batching reduces chattiness, uses network bandwidth more efficiently, and improves the responsiveness of your applications. In order to use batching, you simply submit multiple queries at the same time using the **Data ServiceContext.BeginExecuteBatch** method.

C#
```
context.BeginExecuteBatch(DisplayParts, context, invQuery, partsQuery);
```

In this example, two queries are submitted: **invQuery** and **partsQuery**. The list of queries submitted is variable, so while this example shows two queries, additional queries could be added. When the server finishes executing a batch of requests, it returns a collection of results to the client. This is illustrated by the following code example.

C#
```
// Get the batch response.
DataServiceResponse Response = context.EndExecuteBatch(result);

// Loop through each operation.
foreach (QueryOperationResponse operation in Response)
{
  if (operation.Error != null)
  {
    throw operation.Error;
  }
  if (oOperation is QueryOperationResponse<InventoryLocationsItem>)
  {
    ProcessInventoryLocation(operation);
  }
  if (operation is QueryOperationResponse<PartsItem>)
  {
    ProcessParts(operation);
  }
}
```

The service proxy sends batch requests in a multi-part message (MIME) format to the REST service. Although you'll never need to manipulate these HTTP requests and responses manually, it can be instructive to take a look at how they are formed. Notice that the message contains two GET requests, one for Inventory Locations and one for Parts.

HTTP Request
```
POST http://contoso/sites/sharepointlist/_vti_bin/listdata.svc/$batch HTTP/1.1
Content-Type: multipart/mixed; boundary=batch_16c7085d-ad1e-4962-b5e3-e7c83452b95a
Accept-Language: en-US

Note: Some header content has been removed for brevity.

--batch_16c7085d-ad1e-4962-b5e3-e7c83452b95a
Content-Type: application/http
Content-Transfer-Encoding: binary
```

```
GET http://contoso/sites/sharepointlist/_vti_bin/listdata.svc/InventoryLocations()
?$filter=startswith(Part/SKU,'sku11')&$orderby=Part/SKU&$expand=Part&$select=
BinNumber,Quantity,Title,Id,PartId,Part/SKU,Part/Title HTTP/1.1
DataServiceVersion: 2.0;NetFx


--batch_16c7085d-ad1e-4962-b5e3-e7c83452b95a
Content-Type: application/http
Content-Transfer-Encoding: binary


GET http://contoso/sites/sharepointlist/_vti_bin/listdata.svc/Parts()?$filter
=startswith(SKU,'sku11')&$select=Title,SKU,Id,Description HTTP/1.1
DataServiceVersion: 2.0;NetFx


--batch_16c7085d-ad1e-4962-b5e3-e7c83452b95a--
```

The response to the batch execution also uses MIME formatting, and it contains two HTTP responses, one for each query submitted.

HTTP Response

```
HTTP/1.1 202 Accepted
Cache-Control: no-cache
Content-Type:
  multipart/mixed; boundary=batchresponse_8ad6352b-ac02-4946-afc5-1df735bb7f55
Server: Microsoft-IIS/7.5
SPRequestGuid: 5f0f516c-78cf-4ffe-b37e-1c9e7168ef18


Note: Some header content has been removed for brevity.


--batchresponse_8ad6352b-ac02-4946-afc5-1df735bb7f55
Content-Type: application/http
Content-Transfer-Encoding: binary


HTTP/1.1 200 OK
Cache-Control: no-cache
DataServiceVersion: 2.0;
Content-Type: application/atom+xml;charset=utf-8


<?xml version="1.0" encoding="utf-8" standalone="yes"?>
<feed xml:base="http://contoso/sites/sharepointlist/_vti_bin/listdata.svc/"
  xmlns:d="http://schemas.microsoft.com/ado/2007/08/dataservices"
  xmlns:m="http://schemas.microsoft.com/ado/2007/08/dataservices/metadata"
  xmlns="http://www.w3.org/2005/Atom">
  <title type="text">InventoryLocations</title>
  <id>http://contoso/sites/sharepointlist/_vti_bin/listdata.svc/InventoryLocations</id>
  <updated>2010-05-30T16:34:19Z</updated>
```

```
<link rel="self" title="InventoryLocations" href="InventoryLocations" />
<entry m:ETag="W/&quot;1&quot;">
  <id>http://contoso/sites/sharepointlist/_vti_bin/listdata.svc/
    InventoryLocations(18)</id>
  <title type="text"></title>
  <updated>2010-05-21T14:06:13-04:00</updated>
  <author>
    <name />
  </author>
  <link rel="edit" title="InventoryLocationsItem" href="InventoryLocations(18)" />
  <link rel="http://schemas.microsoft.com/ado/2007/08/dataservices/related/Part"
type="application/atom+xml;type=entry" title="Part"
  href="InventoryLocations(18)/Part">
    <m:inline>
      <entry m:ETag="W/&quot;2&quot;">
        <id>http://contoso/sites/sharepointlist/_vti_bin/listdata.svc/Parts(12)</id>
        <title type="text">LOCK WASHERS, 1/2 11</title>
        <updated>2010-05-21T14:06:13-04:00</updated>
        <author>
          <name />
        </author>
        <link rel="edit" title="PartsItem" href="Parts(12)" />
        <category term="Microsoft.SharePoint.DataService.PartsItem"
  scheme="http://schemas.microsoft.com/ado/2007/08/dataservices/scheme" />
        <content type="application/xml">
          <m:properties>
            <d:Title>LOCK WASHERS, 1/2 11</d:Title>
            <d:SKU>SKU11</d:SKU>
          </m:properties>
        </content>
      </entry>
    </m:inline>
  </link>
  <category term="Microsoft.SharePoint.DataService.InventoryLocationsItem"
  scheme="http://schemas.microsoft.com/ado/2007/08/dataservices/scheme" />
  <content type="application/xml">
    <m:properties>
      <d:Title m:null="true" />
      <d:PartId m:type="Edm.Int32">12</d:PartId>
      <d:BinNumber>Bin 0.5.17</d:BinNumber>
      <d:Quantity m:type="Edm.Double">9</d:Quantity>
      <d:Id m:type="Edm.Int32">18</d:Id>
    </m:properties>
```

```
      </content>
    </entry>
</feed>
--batchresponse_8ad6352b-ac02-4946-afc5-1df735bb7f55
Content-Type: application/http
Content-Transfer-Encoding: binary

HTTP/1.1 200 OK
Cache-Control: no-cache
DataServiceVersion: 2.0;
Content-Type: application/atom+xml;charset=utf-8

<?xml version="1.0" encoding="utf-8" standalone="yes"?>
<feed xml:base="http://contoso/sites/sharepointlist/_vti_bin/listdata.svc/"
  xmlns:d="http://schemas.microsoft.com/ado/2007/08/dataservices"
  xmlns:m="http://schemas.microsoft.com/ado/2007/08/dataservices/metadata"
  xmlns="http://www.w3.org/2005/Atom">
  <title type="text">Parts</title>
  <id>http://contoso/sites/sharepointlist/_vti_bin/listdata.svc/Parts</id>
  <updated>2010-05-30T16:34:19Z</updated>
  <link rel="self" title="Parts" href="Parts" />
  <entry m:ETag="W/&quot;2&quot;">
    <id>http://contoso/sites/sharepointlist/_vti_bin/listdata.svc/Parts(12)</id>
    <title type="text">LOCK WASHERS, 1/2 11</title>
    <updated>2010-05-21T14:06:13-04:00</updated>
    <author>
      <name />
    </author>
    <link rel="edit" title="PartsItem" href="Parts(12)" />
    <category term="Microsoft.SharePoint.DataService.PartsItem"
  scheme="http://schemas.microsoft.com/ado/2007/08/dataservices/scheme" />
    <content type="application/xml">
      <m:properties>
        <d:Title>LOCK WASHERS, 1/2 11</d:Title>
        <d:SKU>SKU11</d:SKU>
        <d:Description m:null="true" />
        <d:Id m:type="Edm.Int32">12</d:Id>
      </m:properties>
    </content>
  </entry>
</feed>
--batchresponse_8ad6352b-ac02-4946-afc5-1df735bb7f55--
```

Synchronous and Asynchronous Operations

The service proxy for the SharePoint REST interface supports synchronous and asynchronous calls to the service. The approach to managing asynchronous operations is almost identical to the CSOM experience. As described earlier in this chapter, the **DataServiceQuery<TElement>** class provides a **BeginExecute** method that you can use to asynchronously invoke a REST query. You should use the asynchronous approach in applications where you need to avoid blocking the UI thread. You cannot make a synchronous call to the REST interface from Silverlight or from JavaScript.

Conclusion

This chapter provided technical insights into the two new approaches to client-side data access in SharePoint 2010: the client-side object model (CSOM) and the SharePoint REST interface. The chapter described how each API works under the covers, and reviewed the capabilities, limitations, and efficiency of each approach. The key points were as follows:

- The CSOM provides access to a broad subset of the server-side SharePoint Foundation object model. The CSOM uses a request-batching process in which operations are queued on the client until the **ExecuteQuery** method or the **ExecuteQuery Async** method is called. THE CSOM supports the use of list joins and view projections in CAML queries, which can substantially improve the efficiency of query operations.

- The SharePoint REST interface enables applications to retrieve and manipulate SharePoint list data by sending HTTP requests. Like any RESTful service, the SharePoint REST interface works by exposing data—in this case, SharePoint lists and list items—as addressable resources through URLs. You can generate a WCF Data Services service proxy to interact with the REST interface through strongly-typed code. On the server, REST statements are converted first into LINQ to SharePoint expressions and subsequently into CAML queries. As a result, you have less control over query efficiency. You can batch REST requests to improve the efficiency and user experience of your application.

See It in Action: The Client Reference Implementation in the Developing Applications for SharePoint 2010 online guidance is a fully-documented, downloadable solution that illustrates various approaches to building a user experience for SharePoint clients, together with different techniques for client-side data access. You can deploy the reference implementation to a SharePoint 2010 test environment and explore the source code at your leisure in Visual Studio 2010.

For more information, see Reference Implementation: Client at http://msdn. microsoft.com/en-us/library/ff798454.aspx.

FURTHER INFORMATION

For further background information in addition to the documents below, see the book's bibliography online at http://msdn.microsoft.com/gg213840.aspx.

- "WCF Services in SharePoint Foundation 2010"
- "Using the SharePoint Foundation 2010 Managed Client Object Model with the Open XML SDK 2.0"
- "Data Access in SharePoint 2010"

PART FOUR
APPLICATION
FOUNDATIONS

1   Building Robust SharePoint Applications

There is a world of difference between simply making your code work and writing production-quality applications. If you're designing or developing enterprise-scale Microsoft® SharePoint® applications, it's important to ensure that your solutions are built on solid foundations. This chapter examines how you can improve the quality of your code across the entire spectrum of SharePoint functional areas. It also introduces some of the reusable components that are included in the SharePoint Guidance Library to help you develop better solutions.

So what makes good code? Performance and stability are obviously at the top of the list. However, when you develop code for enterprise-scale applications, other concerns become increasingly important:

- **Testability**. Can you test your classes in isolation? If your code is tightly coupled to a user interface, or relies on specific types, this can be challenging.
- **Flexibility**. Can you update or replace dependencies without editing and recompiling your code?
- **Configuration**. How do you manage configuration settings for your solution? Will your approach scale out to an enterprise-scale deployment environment?
- **Logging and exception handling**. How do you log exceptions and trace information in the enterprise environment? Is your approach consistent with that of other developers on the team? Are you providing system administrators with reliable information that they can use to diagnose problems effectively?
- **Maintainability**. How easy is it to maintain your code in a code base that is constantly evolving? Do you have to rewrite your code if a dependent class is updated or replaced?

Introducing the SharePoint Guidance Library

The SharePoint Guidance Library is a set of reusable components and utility classes, developed by the patterns & practices team at Microsoft, which can help you to build more robust applications for SharePoint 2010. You can download the SharePoint Guidance Library as source code, build the assembly, and use the components in your own applications.

Note: *To download the SharePoint Guidance Library and read the documentation, visit Developing Applications for SharePoint 2010 at http://msdn.microsoft.com/en-us/library/ff770300.aspx.*

The SharePoint Guidance Library includes the following components:

- The **SharePoint Logger**, which can help you to log exceptions and trace information in a consistent, informative way, by providing easy-to-use utility methods that write to the Microsoft Windows® Event log and the ULS (SharePoint Unified Logging Service) trace log.
- The **Application Setting Manager**, which can help you to manage configuration settings, by providing a robust, consistent mechanism that you can use to store and retrieve configuration settings at each level of the SharePoint hierarchy.
- The **SharePoint Service Locator**, which can help you develop testable, modular code, by enabling you to decouple your code from dependencies on external types.

Let's take a brief look at each of these components.

THE SHAREPOINT LOGGER

When you develop business-critical solutions, it is essential to ensure that you make diagnostic information about your application available to administrators and other developers. Providing and consuming diagnostic information involves two distinct activities: logging and tracing. Logging is primarily directed toward system administrators, who typically rely on the Microsoft Windows® event logs to monitor deployed applications. They often use automated tools such as the System Center Operations Manager (SCOM) to monitor the event logs. Tracing, on the other hand, is primarily directed toward developers and field engineers. Trace logs record more detailed information about action taken and problems encountered during the execution of an application, and are typically used by people who are familiar with the implementation details of the application to monitor behavior and diagnose problems.

SharePoint 2010 includes enhanced functionality for logging and tracing. You can now throttle reporting to the Windows Event Log and the Microsoft Office® Server Unified Logging Service (ULS) trace logs by *area* and by *category*:

- Areas correspond to broad areas of SharePoint functionality, such as Access Services, Business Connectivity Services, and Document Management Server.
- The area is used as the event source name in the Windows event logs.
- Each area contains one or more categories, which correspond to more specific areas of functionality. For example, the Document Management Server area includes categories named Content Organizer, Information Policy Management, and Records Center.
- For each category, you can specify the least critical event to report to the event log and the trace log. This sets the default event throttling threshold for that category. These values are also used as the default severity for a trace or log if no severity level is specified.

In addition to areas and categories, SharePoint 2010 brings substantial improvements to event correlation. Every trace log entry now includes a correlation ID that identifies all the events that correspond to a particular action, such as a user uploading a document. Administrators can use tools such as the ULS Viewer to filter the trace logs by correlation ID. The platform also provides a centralized logging database that allows you to consolidate diagnostic information and generate reports. SharePoint 2010 also includes a Health Analyzer tool that administrators can configure to actively monitor the system for error conditions and to address them where possible.

The SharePoint Logger is a reusable component that you can use to write messages to the Windows event logs and the ULS trace log. The SharePoint Logger works by exposing and implementing a simple interface named **ILogger**. This interface defines the two key methods listed in the following table.

ILogger method	Description
LogToOperations	This method writes a message to the Windows event logs and the ULS trace log. Overloads allow you to specify identifiers, categories, severities, and exception details.
TraceToDeveloper	This method writes a message to the ULS trace log. Overloads allow you to specify identifiers, categories, severities, and exception details.

When you write a message to either log, the SharePoint Logger adds contextual information, such as the current URL and the name of the currently logged-on user, which can help the reader to diagnose the problem. The SharePoint Logger also provides a high level of robustness in case the logging fails. For example, if a message cannot be written to the event log, a **LoggingException** is thrown that contains both the original message and the reason for the logging failure.

The following code shows a simple example of how you can use the SharePoint Logger to write a message to the ULS trace log.

C#

```
ILogger logger = SharePointServiceLocator.GetCurrent().GetInstance<ILogger>();
logger.TraceToDeveloper("Unexpected condition");
```

The SharePoint Logger allows you to create and register custom areas and categories for use by your own SharePoint applications. This allows administrators to throttle diagnostic logging from your application, along with all the built-in areas and categories, through the SharePoint Central Administration Web site.

For more information on the SharePoint Logger, see the Developing Applications for SharePoint 2010 online guidance.

THE APPLICATION SETTING MANAGER

All enterprise-scale applications use configuration settings to some extent. Application configuration data provides the information that an application requires to be able to run in a specific deployment environment. For example, configuration data might include a connection string for a database, the location of a dependent SharePoint library or list, or information about the security context of the environment.

Managing application settings in a SharePoint environment introduces challenges beyond those encountered by developers who are familiar with ASP.NET and other platforms. First, the SharePoint environment employs a unique hierarchy that enables configuration at each logical level of its architecture—farm, Web application, site collection, site, and list. Second, developers need to account for the dynamic nature of SharePoint. Users can drop your Web Parts into many different pages and instantiate your templates in many different locations. This can have a major bearing on how you manage configuration options for your solutions.

There are also several different storage mechanisms for configuration settings:

- **Web.config**. You can add configuration data to the configuration file either declaratively or programmatically. This effectively confines your configuration settings to the Web application scope.

- **Hierarchical object store**. You can use the **SPPersistedObject** class to persist strongly typed data at any level of the SharePoint hierarchy.

- **Property bags**. Each level of the SharePoint hierarchy exposes property bags, albeit with slightly different access mechanisms.

- **Lists**. You can persist configuration data to a SharePoint list. This effectively confines your configuration settings to the site collection scope or the site scope.

Each mechanism has advantages, disadvantages, and sometimes risks—for example, SharePoint property bags provide an easy-to-use storage mechanism, but developers risk corrupting the configuration database or the content database if they attempt to persist non-serializable types. You can find links to resources that provide detailed comparisons of these storage mechanisms in the Further Information section at the end of this chapter.

Because of the complexities in choosing and implementing an appropriate strategy for the storage of configuration data, the patterns & practices SharePoint Guidance team has developed a reusable component named the *Application Setting Manager*. This provides a consistent, strongly-typed mechanism that you can use to store and retrieve configuration settings in property bags at the following levels of the SharePoint hierarchy:

- Farm (**SPFarm** class)
- Web application (**SPWebApplication** class)
- Site collection (**SPSite** class)
- Site (**SPWeb** class)

You can use the Application Setting Manager to store simple types, such as integers or strings, as well as more complex types that can be serialized to XML. The Application Setting Manager manages the serialization and deserialization of data types to and from XML.

The Application Setting Manager provides a hierarchical model for the storage and retrieval of configuration settings. This enables you to create an application setting at a broad scope (such as the farm level) and override that setting at a narrower scope (such as the site level). When you retrieve a setting using a key string, the Application Setting Manager will first look for that key at the site (**SPWeb**) level of the current execution context. If the configuration key is not found, the Application Setting Manager will look for the configuration setting at a progressively broader scope, up to and including the farm level. For example, you could use the following code to locate a configuration setting of type **DateTime**, without knowing the level in the SharePoint hierarchy at which the setting is stored.

C#

```csharp
IServiceLocator serviceLocator = SharePointServiceLocator.GetCurrent();
var config = serviceLocator.GetInstance<IHierarchicalConfig>();

DateTime timeApproved;
if (config.ContainsKey("approvedTime"))
    timeApproved = config.GetByKey<DateTime>("approvedTime");
```

In this case, the Application Setting Manager will return the most relevant application setting available with a key string of *approvedTime*. For example, if the current site collection and the current site both contain a value for *approvedTime*, the Application Setting Manager will return the value stored at the site level.

Note: *As illustrated by the code example, you are encouraged to use the SharePoint Service Locator to retrieve and instantiate instances of the interfaces provided by the Application Setting Manager. The SharePoint Service Locator is described later in this chapter.*

The Application Setting Manager uses property bags to store application settings. A property bag is simply a collection of string-based key-value pairs. The Application Setting Manager uses purpose-built property bags for storing settings at the **SPWeb**, **SPWeb Application**, and **SPFarm** level. The extensibility of the Application Setting Manager allows you to configure alternative property bag stores, if necessary.

To be able to allow you to store complex types instead of only string values in the property bag, the Application Setting Manager uses XML serialization to convert complex types into a manageable form for storage. For more information on the Application Setting Manager, see the Developing Applications for SharePoint 2010 online guidance.

THE SHAREPOINT SERVICE LOCATOR

When you develop a class, your code will often depend upon functionality from other classes. A dependency on another class simply means that your code directly instantiates and uses functionality implemented in the other class. As a result, your consumer class is tightly coupled to the specific implementation of the dependency class. If you use an interface to provide a foundation for your dependency classes, you start to decouple the consumer class from the dependency class. You can change or replace the interface implementation without altering how your service is consumed.

So why is it a good idea to remove explicit dependencies on other classes from your code? As your code base becomes more complex and abstracted, it can be difficult to manage references and assembly dependencies that are scattered throughout various projects and solutions. These dependencies often make it challenging to maintain code over time—if you modify one class, you must recompile every project that references that class. This also makes unit testing code in isolation much more complicated. In short, decoupling your code from specific types makes your code more modular, easier to manage, and easier to test.

Service location takes this decoupling process to the next level. When you use a service location pattern, your code can create and use an instance of a class that supports a desired interface without knowing the name or any details of the class that implements the interface. This removes the dependency between the consumer class and the implementation class.

> **Note:** *What do we mean by* service *when we talk about service location? We don't necessarily mean a Web service. In this context, a* service *is any class that provides a service to other classes. The services provided by each class are defined by the interfaces that the class implements.*

The SharePoint Service Locator is a reusable component that provides a simple, easy-to-use implementation of the service locator pattern. You can use it in your own SharePoint applications to decouple the consumers of an interface from the implementations of that interface. Instead of creating an object by invoking the constructor of a class, you request an object with a specified interface from the service locator. The service implementation can now be replaced or updated without altering the consuming class implementation.

At the core of the SharePoint Service Locator is a dictionary of *type mappings*. Each dictionary entry maps an interface and an optional key string to the name of a class that implements the specified interface. The following table illustrates this. These type mappings are included by default to support other components in the SharePoint Guidance library.

Interface	Registered implementation class
ILogger	SharePointLogger
IHierarchicalConfig	HierarchicalConfig
IConfigManager	ConfigManager

The SharePoint Service Locator provides methods that make it easy to add, remove, or modify type mappings. In most cases, you would use a feature receiver class to register type mappings when you deploy or upgrade your solution. When you need to use an external service in your code, rather than creating an object by invoking the constructor of a class, you can request an object with a specified interface from the service locator. The service locator looks up the interface in the dictionary, locates the corresponding implementation class, and returns an instantiated object to the caller. For example, suppose that your class needs an implementation of the **ILogger** interface. You could instantiate a specific implementation of the **ILogger** interface in your code, as shown by Figure 1.

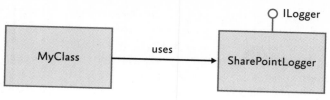

FIGURE 1
Class with a direct dependency on a service

In this case, your code will resemble the following:

C#
```
SharePointLogger logger = new SharePointLogger();
```

This approach has several drawbacks. For example, let's say that your corporate policy changes and you need to enhance your logging functionality to take additional action on critical errors, beyond the default behavior of writing to the event log. If you want to replace the **SharePointLogger** class with an enhanced implementation of the **ILogger** interface, you must edit and recompile your consumer class. Also, as your consumer classes reference **SharePointLogger** directly, it's difficult to replace it with a mock object or a stub implementation of the **ILogger** interface for testing. Finally, you must ensure that the correct version of **SharePointLogger** is available at compile time.

In contrast, the service locator approach allows you to simply request the registered implementation of the **ILogger** interface. You do not need to know the details of the implementation. As a result, you can replace all the direct service dependencies in your class with a dependency on the service locator. This is illustrated by Figure 2.

FIGURE 2
Class using the SharePoint Service Locator to retrieve a service

In this case, your code will resemble the following:

C#
```
IServiceLocator serviceLocator = SharePointServiceLocator.GetCurrent();
ILogger logger = serviceLocator.GetInstance<ILogger>();
```

In this scenario, you can change the implementation of **ILogger** without modifying the consuming class. For example, to unit test your code, you might want to use a stub implementation of **ILogger** named **FakeLogger**. If you want to log events and trace information to a central database, you might create an alternative implementation of **ILogger** named **DatabaseLogger**. In each case, all you need to do is to update the type mapping for **ILogger** in the SharePoint Service Locator, and your consumer classes will continue to work as expected.

Let's examine how this works in practice. Suppose your code requires logging functionality. You want to use the **DatabaseLogger** class, which implements the **ILogger** interface. Your first step would be to register the **DatabaseLogger** class with the service locator as the default implementation of **ILogger**, as shown by the following code example. Typically you would add this code to a feature receiver that runs when you deploy your solution.

```C#
//Retrieve the service locator instance for the local SharePoint environment.
IServiceLocator serviceLocator = SharePointServiceLocator.GetCurrent();

//Retrieve the type mappings associated with the service locator instance.
IServiceLocatorConfig typeMappings =
  serviceLocator.GetInstance<IServiceLocatorConfig>();

//Register a type mapping for the ILogger interface
typeMappings.RegisterTypeMapping<ILogger, DatabaseLogger>();
```

Now that you've registered an implementation of **ILogger** with the service locator, you can use the functionality defined by the **ILogger** interface in your code without knowing the details of the implementation. This is illustrated by the following code example.

```C#
//Retrieve the service locator instance for the local SharePoint environment.
IServiceLocator serviceLocator = SharePointServiceLocator.GetCurrent();

//Instantiate an ILogger implementation.
ILogger logger = serviceLocator.GetInstance<ILogger>();

//Use the ILogger implementation.
logger.LogToOperations("Message");
```

Under the covers, the service locator retrieves the type mapping for the **ILogger** interface, creates a **DatabaseLogger** instance, and returns it to the caller. If you want to use an alternative implementation of **ILogger**, you can simply update the type mapping in the service locator without editing your code. For example, suppose you want all your code to use a class named **AlternativeLogger**. In this case, you would use the following code to replace the registered implementation of **ILogger**.

```C#
IServiceLocator serviceLocator = SharePointServiceLocator.GetCurrent();
IServiceLocatorConfig typeMappings =
  serviceLocator.GetInstance<IServiceLocatorConfig>();

typeMappings.RegisterTypeMapping<ILogger, AlternativeLogger>();
```

When your code requests an implementation of **ILogger**, the service locator will now return an instance of **AlternativeLogger**. In this way, you have broken the dependency between your code and the logging functionality that it uses.

The SharePoint Service Locator contains many other features not described here, such as the ability to add named type mappings and the ability to scope type mappings at the site collection level or the farm level. For more information, see the Developing Applications for SharePoint 2010 online guidance.

Building in Robustness

Building robust, resilient SharePoint applications is a multi-faceted task. You should anticipate problems that might occur and provide appropriate handlers for specific exceptions. You should consider whether you need to implement handlers at system boundaries for otherwise unhandled exceptions. Finally, you should consistently and methodically write information to the Windows event logs and the Unified Logging Service (ULS) trace logs to help administrators and developers diagnose problems.

Earlier in this chapter, we discussed logging and tracing in SharePoint 2010 and we described how you can use the SharePoint Logger to simplify these processes. Now, let's take a closer look at exception handling in SharePoint 2010. Most general guidelines for exception management in Microsoft .NET applications are equally relevant to SharePoint applications. In this section we revisit some of these broader guidelines before looking at some SharePoint-specific exception management issues.

Catch Only Exceptions That You Handle

In general you should only catch an exception if you're going to take remedial action of some kind. Depending on the nature of the exception, this action can take various forms:

- **Take an alternative course of action**. In some cases, the exception represents a correctable situation. For example, if you try to call a Web service and it is too busy to handle the request, you could use the exception handler to repeat the operation a few more times.

- **Record the exception**. If you encounter an unexpected exception, it's often best to write the exception information to the Windows event log and then allow your application to fail gracefully. For less critical exceptions, and exceptions with a known, correctable cause, it may be better to write the information to the trace log for debugging purposes.

- **Display an error message**. If an exception requires action by the end user—for example, they lack required software or their client environment is not configured correctly—you should display an informative message. If an unknown or unexpected error occurs, you should display a generic error message to the user.

- **Throw a more abstract exception**. In some cases you may want to allow an exception to propagate up the call stack. In these circumstances, you should consider wrapping the exception in a more abstract exception that contains more information on the task being performed.

Catch the Most Specific Type of Exception

You should always try to catch the most specific types of exceptions first. In most cases, you should not catch the general **Exception** type, as this can cause unexpected behavior and lead to bugs that are hard to diagnose.

Avoid Empty Catch Blocks

You should avoid catching exceptions with an empty catch block. In particular, never catch the general **Exception** type with an empty catch block, as this can lead to bugs that are very hard to find. For example, suppose another thread tries to abort the current thread by raising a **ThreadAbortException**. The empty catch block will intercept and handle the **ThreadAbortException**, thereby preventing the thread from being aborted and producing some unexpected behavior. As the empty catch block neither logs the exception nor displays an error message, this bug will be extremely difficult to diagnose.

Implement a Handler for Unexpected Exceptions

Even if you have years of experience and exceptional programming skills, it's not possible to anticipate every error that your solution could encounter. In some cases it's appropriate to implement exception handlers at system boundaries to catch otherwise unhandled exceptions.

For example, suppose an exception occurs in a Web Part. If the Web Part doesn't handle the exception, the exception propagates to the page that hosts the Web Part. The unhandled exception handler for the page then redirects the user to an error page that may or may not display more information about the problem. As a result, an unhandled exception in a Web Part can prevent the Web page as a whole from being displayed. In some situations this might be the desired outcome, since unhandled exceptions can potentially corrupt data on the page. In other scenarios, it may be better to trap unhandled exceptions at the Web Part boundary. Using this approach, the problematic Web Part can display an error message while all other Web Parts on the page continue to function normally.

When you trap unhandled exceptions at the Web Part boundary, you'll typically aim to complete the following steps:

- Catch the exception.
- Log the exception to the Windows event log and the ULS trace log.
- Replace the entire UI of the Web Part with an informative error message.

If you use the *Model-View-Presenter* (MVP) pattern in your Web Part design, one approach to trapping unhandled exceptions is to include an *error visualizer* component. The view is a child control of the error visualizer, which in turn is a child control of the Web Part. This is illustrated by Figure 3.

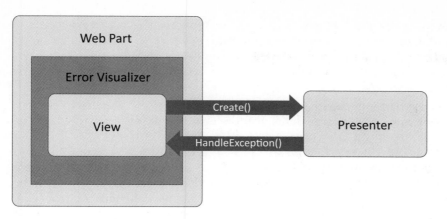

FIGURE 3
Using an error visualizer control

In this approach, if an unhandled exception occurs in the presenter logic, the presenter instructs the error visualizer to handle the exception. Since the view is a child control of the error visualizer, the error visualizer is able to suppress the rendering of the view and instead display an appropriate error message. For a practical example of using an error visualizer, see the Sandbox Reference Implementation in the Developing Applications for SharePoint 2010 online guidance.

Providing Testability and Flexibility

When you write a unit test, you are aiming to isolate a piece of code in order to test it with known inputs. You typically need to substitute dependencies—such as external code, data sources, and the user interface—with fake implementations that provide the specific conditions that you want to test. These fake implementations are referred to by various names, but most often they are known as mocks or stubs.

When you write flexible, modular code, you are also aiming to isolate your code from the implementation details of external classes, data sources, and the user interface. Ideally, you should be able to amend or replace dependencies without editing and recompiling your code. Consequently, testability and flexibility go hand in hand. To write fully testable code is to write flexible, pluggable code.

There are several well-known design patterns that can help you to isolate your code in this way:

- The *Service Locator* pattern discussed earlier in this chapter enables you to request an implementation of an interface without knowing the details of the implementation. This allows you to replace dependencies with alternative implementations or mock implementations without editing or recompiling your code.

- The *Model-View-Presenter* (MVP) pattern allows you to isolate the business logic in your application from the user interface, which enables you to test your business logic in isolation. You can also make the business logic easier to understand and maintain by removing user interface-specific implementation details.

- The *Repository* pattern allows you to isolate your application's data access code from the business logic. You can use the Repository pattern to wrap any data source, such as a database or a SharePoint list. This allows you to test the data access code in isolation and to substitute the data access implementation to unit test your business logic.

We'll look at these patterns, together with other patterns that you can use to improve the modularity of your code, in more detail over the next few pages.

Removing Dependencies from Your Code

At the start of this chapter we described the SharePoint Service Locator, which uses the service location pattern to decouple your classes from the services they consume. However, there are many other patterns you can also use to remove dependencies from your code. One simple approach is to use a *dependency injection* pattern, such as *constructor injection*. In this approach, you use your class constructor to instantiate an implementation of an interface. The class itself has no knowledge of the implementation, as shown by the following code example.

```C#
class MyClass
{
  private ILogger logger;

  public MyClass(ILogger logger)
  {
    this.logger = logger;
  }
  ...
}
```

In this scenario, the calling class can instantiate your class by providing any object that implements the **ILogger** interface. In your production code, you might pass in a **Share PointLogger** instance. In a unit test, you might instantiate your class with a stub implementation of **ILogger** named **FakeLogger**.

Constructor injection and other similar approaches (such as *method injection* and *property injection*) only isolate your code from its dependencies in one direction. In other words, while your class (the service) doesn't need to know the details of the **ILogger** implementation, the code that instantiates your class (the consumer) must provide a concrete implementation of **ILogger**. You can use more advanced dependency injection containers, such as the patterns & practices Unity Application Block, to avoid this limitation. However, this approach is beyond the scope of this book.

So, when should you use the service locator and when should you use a dependency injection approach? When you request an interface implementation from the service locator, the service locator will construct a new object. You can't use the service locator to pass an existing object, with any relevant stateful information, into your code. In some cases you will want to inject an instance of an object that already exists, such as the

SPSite or **SPUser** instance from the current context. In these cases you will need to use a dependency injection approach to pass the instance to your code, or create a more complex scheme to relay the stateful context to the constructed objects.

ISOLATING USER INTERFACE LOGIC

When you design a solution, you should aim to separate your business logic from the implementation details of your user interface (UI). This is good design practice for any application. However, it can be particularly challenging for developers of ASP.NET pages (and related technologies such as SharePoint), where the code-behind programming model tends to encourage the mixing of business logic and UI logic. This makes testing or updating your applications much more difficult. You can't update your business logic without affecting your UI implementation, and vice versa. The solution is to use a design pattern that provides a clean separation of business logic and UI logic. There is a class of design patterns, known as *Separated Presentation* patterns, which aim to provide this separation. Within this group of patterns, different individual patterns have evolved to meet the needs of different development platforms. For example, the *Model-View-Presenter* (MVP) pattern is well suited to the stateless, request-response–driven ASP.NET programming model, while the *Model-View-ViewModel* (MVVM) pattern is designed for stateful platforms with two-way data binding and a rich eventing infrastructure, such as Microsoft® Silverlight® and the Windows Presentation Foundation (WPF) framework. Both of these patterns are useful tools in the arsenal of the SharePoint 2010 developer.

The Model-View-Presenter Pattern

When you implement an MVP pattern, the classes in your solution are divided into the following roles:

- **Model** classes encapsulate the data access part of your solution. You should be able to change the way the model retrieves data—for example, to use an alternative data source—without changing any other components in your solution.

- **View** classes encapsulate the user interface of your solution. View classes are typically passive and simply allow presenter classes to insert data into them. You should be able to change the way your user interface is displayed without changing any other components in your solution.

- **Presenter** classes encapsulate the business logic of your solution. The presenter class is responsible for retrieving data from the model and pushing it into the view. Presenter classes should not contain data access logic or UI logic.

The best way to understand how this works in the context of SharePoint development is to look at an example. The following example is taken from the Sandbox Reference Implementation in the Developing Applications for SharePoint 2010 online guidance. The reference implementation demonstrates how to create a Web Part—the *Aggregate View* Web Part—that collates documents, including estimates and statements of work (SOWs), from document libraries across a site collection. The class diagram in Figure 4 illustrates the structure of the Aggregate View Web part.

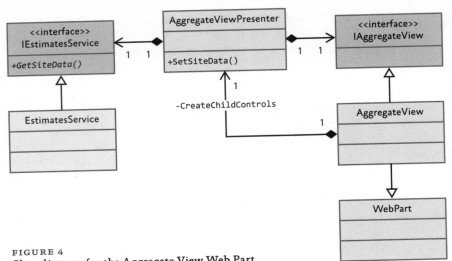

FIGURE 4
Class diagram for the Aggregate View Web Part

The **AggregateViewPresenter** class represents the *presenter* component in the MVP pattern. This class performs the following tasks:
- It retrieves a **DataTable** from the model represented by the **IEstimatesService**.
- It sets the **DataTable** as the data source in the view represented by **IAggregate View**.

The **AggregateView** class represents the *view* component in the MVP pattern. This class is the actual Web Part. This class performs the following tasks:
- It instantiates the Presenter object represented by the **AggregateViewPresenter**. To do this, it creates an instance of the Model represented by **EstimatesService**, and then it constructs the **AggregrateViewPresenter**, passing in itself as the View and the **EstimatesService** as the Model. This is an example of constructor injection.
- It renders the data supplied by the presenter to the UI.

Finally, the **EstimatesService** class represents the *model* component in the MVP pattern. This class performs the following tasks:
- It executes a query to retrieve data from the Estimates list on each subsite.
- It returns the data to the caller in a **DataTable**.

The use of the MVP pattern increases the modularity, flexibility, and testability of the application. If you want to display the data differently, you can modify or replace the view, without changing any of the business logic, by providing an alternative implementation of **IAggregateView**. In other words, you can create a view that displays the data in any way you want, as long as it exposes a public write-only property of type **DataTable** named **RollupTable**. Similarly, if you change the way you store your SOWs and estimations, you can provide an alternative implementation of **IEstimatesService** without editing the view or the presenter. Finally, the design makes it easy to test your presenter logic by providing mock implementations of **IEstimatesService** and **IAggregateView**.

Figure 5 shows how execution passes between the View, Model, and Presenter classes.

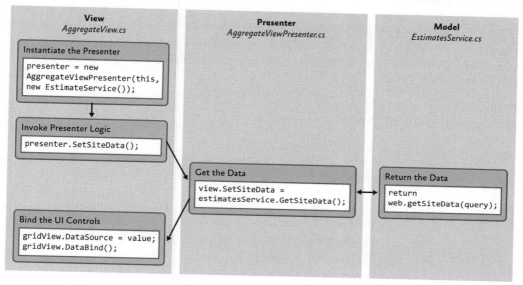

FIGURE 5
Flow of execution in the Aggregate View Web Part

It is important to note that the view is relatively passive and is entirely driven by the presenter logic. The view class simply provides a forward-only property setter that the presenter can use to set the data source for the view. Let's take a closer look at each of these three roles.

View Classes

In terms of contracts, the sole responsibility of a view class is to expose public properties that enable a presenter class to insert data into the view. What the view class does with the data is of no concern to the presenter. Because of this, the interface that underpins the view class, **IAggregateView**, simply defines a write-only property of type **DataTable**.

C#
```csharp
public interface IAggregateView
{
  DataTable RollupTable { set; }
}
```

In this case, the view class should be a Web Part. In addition to implementing the **IAggregateView** interface, the **AggregateView** class must inherit from the abstract **Web Part** class. This class provides the functionality that enables the **AggregateView** class to plug into the SharePoint Web Part framework.

```C#
public class AggregateView : WebPart, IAggregateView
```

Because the Web Part provides the entry point for the application, the **Aggregate View** class must instantiate the **Presenter** class. You can do this in the **CreateChild Controls** method, which is called early in the page life cycle before the Web Part is rendered. You can then call the **SetSiteData** method on the **Presenter** object, which invokes the presenter logic.

```C#
private AggregateViewPresenter presenter;

protected override void CreateChildControls()
{
  base.CreateChildControls();

  // Configure the grid view.

  presenter = new AggregateViewPresenter(this, new EstimatesService());
  presenter.SetRollupData();

  Controls.Add(gridView);
}
```

The **AggregateView** class provides an implementation of the **SetRollupData** property setter that performs two tasks:

- It extracts column names from the passed-in data table and creates corresponding data columns in the grid view.
- It binds the grid view to the passed-in data table.

This property setter is used by the **presenter** class to provide the **view** with a data source. The following code example shows the **RollupTable** implementation in the **AggregateView** class.

```C#
public DataTable RollupTable
{
    set
    {
        PresenterUtilities.FormatGridDisplay(gridView, value);

        gridView.DataSource = value;
        gridView.DataBind();
    }
```

Finally, it is worth noting that the **Presenter** class simply requires a view object that implements **IAggregateView**. In unit testing scenarios, you can instantiate the presenter class using a mock implementation of **IAggregateView**, such as the **MockAggregateView** class shown in the following code example.

```C#
class MockAggregateView : IAggregateView
{
  public DataTable Data { get; set; }

  public DataTable RollupTable
  {
    set { this.Data = value; }
  }
}
```

This ability to substitute a fake view class allows you to test your presenter logic in isolation, without any dependencies on the SharePoint environment or the implementation details of the user interface (UI). In the assert phase of your unit test, you can simply read the **Data** property of the **MockAggregateView** object to verify that the presenter class is sending valid data to the view.

Presenter Classes

Presenter classes have one primary task: to retrieve data from the model and to send that data to the view. When you create a presenter class, you must pass in a view object and a model object. The following code example shows the constructor of the **Aggregate ViewPresenter** class.

```C#
private IAggregateView view;
private IEstimatesService estimatesService;

public AggregateViewPresenter(IAggregateView view,
                              IEstimatesService estimatesService)
{
  this.view = view;
  this.estimatesService = estimatesService;
}
```

The **AggregateViewPresenter** class has no knowledge of how the view class and the model class are implemented; it simply requires that they implement the specified interfaces:

- **IAggregateView**. This interface defines a single write-only property named **RollupTable** that requires an object of type **DataTable**.

- **IEstimatesService**. This interface defines a single method named **GetSiteData** that returns an object of type **DataTable**.

This is an example of the *constructor injection* pattern we described earlier in this chapter.

In the **AggregateViewPresenter** class, the presenter logic is contained in a method named **SetRollupData**. In the reference implementation, this method is invoked by the view class. However, you could just as easily invoke this method from a unit test.

```C#
public void SetRollupData()
{
  try
  {
    view.RollupTable = estimatesService.GetSiteData();
  }
  catch (Exception ex)
  {
    // The exception shielding logic is removed from here for simplicity.
  }
}
```

As you can see, the presenter logic itself is extremely straightforward and consists of a single line of code. However, in many real-world examples, the presenter class will include substantial business logic and is likely to be larger and more complex.

Model Classes

The responsibility of a **Model** class is to interact with the underlying data source and to hide the details of that interaction from the presenter. The interface that underpins the **Model** class in the sandbox reference implementation defines a single method that returns a **DataTable** object.

The interface that underpins the **Model** class, **IEstimatesService**, defines a single method that returns a **DataTable**.

```C#
public interface IEstimatesService
{
  DataTable GetSiteData();
}
```

The interface specifies nothing of the location or format of the data, so you can easily provide alternative implementations of **IEstimatesService** that retrieve data in different formats or from alternative locations. Also, you can easily create mock implementations of **IEstimatesService** to test the presenter logic.

The **EstimatesService** class provides a simple implementation of **IEstimatesService**. When the **EstimatesService** class is instantiated, it builds an **SPSiteDataQuery** object. The implementation of the **GetSiteData** method simply runs the query.

```csharp
C#
public class EstimatesService : IEstimatesService
{
  private SPSiteDataQuery query;

  public EstimatesService()
  {
    query = new SPSiteDataQuery();
    query.Lists = "<Lists BaseType='1' />";
    query.ViewFields = "<FieldRef Name='SOWStatus' />" +
                       "<FieldRef Name='EstimateValue' />";
    query.Query = "<OrderBy><FieldRef Name='EstimateValue' /></OrderBy>";
    query.Webs = "<Webs Scope='SiteCollection' />";
  }

  public System.Data.DataTable GetSiteData()
  {
    SPWeb web = SPContext.Current.Web;
    return web.GetSiteData(query);
  }
}
```

The Model-View-ViewModel Pattern

The Model-View-ViewModel (MVVM) pattern is an application pattern that isolates the user interface from the underlying business logic. In many ways the MVVM pattern is similar to the Model-View-Presenter (MVP) pattern described previously—both patterns are variants of the Model-View-Controller (MVC) pattern, both are Separated Presentation patterns, and both are designed to isolate the details of the user interface from the underlying business logic in order to enhance manageability and testability. However, whereas the MVP pattern is best suited to traditional server-rendered Web pages and the request/response paradigm, the MVVM pattern is optimized for stateful rich-client applications where client-side business logic and application state is maintained through user or service interactions. The pattern enables you to capitalize on the features of WPF and Silverlight, such as two-way data-binding functionality, events, and stateful behavior.

The MVVM pattern consists of the following parts:

- **Model** classes provide a view-independent representation of your business entities. The design of the model is optimized for the logical relationships and operations between your business entities, regardless of how the data is presented in the user interface.

- **View** classes define the user interface. They display information to the user and fire events in response to user interactions.

- **ViewModel** classes provide the link between the view and the model. Each View class has a corresponding ViewModel class. The ViewModel retrieves data from the Model and manipulates it into the format required by the View. It notifies the View if the underlying data in the model is changed, and it updates the data in the Model in response to UI events from the View. Declarative data binding is typically used to bind the View to the corresponding ViewModel.

Figure 6 illustrates the relationship between the View, the ViewModel, and the Model in the MVVM pattern.

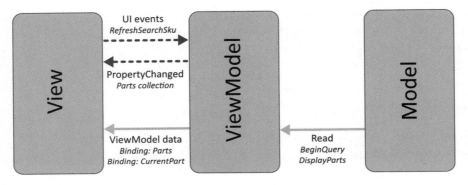

FIGURE 6
The MVVM pattern

Implementations of the MVVM pattern have the following characteristics:

- The View class generates events in response to user interactions. These events are handled by the corresponding ViewModel class. The View class has no knowledge of how the events are handled, or what impact the events will have on the Model.

- The ViewModel class determines whether a user action requires modification of the data in the Model, and acts on the Model if required. For example, if a user presses a button to update the inventory quantity for a part, the View simply notifies the ViewModel that this event occurred. The ViewModel retrieves the new inventory amount from the View and updates the Model. This decouples the View from the Model, and consolidates the business logic into the ViewModel and the Model where it can be tested.

- The Model notifies the ViewModel if the data in the underlying data store has changed. Generally, when you work with a stateless request/response model, you don't need to worry about whether data has changed while the request is being processed, since the window of time is small. With Rich Internet Application (RIA) approaches, the Model data typically stays in memory for longer, and multiple active Views may share the Model data. A user may make changes in one View that affects a different View within the application. The Model fires events to notify any active ViewModels of data changes.

- The ViewModel notifies the View when information has changed. This is typically automated through the two-way binding infrastructure described previously.

The Client Reference Implementation in the Developing Applications for SharePoint 2010 online guidance includes a fully-documented Silverlight implementation of the MVVM pattern for SharePoint data.

ISOLATING DATA ACCESS LOGIC

Many developers combine business logic with data access logic. The business logic interacts directly with data sources such as SharePoint lists, external databases, and Web services. There are several drawbacks to this approach:

- It's hard to test your business logic in isolation if it's dependent on a specific data source (or a specific type of data source).
- It's hard to avoid duplicating data access code, and any changes to the data source require multiple updates to business logic.
- It's hard to optimize data access logic, or implement data-related policies such as caching, if the data access code is distributed throughout the application.
- It's hard to build strongly typed business entities around data access logic.

The solution to these problems is to build a centralized data repository that encapsulates the data access code. This provides a clean separation between business logic and data access logic. Essentially, the repository maps business entities to underlying data structures. The business tier performs create, read, update, and delete (CRUD) operations on the repository, and the repository performs CRUD operations on the underlying data source. This is illustrated by Figure 7.

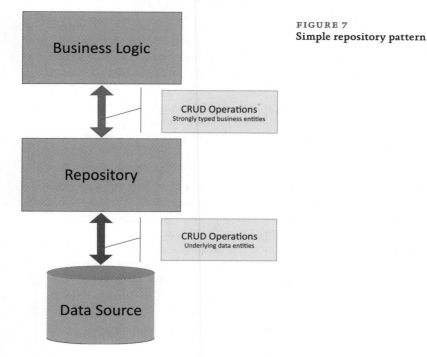

FIGURE 7
Simple repository pattern

Building a centralized data repository in this way makes your applications easier to update, easier to test, and more flexible. If your data schema evolves over time, or you switch to an alternative data source, you need only update your data access code in one location. If you want to unit test your business logic, you can easily switch your repository class with a mock implementation. In short, you can update, modify, and optimize your data access logic without editing any code in the business tier. To support substitution for unit testing, you should build your repository class as an implementation of an interface.

Note: *The SharePoint List Data Models Reference Implementation in the Developing Applications for SharePoint 2010 online guidance includes an example of LINQ to SharePoint-based repository class. For more general information on repository classes in SharePoint applications, see The Repository Pattern at http://msdn.microsoft.com/en-us/library/ff649690.aspx.*

Conclusion

This chapter provided an overview of some of the broader issues relating to the designing of SharePoint 2010 solutions with testability, flexibility, and robustness in mind. In particular, the following aspects of solution design were discussed:

- You should aim to remove dependencies between classes wherever possible. There are various patterns, such service location and constructor injection, that can help you to achieve this. The SharePoint Service Locator provides a reusable implementation of the service location pattern for SharePoint applications.

- You should aim to isolate presentation logic from business logic. The separated presentation class of patterns can help you to achieve this. The Model-View-Presenter (MVP) pattern is well-suited to the development of server-side Web Parts and Web pages, and the MVVM pattern is useful for client applications built using Windows Presentation Foundation Silverlight.

- You should aim to isolate data access logic from business logic. Building a repository class can help you to achieve a clean separation between data access code and business logic, and enables you to encapsulate data access logic in one location for ease of maintenance. The repository pattern also makes it easier to test your business logic, by providing a single point of substitution for data access code.

- You should carefully consider how you manage configuration data for your SharePoint solutions. SharePoint supports multiple mechanisms for the storage and retrieval of configuration settings, including the Web.config file, the hierarchical object store, property bags, and SharePoint lists. You can also configure settings at multiple levels of the SharePoint hierarchy, from individual sites to entire farms. The SharePoint Guidance Library includes a reusable component named the Application Setting Manager that can simplify the management of configuration data.

- You should follow general good practice guidelines for exception management. In particular, you should aim to catch unhandled exceptions at system boundaries where appropriate. Log relevant information to the Windows event logs and the ULS trace log. The SharePoint Guidance Library includes a reusable logging component, the SharePoint Logger, than can simplify the implementation of logging functionality.

FURTHER INFORMATION

For further background information in addition to the documents listed below, see the book's bibliography online at http://msdn.microsoft.com/gg213840.aspx.

- "Providing Application Diagnostics"
- "Managing Application Configuration"
- "Managing Custom Configuration Options for a SharePoint Application"

2 Testing SharePoint Solutions

SharePoint developers have traditionally been slow to adopt modern approaches to software testing. There are various reasons for this. First, solution development for Microsoft® SharePoint® is often a specialized, fairly solitary process that isn't automated or streamlined to the same degree as mainstream software development. Second, the ASP. NET programming model that underpins SharePoint development does not naturally lend itself to automated testing. Finally, most of the classes and methods in the SharePoint API do not implement interfaces or override virtual methods, making them difficult to "stub out" using conventional mocking techniques. However, automated, robust testing is an increasingly essential part of enterprise-scale SharePoint development. This chapter first provides a brief overview of the different types of testing that you are likely to encounter when you work on enterprise-scale applications, and then provides more detailed information about unit testing for SharePoint applications. In particular, it demonstrates the use of a new isolation framework, Moles, for unit testing SharePoint solutions.

Testing Concepts and Phases

Before you look at the mechanics of unit testing SharePoint solutions, it's useful to have a broader understanding of the many different types of software testing in popular use and how they relate to each other. This section provides a conceptual overview of the most common approaches to code testing. It introduces some of the key terminology and identifies the scenarios in which each type of test may be appropriate.

UNIT TESTING

Unit tests are automated procedures that verify whether an isolated piece of code behaves as expected in response to a specific input. Unit tests are usually created by developers and are typically written against public methods and interfaces. Each unit test should focus on testing a single aspect of the code under test; therefore, it should generally not contain any branching logic. In test-driven development scenarios, you create unit tests before you code a particular method. You can run the unit tests repeatedly as you add code to the method. Your task is complete when your code passes all of its unit tests.

A unit test isolates the code under test from all external dependencies, such as external APIs, systems, and services. There are various patterns and tools you can use to ensure that your classes and methods can be isolated in this way, and they are discussed later in this section.

Unit tests should verify that the code under test responds as expected to both normal and exceptional conditions. Unit tests can also provide a way to test responses to error conditions that are hard to generate on demand in real systems, such as hardware failures and out-of-memory exceptions. Because unit tests are isolated from external dependencies, they run very quickly; it is typical for a large suite consisting of hundreds of unit tests to run in a matter of seconds. The speed of execution is critical when you are using an iterative approach to development, because the developer should run the test suite on a regular basis during the development process.

Unit tests make it easier to exercise all code paths in branching logic. They do this by simulating conditions that are difficult to produce on real systems in order to drive all paths through the code. This leads to fewer production bugs, which are often costly to the business in terms of the resulting downtime, instability, and the effort required to create, test, and apply production patches.

INTEGRATION TESTING

While unit tests verify the functionality of a piece of code in isolation, integration tests verify the functionality of a piece of code against a target system or platform. Just like unit tests, integration tests are automated procedures that run within a testing framework. Although comprehensive unit testing verifies that your code behaves as expected in isolation, you still need to ensure that your code behaves as expected in its target environment, and that the external systems on which your code depends behave as anticipated. That is the role of integration testing.

Unlike a unit test, an integration test executes all code in the call path for each method under test—regardless of whether that code is within the class you are testing or is part of an external API. Because of this, it typically takes longer to set up the test conditions for an integration test. For example, you may need to create users and groups or add lists and list items. Integration tests also take considerably longer to run. However, unlike unit tests, integration tests do not rely on assumptions about the behavior of external systems and services. As a result, integration tests may detect bugs that are missed by unit tests.

Developers often use integration tests to verify that external dependencies, such as Web services, behave as expected, or to test code with a heavy reliance on external dependencies that cannot be factored out. Testers often also develop and use integration tests for more diverse scenarios, such as security testing and stress testing.

In many cases, organizations do not distinguish between integration and unit testing, because both types of tests are typically driven by unit testing frameworks such as nUnit, xUnit, and Microsoft Visual Studio® Unit Test. Organizations that employ agile development practices do, however, make this distinction, since the two types of tests have different purposes within the agile process.

Note: *In the Visual Studio 2010 release, there is a limitation that prevents you from running integration tests against SharePoint assemblies using Visual Studio Unit Test. Unit tests created for Visual Studio Unit Test must be developed using the Microsoft . NET Framework 4.0 in Visual Studio 2010, whereas SharePoint 2010 assemblies are based on .NET Framework 3.5. In many cases, this is not an issue—.NET Framework 4.0 assemblies are generally compatible with .NET Framework 3.5 assemblies, so you can run a .NET Framework 4.0 test against a .NET Framework 3.5 assembly. However, the way in which SharePoint loads the .NET common language runtime (CLR) prevents the runtime from properly loading and running the tests within Visual Studio Unit Test.*

This limitation prevents you from running integration tests with SharePoint within Visual Studio Unit Test. Integration tests execute real SharePoint API logic instead of substituting the logic with a test implementation. Two isolation tools discussed in the following sections, TypeMock and Moles, will continue to work because they intercept calls to the SharePoint API before the actual SharePoint logic is invoked. You can execute integration tests using a third-party framework such as xUnit or nUnit. Coded user interface (UI) tests against SharePoint applications will run without any issues from within Visual Studio 2010.

CONTINUOUS INTEGRATION TESTING

Continuous integration (CI) is a process that provides a continual verification of code as it is checked into the source repository. This process ensures that the quality of the code that's checked in is always high, because developers do not want to be responsible for breaking the team build. It also ensures that any problems are quickly identified and addressed—on many agile teams, if the CI server is "red," development stops until the issue is resolved.

Typically, development teams run CI in response to a check-in event when code is added or changed, although it may also run periodically at a regular interval, such as every couple of hours. The CI process builds the code and runs all of the unit tests. The CI process can also run additional checks, such as static analysis. For example, when you work with SharePoint solutions, a recommended practice is to run the SPDisposeCheck utility to check for improper disposal of SharePoint objects.

Typically, CI servers use a commercial tool, such as Team Foundation Build, or an open source tool, such as Cruise Control, to help automate the build and test process. These tools simplify the setup and execution of the CI process and provide reporting on build and test results.

WEB TESTING

Web testing simulates the interaction between a user and a Web-based user interface. The Web test sends HTTP requests to your solution and verifies that the HTTP response it receives is as you expect. Even with sophisticated tools, writing a robust, repeatable Web test can be challenging and time consuming for complex user interfaces. Within Visual Studio, Web tests are known as coded UI tests.

STRESS TESTING

Stress tests run an isolated component under excessive load conditions. The purpose of a stress test is to drive the component beyond its normal operating conditions to ensure that it degrades gracefully. Usually, you will use integration tests to conduct stress testing, although you can also use coded UI tests. Stress tests are a useful way to detect certain classes of problems, including memory leaks due to improper disposal, and threading-related issues such as deadlocks or resource contention. When you conduct stress testing, you need to make sure that you stay within the limits of the underlying hardware and operating system, because, inevitably, failures will arise as you exceed the capacity of the infrastructure.

FUNCTIONAL TESTING

Functional testing refers to any procedure that tests the functionality of an application from the perspective of a user. Functional tests can include manual tests, Web tests, and integration tests. Integration tests are included in functional testing because systems often expose APIs for extensibility or for programmatic use. In this case, the target user is a developer.

BUILD VERIFICATION TESTING

Build verification tests (BVTs) work in a similar way to continuous integration, and typically use the same tools. However, while continuous integration ensures that code builds successfully and passes unit tests, BVTs are used to determine whether code satisfies a representative subset of the functionality expected by end users. Typically, BVTs use a combination of integration tests and coded UI tests. A BVT process builds, installs, deploys, and tests an application on a regular basis. BVTs must often perform extensive scripted configuration of the deployment environment before running intensive test processes; because of this, they can take tens of minutes to complete.

BVTs provide a baseline measure of confidence in the quality of a build against a real system before it is deployed more widely into other testing environments. BVTs should be conducted in addition to rather than instead of unit testing, because unit tests do not catch bugs related to the behavior of a system at run time. A build can be "green" on the CI server yet still not function in the production environment.

LOAD OR SCALE TESTING

Load or scale testing measures the performance of a solution against a specific set of resources. Ideally, you should run load or scale testing on a test farm that replicates the conditions of your production environment. The idea is to ensure that your system behaves well under normal high-end load conditions and to understand how your application scales as load increases. Load or scale testing uses coded UI tests, often with multiple computers running client test agents to simulate requests and measure responses. Preparing and running load or scale tests is a time-consuming and resource-intensive process.

USER ACCEPTANCE TESTING

User acceptance testing is any process that tests your solution from the user's perspective, such as load testing and functional testing procedures. In many agile development methodologies, the business owner for the system is also required to test the solution to ensure that business needs are being met. Functional testing by business owners is considered to be a part of user acceptance testing.

Unit Testing for SharePoint Applications

In Chapter 10, "Building Robust SharePoint Applications," we identified several reasons why you should avoid writing classes that have direct dependencies on other services. We also introduced various patterns that you can use to avoid direct dependencies in your code. One of the key reasons for removing direct dependencies is to make your classes suitable for unit testing. The previous section describes how unit testing involves isolating specific components of your code, usually individual methods, to be able to verify that the code under test provides expected outputs in response to known inputs. This section describes how unit testing actually works for SharePoint applications.

Suppose you want to design a Web Part that enables users to view and query product details from a catalog. In a rough, proof-of-concept approach, you might create a Visual Web Part and put all your logic in the code-behind file for the user control. However, this makes it almost impossible to unit test your business logic. Your code is tightly coupled to the user interface, the SharePoint environment, and the data source. To make your logic testable, there are several design changes you can introduce:

- Use the Model-View-Presenter (MVP) pattern to isolate your business logic from the user interface and the data source. You create a view class to render your user interface and a repository, or model, class to interact with your data source. All your business logic goes in the presenter class.

- Implement interfaces for your view classes and your services (such as repository classes). This enables you to replace the real classes with a fake class, typically known as *stub classes* or *mock classes*. Later sections describe these concepts in more detail.

- Use the Service Locator pattern to decouple your presenter class from specific implementations of the services that your presenter uses (such as your repository class). This provides an "interception" point where you can replace the real implementation that your presenter depends on with a fake implementation during test execution.

Suppose you develop a Web Part that retrieves and displays product details from a catalog. You use the MVP pattern to isolate your business logic in a presenter class, and you define your model and your view classes as interface implementations. This allows you to test your business logic in isolation by substituting mock implementations of the model and the view, as illustrated by Figure 1.

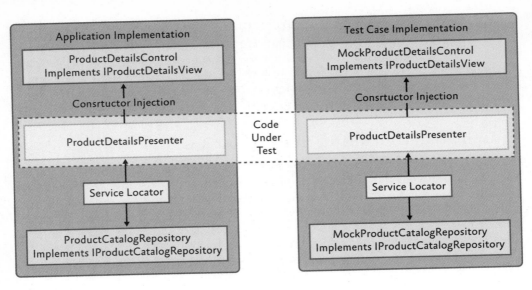

FIGURE 1
Designing Web Parts for ease of testing

Let's review what happens when you unit test the **ProductDetailsPresenter** class. First, you develop two fake classes, the **MockProductDetailsView** and the **MockProduct CatalogRepository**. The first class, **MockProductDetailsView**, implements the view interface. The test creates an instance of the **MockProductDetailsView** class. The view class instantiates the presenter class, and then it passes itself as the argument to the constructor for the presenter class. This approach is known as *constructor injection*. However, the test still needs to replace the actual repository class with the mock repository class. To achieve this, the test configures the service locator to return the test implementation to the presenter. The end result is that the presenter executes its logic without ever knowing that it is using fake implementations of the view and the repository.

STUBS AND MOCKS

So what do the terms *stub classes* and *mock classes* mean? In a unit test, you test one specific piece of code. If your code makes calls to other classes and external assemblies, you introduce complexity and uncertainty into the test—you do not know whether your code is failing the test or whether the dependency classes are behaving in an unexpected way. To remove this uncertainty, you replace the dependency classes with fake implementations. These fake implementations are known as *fakes, mocks,* and *stubs*. The nuanced differences between fakes, mocks, and stubs are not very important to this section, vary according to who you ask, and often evolve into complex discussions around topics such as behavioral and state-based testing. As your approach to testing becomes more sophisticated these nuances are good to understand, but for now they cloud the issues. Mock has become a popular term and is often used today to represent any type of test class substituted for a real implementation. Fake is a more generic term in increasingly common use and has less controversy surrounding it, so the remainder of this section refers to these substitute test implementations as fakes.

Substituting classes that are required by the code under test is challenging. For example, your presenter class calls into your repository class. How do you replace the repository implementation with a fake class without editing the presenter class? This is where service location (or a more sophisticated dependency injection approach) comes in. Your presenter class uses service location to get a repository implementation, and when you run the test, you configure the service locator to return your fake implementation instead.

Service location is driven by interfaces and interface implementations. To use service location, you must design your dependency classes to implement relevant interfaces. For example, by defining the **IProductCatalogRepository** interface as the basis for your repository class, and by calling **IProductCatalogRepository** methods from your presenter class, you make it possible to supply fake implementations of **IProductCatalog Repository** without editing your presenter logic.

Using fake classes is straightforward if you create the dependency classes yourself, because you have full control over how they are implemented. It can be more challenging if you need to provide substitutes for external classes. The SharePoint object model is a case in point. SharePoint integration is problematic in unit tests for the following reasons:

- Most classes in the SharePoint object model do not implement interfaces or virtual methods that you can override to create substitute implementations.

- Many SharePoint classes are sealed with private constructors, so you cannot derive from them or even create them directly.

This makes these classes impossible to substitute with conventional mocking techniques. Providing substitute implementations of SharePoint classes for unit testing requires a more sophisticated toolset, in the form of a *detouring framework*. Essentially, a detouring framework intercepts calls to APIs and redirects the calls to mock implementations. The best known detouring framework is probably TypeMock, a third-party product that provides highly effective mocking functionality when you work with SharePoint 2010. In this chapter, we look at the use of a new Microsoft detouring framework named *Moles*. However, the broader concepts we describe are applicable to many testing platforms.

THE MOLES FRAMEWORK

The Moles framework emerged as part of a larger Microsoft Research project named *Pex*, which aims to provide a systematic, automated approach to unit testing. Pex provides comprehensive test automation based on parameterized unit tests, and is not covered in this brief overview. Moles also includes many features that are beyond the scope of this document. Moles is a Visual Studio Power Tool—it's available as a free download from Visual Studio Gallery, and supports both Visual Studio 2010 and Visual Studio 2008. Pex is available for MSDN subscribers as a subscriber download.

The Moles framework actually supports two different kinds of substitution classes—*stub types* and *mole types*. These two approaches allow you to create substitute classes for code dependencies under different circumstances:

- Stub types provide a lightweight isolation framework that generates fake stub implementations of virtual methods and interfaces for unit testing.
- Mole types use a powerful detouring framework that uses code profiler APIs to intercept calls to dependency classes and redirect the calls to a fake object.

Generally speaking, you should use stubs (or an alternative mocking framework) to create substitute implementations for your own code and for any third-party code that exposes virtual methods and interfaces that you can override. When it is not possible to create stubs for third-party code, such as when the code uses sealed classes or static, non-virtual methods, you should use moles to redirect calls to the code. Later sections provide more guidance on when it is appropriate to use stubs and moles. First, the next sections describe how you can use these two components.

USING STUBS

When you use a stub, the Moles framework generates stub implementations of dependency methods and classes for unit testing. This functionality is similar to that of many conventional isolation frameworks such as **Moq, NMock2, and Rhino Mocks**. The stub types are automatically generated classes that run very quickly at execution and are simple to use. However, stubs lack many of the capabilities of the conventional mocking frameworks and may require some additional coding. Moles can automatically generate stub types for your own code and for third-party assemblies you are using, including assemblies in the .NET Framework or SharePoint. By default, stubs are generated for all interfaces and abstract classes, although you can also configure Moles to generate stubs for non-abstract classes that expose virtual methods. Note that in some cases, it may be easier to manually implement mocks or stubs for your own code instead of using the stub class generated by the Moles framework.

The following example shows how to consume a stub object generated by the Moles framework within a test class. In this example, we want to test the **ServiceLocatorConfig** class, a key component of the SharePoint Service Locator. The **ServiceLocatorConfig** class depends on implementations of the **IConfigManager** interface to manage the storage of configuration settings. In this case, the **IConfigManager** instance is provided by a stub implementation named **SIConfigManager**.

```csharp
C#
[TestMethod]
public void SetSiteCacheInterval_WithValidValue_UpdatesConfiguration()
{
  // Arrange
  int expected = 30;
  string expectedKey =
    "Microsoft.Practices.SharePoint.Common.SiteLocatorCacheInterval";
  var bag = new BIPropertyBag();
  int target = -1;

  var cfgMgr = new SIConfigManager();
```

```
cfgMgr.SetInPropertyBagStringObjectIPropertyBag =
  (key, value, propBag) =>
  {
    if(key == expectedKey)
      target = (int) value;
  };


cfgMgr.GetPropertyBagConfigLevel = (configlevel) => bag;

var config = new ServiceLocatorConfig(cfgMgr);

// Act
config.SetSiteCacheInterval(expected);

// Assert
Assert.AreEqual(expected, target);
}
```

There are a few key points you need to be aware of to fully understand this test method. First, the following describes the naming conventions used for the generated stubs.

- The generated stub class, **SIConfigManager**, provides stubs for the interface **IConfigManager**. The naming convention precedes the name of the interface or abstract class with the letter "S."

- The stub class is created in the **Microsoft.Practices.SharePoint.Common. Configuration.Moles** namespace. Stub classes are created in **.Moles**, a sub-namespace of the namespace that contains the interface or abstract class being stubbed. In this case, the interface in question, **IConfigManager**, is in the **Microsoft.Practices.SharePoint.Common.Configuration** namespace.

The **Arrange** section of the code example is the setup phase of the test. You can see that the stub object is passed in to the constructor of the class under test, **ServiceLocator-Config**, which requires an argument of type **IConfigManager**. This is an example of *constructor injection*, which is a type of *dependency injection*. Whenever you use a fake object, you need a way to provide the fake object to the code under test, and you typically do this by using some form of dependency injection.

So how do you make your stub object instance simulate the behavior you require for the unit test? One of the key tenets of the Moles framework is that you can override virtual methods or interface methods in a flexible way, by attaching delegates to the corresponding method in the stub class. When the object under test calls interface methods on the stub object, the stub object will invoke your delegate. In the **Arrange** section, you can see that lambda expressions are used to specify implementations for two delegates, **SetInPropertyBagStringObjectIPropertyBag**, and **GetPropertyBagConfigLevel**. The following conventions and approaches are used when defining delegate test implementations for a stub class:

- The name of each delegate on the stub class indicates the name of the method on the interface, together with the parameters that it takes. This naming convention is intended to make the name of the delegate unique; a method may have multiple overloads, so adding parameter types makes the delegate name specific to an individual method overload. In the first example, the method name is **SetIn PropertyBag** and the parameter types are **String**, **Object**, and **IPropertyBag**. Hence the delegate is named **SetInPropertyBagStringObjectIPropertyBag**.

- Each lambda expression defines an anonymous method that will be invoked by your delegate. The stub class invokes this delegate when the code under test calls the corresponding actual method on the interface.

The following code shows the first delegate implementation for the **SIConfigManager** stub class:

```C#
cfgMgr.SetInPropertyBagStringObjectIPropertyBag =
  (key, value, propBag) =>
  {
    if(key == expectedKey)
      target = (int) value;
  };
```

This example specifies the logic to invoke when the **IConfigManager. SetInPropertyBag(string, object, IPropertyBag)** method is called. If the provided key matches the expected key, then the value is saved in the local integer variable named **target**. If the provided key does not match the expected key, no action is taken. Reading and writing local variables within your lambda expressions provides a convenient way to record what occurs during the test, and allows you to check the values during the *Assert* phase of the test.

The following code shows the second delegate implementation for the **SIConfig-Manager** stub class:

```C#
cfgMgr.GetPropertyBagConfigLevel = (configlevel) => bag;
```

This example specifies the behavior for the method **GetPropertyBag(ConfigLevel)** and will always return a reference to the local variable named **bag**. A common mistake is to return a new value every time a lambda expression is evaluated. Often the code under test will expect the same value to be returned, and by defining a local variable you can ensure that the object is created once and the same value returned each time the test code is invoked.

> **Note:** *The* **bag** *local variable is an instance of* **BIPropertyBag***, which is an example of another type of fake object known as a* **behaved type***. Behaved types are described later in this chapter.*

You can configure the Moles framework to respond in various ways if the code under test calls a stub method for which a test implementation has not been defined. By default, the framework will throw an exception indicating that the method has not been defined:

Microsoft.Moles.Framework.Behaviors.BehaviorNotImplementedException:
SIConfigManager.global::Microsoft.Practices.SharePoint.Common.Configuration.
IConfigManager.GetPropertyBag(ConfigLevel) was not stubbed.

A common approach to discovering which methods you need to stub for your test is to run the test, see if the exception is thrown for a missing stub method, then implement the stub method. The Moles framework also supports a **BehaveAsDefault** approach, in which case any stub methods that you have not implemented will return a default value for the return type of the method.

The remainder of the test class uses the same approach as any other unit test. The **Act** section performs one more action on the code that you want to test. The **Assert** section verifies that the code under test behaved as expected.

USING MOLES

Moles is a detouring framework. It uses the powerful profiling features of the CLR's just-in-time compiler to redirect method calls to custom delegates.

A common problem that demonstrates the need for a detouring framework, such as Moles, occurs when you want to run unit tests on code that depends on the **DateTime. Now** static property. You cannot use **DateTime.Now** to test specific conditions, because the value always returns the current date and time from your system clock. You also cannot directly override the **DateTime.Now** property to return a specific value. In this situation, you can use the Moles framework to detour the **DateTime.Now** property getter to your own custom delegate. This custom delegate is known as a mole.

When execution enters a method, such as the **DateTime.Now** property getter, the Moles framework checks to see whether the test class has defined a detour for that method. If a detour is defined, the framework redirects the call to the detour delegate. If a detour is not defined, then a not-implemented exception will be thrown. Alternatively you can configure moles to direct the call to the real implementation of the method or return a default value. For example, if a detour for the **DateTime.Now** property getter is defined, the method call returns the result of the detour expression. Otherwise, it uses the real implementation of the property getter to return the current date and time.

The following code example shows a test method that uses Moles to create a detour for the **SPFarm.Local** static property. This is a unit test for the **SharePointService Locator** class. The goal of this test is to verify that calls to **SharePointServiceLocator. GetCurrent()** fail if a SharePoint context is unavailable.

C#

```
[TestMethod]
[HostType("Moles")]
public void GetCurrent_CallWithoutSharePoint_ThrowsNoSharePointContextException()
```

```
{
  // Arrange
  MSPFarm.LocalGet = () => null;
  bool expectedExceptionThrown = false;

  // Act
  try
  {
    IServiceLocator target = SharePointServiceLocator.GetCurrent();
  }
  catch(NoSharePointContextException)
  {
    expectedExceptionThrown = true;
  }

  // Assert
  Assert.IsTrue(expectedExceptionThrown);
}
```

This section describes the key points of interest in this test method. First, note that a **HostType** attribute has been added to the method. This instructs the test runtime to execute this test within the Moles environment, which runs in a separate process. This attribute is necessary only when you use a mole, because moles rely on the profiler to detour method calls. Stubs do not involve detours, so they can run in the standard test environment.

In this test method, **MSPFarm** defines a mole for the **SPFarm** class. The naming convention for a mole is to prefix the name of the class with the letter "M." Just like stubs, moles are created in a sub-namespace, **.Moles**, of the namespace that contains the class you are detouring. In this case, the **MSPFarm** mole is defined in the **Microsoft.Share Point.Administration.Moles** namespace.

In this case, the test creates a delegate for the **SPFarm.Local** property getter. The delegate signature, **LocalGet**, indicates that you are overriding the property getter for the **Local** property. If you could set the **Local** property, the mole would also have a **LocalSet** delegate. Because **SPFarm.Local** is a read-only property, the **LocalSet** delegate is not defined. The lambda expression, **() => null**, specifies that detoured calls to the **SPFarm. Local** property getter will return **null**.

BEST PRACTICES FOR STUBS AND MOLES

When you work with the Moles framework, it is important to understand when you should use stub types and when you should use mole types. The following guidelines apply to the majority of test scenarios:

- Use *stub types* (or an alternative mocking framework) and hand-coded mock classes for replacing components you control.

- Use *mole types* (or an alternative detouring framework) for mocking static methods and classes that you do not control, such as SharePoint classes. Do not use mole types to implement interfaces, abstract classes, or virtual methods that you can easily mock using stub types.

- Structure your unit tests into areas of Arrange, Act, and Assert for clarity:
    - Put the setup and configuration tasks for your test in the Arrange section.
    - Perform the actions that you want to test in the Act section.
    - Verify the results of your actions in the Assert section.

- Test a single behavior in your unit test. If you have branching logic in your unit test, it is often a good indicator that you should have more tests.

- Assert multiple results when it makes sense to do so. Often, a single behavior can result in multiple changes in state.

- Use the SharePoint Service Locator, or an alternative implementation of the service location pattern, to decouple your classes from dependencies and to substitute interface implementations for unit testing.

Undoubtedly, you will encounter scenarios in which these guidelines do not apply. For example, suppose you create a class that derives from a base class that you do not own. In this case, it may be difficult to get full test coverage through the use of only simple mocking techniques. You can sometimes avoid this problem by adding virtual methods that you can override in a test implementation, but in other cases, you will need to create detours for your own methods through Moles or TypeMock.

There are many more sophisticated examples that illustrate the use of stub types, manual mocks, and mole types in the SharePoint Guidance Library and the accompanying reference implementations.

BEHAVIORAL MODELS

When you start using a framework such as Moles or TypeMock for unit testing, you may find that your unit tests often break when you change the way your logic is implemented. When your unit test dictates a specific response for each method call to a mock object, your unit test must reflect the state and behavior of the types that you are substituting. If you edit the code under test to use alternative methods, or even to call the same methods in a different order, you may find that your unit test no longer provides an accurate snapshot of the behavior of the dependency class—even though the functionality remains outwardly unchanged. Your unit tests become susceptible to frequent breaking changes, and risk becoming a reflection of the implementation details instead of a pure test of output conditions.

One approach to mitigating this problem is to implement *behaved types* that provide a more general representation of the class that you are faking. This allows you factor the behavior logic for dependency types out of your individual unit tests and into a single behaved type definition that you can reuse in multiple unit tests. For example, suppose you edit the way your code under test retrieves a list item—instead of using the **GetItems** method, you use the list indexer. Instead of updating every unit test to mock this new behavior, you would simply edit the behaved type for the list to ensure that it supports the new retrieval method. If a behaved type doesn't have the functionality required for your test, you can simply update the behaved type once and all future tests will benefit from the updated functionality.

Behaved types support the concept of *state-based testing*. In your unit tests, you assign values to the behaved type—for example, you might add a list item to a behaved type that represents a list. The behaved type will always return the same item, regardless of whether the code under test uses an indexer or a query to retrieve the item. This breaks the dependency between the overall functionality of the test code and the underlying implementation details of the test code. In other words, your unit tests simply set the *state* of the fake object, while the underlying *behavior* of the fake object is encapsulated within the behaved type. The use of behaved types leads to simpler and more resilient unit tests, and it's preferable to use behaved types instead of moles wherever possible.

The Moles installer includes many behaved type implementations for SharePoint and .NET Framework classes. The following example shows a test method that uses the behaved type implementations of the **SPWeb**, **SPList**, **SPListItem**, and **SPField** classes—**BSPWeb**, **BSPList**, **BSPListItem**, and **BSPField**, respectively—which are provided by the Moles framework. The example tests the presenter class logic in a simple Web Part that implements the Model-View-Presenter (MVP) pattern.

```csharp
C#
[TestMethod]
[HostType("Moles")]
public void DoMagic_WithOneAnswer_ReturnsAnswer()
{
    //Arrange
    string answer = null;
    string error = null;

    // First, set up a stub class to represent the view passed to the presenter.
    var view = new SIMagicEightBallView();
    view.DisplayAnswerString = (s) => answer = s;
    view.DisplayErrorString = (e) => error = e;

    //Set up a behaved type for a web, add a list, and add an item to the list.
    BSPWeb web = new BSPWeb();
    BSPList list = web.Lists.SetOne();
    // add the field that will be used to the list fields.
    BSPField field = new BSPField();
    field.Id = MagicEightBallConstants.AnswerFieldId;
    list.Fields.SetOne(field);

    BSPListItem item = list.Items.SetOne();
```

```
    item.ID = 0;
    list.Title = MagicEightBallConstants.EightBallListName;
    item.Items.SetOne("answer.123");


    //Act
    var presenter = new MagicEightBallPresenter(view, web);
    presenter.DoMagic("Ask a question");

    //Assert
    Assert.IsTrue(answer != null);
    Assert.IsTrue(error == null);
    Assert.IsTrue(answer == "answer.123");
}
```

As you can see from the example, the use of behaved types simplifies the test method and makes it easier to read and understand. In many cases, it also obviates the need for the developer to create moles for SharePoint types, which is beneficial as mole types can be complex to develop. The naming convention for a behaved type is to prefix the name of the class with the letter "B." This test performs the following actions:

- It instantiates a behaved type to represent an **SPWeb** instance.
- It creates a single list for the Web by calling the **web.Lists.SetOne()** method.
- It assigns values for the **ID** field, the **Title** field, and a custom answer field to the list item.
- It adds a single item to the list by calling the **list.Items.SetOne()** method.

This allows you to test the logic of the presenter class; in short, you are able to verify that the presenter class returns the expected answer when you ask it a question.

It's worth taking time to explore some of the built-in behaved type implementations. Behaved types typically contain moles that define the functionality of the type. For example, the constructor of the **BSPList** class instantiates a new mole, of type **MSPList**, to represent the **SPList** class. Just like any other mole class implementation, the behaved type attaches several delegates to the mole class to define the behavior of particular methods. For more advanced scenarios, you can override the behavior of a behaved type by wrapping it with an additional mole. For example, the following example overrides the behavior that the **BSPWeb** behaved type defines for the **SPWeb.CurrentUser** property getter.

C#
```
BSPWeb web = new BSPWeb();
MSPUser testUser = new MSPUser();
testUser.NameGet = () => "test name";
MSPWeb web1 = new MSPWeb((SPWeb)web);
web1.CurrentUserGet = () => testUser;
```

In general, you can build up the functionality in your behaved types progressively over time, as additional unit tests call for additional behavior definitions. However, you should avoid making the behaved type overly specialized or complex. If a particular unit test requires highly specialized behavior, you can still use the behaved type and override particular behaviors from within your unit test setup phase.

> **Note:** *The Moles Start Menu includes an option to build the behaved types using Visual Studio 2010. Selecting this option builds the behaved types to your user directory. You must perform this action before running the Moles-based tests provided with the Share-Point Guidance Library. The use of behaved types in the SharePoint Guidance Library is limited, as the Moles framework was still under development when the SharePoint Guidance Library components were implemented.*

Conclusion

This chapter identified some of the challenges that face developers who want to run unit tests against SharePoint solutions, and described how you can use a combination of design patterns and testing frameworks to meet these challenges. The key points discussed in the chapter were as follows:

- Unit testing isolates a small amount of code, typically a single method or class, and tests the behavior of that code against specific inputs. Any dependencies within the code under test are replaced by fake objects.

- You can use design patterns such as Model-View-Presenter (MVP), service location, and constructor injection to isolate business logic for testing purposes.

- Conventional mocking techniques are not effective in many SharePoint scenarios. This is because most classes in the SharePoint object model do not implement interfaces or virtual methods that you can override to create substitute implementations. Also, many SharePoint classes are sealed with private constructors, so you cannot derive from them or even create them directly. In this case, you need to use a detouring framework such as TypeMock or Moles to test your logic effectively.

- You can make your unit tests more robust by creating behaved types, rather than conventional mocks or stubs, to represent the classes that you are faking. Behaved types simulate the behavior of the class you are faking, which means you don't need to specify behavior in your unit tests.

See It in Action: *The Developing Applications for SharePoint 2010 online guidance includes several downloadable reference implementations that illustrate various facets of SharePoint 2010 development. In the download, there are two Visual Studio 2010 solutions for each reference implementation—one with unit tests, and one without. You can explore the solutions with unit tests to see practical examples of how to test real-world SharePoint applications.*

For more information, and to download the reference implementations, see Developing Applications for SharePoint 2010 at http://msdn.microsoft.com/en-us/ library/ff770300.aspx.

FURTHER INFORMATION

For information on testing, see the documents listed below along with the additional resources listed in the book's online bibliography at http://msdn.microsoft.com/gg213840. aspx.

- "How to Build SharePoint Projects with TFS Team Build"
- "Improving Application Quality Through Testing"
- "Visual Studio 2010 Moles x64 – Isolation Framework for .NET"
- "Unit Testing SharePoint Services with Pex and Moles"

Index

mC

2/11